HUNTING TALES

HUNTING TALES

*A Timeless Collection of Some of the Greatest
Hunting Stories Ever Written*

EDITED BY LAMAR UNDERWOOD

LYONS
PRESS

Essex, Connecticut

An imprint of Globe Pequot, the trade division of
The Rowman & Littlefield Publishing Group, Inc.
4501 Forbes Blvd., Ste. 200
Lanham, MD 20706
www.rowman.com

Distributed by NATIONAL BOOK NETWORK

British Library Cataloguing in Publication Information available

Library of Congress Cataloging-in-Publication Data available

ISBN 978-1-4930-7291-0 (paperback)
ISBN 978-1-4930-7292-7 (epub)

∞™ The paper used in this publication meets the minimum requirements of American National Standard for Information Sciences—Permanence of Paper for Printed Library Materials, ANSI/NISO Z39.48-1992.

Alone far in the wilds and mountains I hunt,
Wandering amazed at my own lightness and glee,
In the late afternoon choosing a safe spot to pass the night,
Kindling a fire and broiling the fresh-kill'd game,
Falling asleep on the gather'd leaves with my dog and gun by my side.

—Walt Whitman
Song of Myself

Contents

Contents

About This Book

by Lamar Underwood

WHAT ROBERT RUARK CALLS "THE HORN OF THE HUNTER" SOUNDS early in life for some of us, for others never at all. I do not envy those folks.

Like fishing, hunting has been part of my life for so long that imagining a void for these activities seems as unfathomable an idea as trying to come to grips with imagining the size of the universe.

In the first place, I like being outdoors more than indoors. I like being a countryman, to the extent that I can considering my family, job, and other responsibilities, including finances. If I could, I would grow, raise, catch, and shoot all of my family's food, taking the lean times with the fat. But that is not possible, because I am very much part of an urbanized world and can find no escape from it.

A quote from Chief Sitting Bull I've always liked really hits home: "When the buffalo are gone, we will hunt mice, for we are hunters and we want our freedom."

The best hunters and anglers I have ever known—and all the writers—have deep and abiding interest in the natural world. They would not spend five seconds in the company of the so-called "slob hunter" who only wants to blast things, knowing nothing, appreciating nothing, learning nothing. Such "hunters" do not deserve the name. Most of the time, they are violating the law as well as denigrating the activity.

Even further disdain goes out to the sanctimonious pundits who claim they hate hunting because they love nature, yet would not know the difference between a loon and a Canada goose, or a sandhill crane and a great blue heron. I suppose what they think they love is the "idea" of nature, as shown in Bambi-like fantasy movies, and not the real thing itself, which they never bother to see or learn about.

But, we are all hunters here, and it's time to get on with some of the stories that brought us together. The pages ahead will take you hunting for all sorts of game and in places that range from mountain peaks to lowland swamps. The best writers I have ever read will be your guides, and I promise you that their prose will become part of your hunting memories and ignite recollections of your own experiences that make up the hunting scrapbook of your mind.

It has always been my belief that one of the things that makes hunting and fishing so special is that on any given day, things can happen that you will never forget. Very few things in everyday life are like that. Births, deaths, marriages, graduations, promotions—all those important events that you never forget—come along very infrequently.

There is nothing remarkable about most days of our lives, as far as storing memories are concerned. But on any day you step out the door with a rod or gun to put in the truck, something really big can happen. Perhaps the day will someday come when nobody you know will care to hear what that something was—a shot well made, a dog's first point or retrieve, the time you turned the big flock of mallards with your calls, the morning you bagged a buck. No matter. You found what you were looking for, and you're keeping it.

Editor's Note

To help make this book as authentic as possible, in preserving the voices of the authors, the stories here are presented without being copyedited for misspelling and grammatical errors. When Theodore Roosevelt spells grizzly as "grisly" we let it stand as written. Also, in certain places, irrelevant and outdated language has been deleted.

With two exceptions, the stories in this book are not new. They have previously appeared in magazines and in various editions of my previous anthologies, including *The Greatest Hunting Stories Ever Told*, *Classic Hunting Stories*, *Great American Hunting Stories*, *Gun Dog Hunting Stories*, and *Roosevelt on Hunting*.

The completely new stories are my "'All-In' for Doves" and the quail-hunting story, "'Yonder They Are.'" These were originally published in *The American Frontiersman* magazine and have never been collected in an anthology. If you will permit me to "blow my own horn" for a moment, I really believe these are two of the best stories I've ever written.

With new stories and previously published ones, I think you will find this big collection of Hunting Tales to be a worthy addition to your personal library.

—Lamar Underwood

I

Tracks to Remember

by Tom Hennessey

There must have been something in the air up there in Bangor, Maine. Or maybe it was the water. I don't know, but the fact is that two really fine writers lived only a few blocks from each other and year after year keep turning out the kind of prose people want to read. One writer is the mega-bestseller novelist Stephen King, still internationally famous. The other was the late Tom Hennessey, outdoor columnist for the Bangor Daily News, *whose fame will never match Stephen King, of course, but who wrote memorable pieces appreciated by Maine readers for many years. "Tracks to Remember" is a little gem of a whitetail-hunting story and is one of the pieces collected in Tom's book* Feathers 'n Fins, *published by Amwell Press in 1989. Tom's talent does not end with his writing. He was an artist whose paintings, prints, and drawings were eagerly sought by collectors.*

STEEPLE-LIKE SPRUCES WERE SILHOUETTED AGAINST A SKY OF GUN-metal gray as Hank Lyons slipped five 170-grain cartridges into the magazine of his .30-30 carbine. Fully loaded, the magazine held six of the flat-nosed .30s. Somewhere long ago—probably because he liked the lines, angles, and curve of its configuration—Hank had decided that five was his lucky number. With a flip of the lever action he chambered a round, then eased the cocked hammer onto the safety position. At a brisk pace, he began hiking the grown-up tote road that would cross a brook about a mile into the woods.

You'd have thought it was springtime. Two days earlier, Ol' Man Winter had thrown one of his white-with-rage tantrums. Shortly thereafter, he began running a temperature and now the woods were shrouded with ground fog. Every bough and branch wore beads of moisture.

Arriving at the brook, Hank wasn't surprised to see that the log bridge had partially collapsed under the constant weight of time. The makeshift span had been old when, years before, he first crossed it while bird hunting. A short distance beyond the brook, several sets of deer tracks crisscrossed the road.

"Does," Hank allowed. "At least a couple. Maybe a fawn with 'em— got to be a buck around somewhere." The tracks indicated that deer were using the mixed growth to the left of the road, and a fir thicket to the right.

The mixed growth climbed a knoll whose top was crowned with apple trees glowing with "golden nuggets." Quietly, Hank worked his way up the slope until he had a commanding view of the area. "As good as any and better than most," he said as he brushed the snow from a wind-toppled spruce.

Sitting among the boughs, he checked the hammer of the carbine. Hank Lyons could sit all day in a duck blind, but he found it difficult to stay anchored for more than an hour on a deer stand. For that reason he had waited until afternoon to enter the woods. Within an hour and a half at the most, dusk would demand his departure. Along the ice-rimmed brook, the ground fog was more concentrated. Thickening and thinning, it swirled like ghosts rising from snow-covered crypts. Directly across from where Hank was sitting—about sixty yards away—a leaning birch opened a white gash in the gray-green timber. Slightly to the right of the birch squatted the stub of what was once an immense pine.

Now and then, the ground fog became so cottony that those objects were momentarily obscured from Hank's view. The wind must have been weary—it never so much as sighed in the tops of the spruces.

"There ain't no sense in sittin' out a deer," Hank had been told early on, "if you can't sit still." That much he had learned. Any movement he made was slower than a Southern drawl. The carbine was cradled across his lap. Slush slid off a bough and stabbed coldly down his neck. Hurry up and wait.

A drizzle that came close to rain began falling and watercolored the woods a shade darker. It seemed that Hank watched the second-hand of his watch sweep the next half hour away. He had about convinced himself that he was wasting his time when he saw a flicker of movement. Near the tote road, the tip of a fir bough nodded. An instant later a dark-furred animal made a swift crossing and disappeared into the fir thicket. "Fisher," Hank observed.

"Probably squirrel hunting. He'll do a hell of a lot better than I will." Again he glanced at his watch. Again he slowly scanned the steamy surroundings.

When his eyeballs locked up, he felt it all the way down to his toes. Squarely in front of the pine stub stood a deer—wearing horns. Just like that. No sight. No sound. Just there. When it comes to quiet, they'd put a shadow to shame. In a situation like that, it takes a second or so to sort things out. From its coiled-tight posture, Hank knew this was no young buck blinded by doe scent, and there was no mistaking that the eight-pointer sensed his presence. Statue-still, and with a tautness almost tangible, hunter and hunted stared.

"If I make a wrong move," Hank thought, "his mainspring will unwind all at once." Directly the buck eased his nose forward, slowly lowered his head and turned it to one side—like a bird dog sifting scent. Hank's thumb cocked the hammer of the carbine. To him, the muffled click sounded like a rock being dropped through shell ice. Taking a step backward, the buck blew. "Please, God."

So slowly it was painful, Hank began lifting the carbine from his lap. To his left—thicker than smoke from a smudge—a bank of fog was following the brook. Like a curtain of white being drawn across a dimly lit stage, it drifted between them, obliterating the buck from Hank's view. Seizing the opportunity, he snapped the carbine to his shoulder, snugged his cheek onto the stock, and squinted through the drizzle-fuzzed sights. Long moments later, the birch leaned. "Right . . . about . . ." The pine stub squatted. Shocked, Hank lifted his head and stared into the dripping, dusky woods. No antlers. No ears. No rut-swollen neck. Not to be outdone, the woods-wise buck also had taken advantage of the well-timed "smoke screen."

Springing to his feet, Hank searched for movement. Not a sign. Hoping for a last-chance shot, he hurried down the slope and crossed the brook. Locating the buck's tracks, he followed them. The wary whitetail had exited through the same door he used for his entrance. In the woods, dusk means darkness. Disappointed as he was, Hank, with a steamy expulsion of breath, conceded, "Just as well. If I wounded him I wouldn't have had time to trail him, and it's a pretty good bet the coyotes would catch up with him during the night—just as well."

If you've never been in the woods on a wet November night, then you don't know the meaning of darkness. Hank's spirits were brightened, however, and his strides lengthened as he recalled the words of a now-departed deer hunter: "You'll soon forget the ones you drag out," his grandfather had said, "but the ones that outfox you will leave tracks on your mind."

2

"All-In" for Doves

by Lamar Underwood

The editor is back at his typewriter, this time revealing one of the most important aspects of his Georgia upbringing, one that has lasted long after he left Georgia.

My right hand—a frozen, ham-fisted thing—was jammed into the pocket of my bird-shooting vest. Vaguely, I felt the shapes of 20-gauge shells, but my fingers refused to close on a single load. With my thoughts screaming *Hurry! Here they come,* my eyes stayed locked on a cluster of birds just crossing the tree line that edged the field. Sharp and clear against a background of lowering clouds, the cluster was changing into the distinct hurtling shapes of mourning doves, riding a stiff northeast breeze that was tossing the tops of the pines.

I glanced down at the open barrels of my over-under. They were waiting to be fed. My hand closed around a wad of shell-shapes. My eyes were back on the birds as I let the wad of shells fall to the ground. The doves were headed my way—ten or more . . . many, many—a chance for a double. I forced myself to focus on picking up a single shell. I dropped it into the bottom barrel. A warning stabbed into my thoughts: *Go ahead, a single shot.* But the sight of so many birds forced my hand back down for another shell. I felt my palm grasp a shell and brought it toward my gun. It didn't feel right. I glanced down and saw I was trying to load a tube of Vicks ChapStick.

Wings whistling as they flared in easy range, the doves had a swept-wing, falcon-like look of speed and strength that instantly ruined my fantasy of getting a single bird, much less a double. I would have missed. No doubt about it. ChapStick in hand, one unused shell in the gun, I watched the gray speedsters vanish into the gloom.

That December afternoon I was crouched in a clump of weeds along-side a stubble field of cut soybeans. Shivering, with frozen hands, because I was dressed for the mild weather I had set out into at noon. Now, a surprise nor'easter was flexing its muscles over the normally benign southeast Georgia skies. My late-season dove hunt had become a mixture of exhilaration and frustration.

I say "hunt" with great deliberation. As experienced followers of the lure of shooting action and table fare created by split dove seasons will attest: There is a great deal of difference between dove "hunts" and dove "shoots."

The only hunting in big dove shoots comes in finding your stand.

To *hunt* doves, you, and perhaps a buddy, must scout out as many locations as you can gain access to. Feeding sites, watering holes, flight lanes—all the spots likely to hold doves during their daily jaunts between food, water, and sheltered nooks to loaf and dust. Migration habits come into your game plan. Sometimes it's not even a case of "here today, gone tomorrow." It's more like here this morning, gone this afternoon. Free-lance hunting for doves, working your available spots, picking up a bird here or a couple there, may lack the glamour and bags of deluxe shoots, but it forms a comfort zone in my hunting season I can't resist. This dove addict is in the game for keeps. Early season, late season . . . I check no bets. I keep pushing in all the chips I have.

Dove shoot fun begins in the shirt-sleeve weather of the September season opener. You meet a group of kindred spirits early in the after-noon—perhaps over barbecue—and take stands alongside fields legally planted to attract doves. The action begins with the occasional shout, "Over your head!", followed by the steady *pop, pop, pop* sounds of scatter-guns at work. On the best shoots, the *pop, pop, pop* grows into a war-like din, with guns going off everywhere around you amid the stirring sights of doves flying just about everywhere. This is how Nash Buckingham and other scribes of wingshooting's halcyon days shot doves. Such shoots still form the core of today's dove action. To get in on one, you have to know somebody. Or have a good buddy who knows somebody. Without that, your only option for the real-deal dove shoot, one like Mister Nash enjoyed, is a pay-for-play shoot costing somewhere around $250 for an afternoon. OK, you can't handle that either, and you still want to get in on an old-time shoot that begins with friends gathering over barbecue, then enjoying shooting so good your gun barrels get hot . . .

Sorry, but without connections or money, the only way you're going to be popping caps in shoots like the old-timers enjoyed is to be born again.

I'm in the same fix, but I don't let it break my dove-hunting stride. I'll grab an invitation to a big shoot whenever such luck comes my way. Meantime, I'm a freelance dove hunter, and I love every minute of it.

Seconds before my misadventure with numb fingers, I was swinging the long tubes of my 20-gauge into the high, sweeping arch of a single bird. This wasn't a true incomer, set to land, but a traveler with an express ticket. The high straight-overhead shot is my nemesis. I seldom get it right, even though I've been coached repeatedly: *Pull through and past the bird, blotting it out as you swing*. So shaky am I with this shot, that one September afternoon, swinging the gun directly overhead at a high and fast target toppled me backward off my Cool-Stool. This time, I didn't sprawl over backward, but my wood-like fingers slapped the trigger twice without the dove changing its wingbeat. The familiar rolls, dips, and jinks of escaping birds weren't necessary for this bird.

As I unbreeched the double, the image of that dove burned through my thoughts. This was one of those big, fully-fledged, powerful birds that make second-season dove hunting such an important part of the upland gunner's year. With winter wind gusts behind them, late-season doves will bring out the best, or worse, of any smoothbore shooter.

I had discovered this spot the day before while quail hunting on the far side of the sprawling bean field. With my pointer working close, hunting singles of a scattered covey, I caught sight of a half-dozen doves pitching into the far corner of the field.

Investigating, scattering the doves while pointer Mack cruised over the scent pools the birds had left, I was puzzled at first. Why had this little beanfield corner become a dove convention center? The combine had cut the beans so clean and close that (in the words of one of my Georgia uncles) "A chicken following along behind it would starve to death." Even sparrows could not be attracted to such billiard-table-clean fields. This one had pulled doves. There had to be a reason.

And there it was: A small area with curving white bands amid the chaff and bits of husk in the bean stalks. The combine had made sharp turns here, leaving streaks of spilled beans, a mother lode of feed to pull hungry December doves from the cold skies.

At noon today, I had felt like a kid at Christmas as I left my truck and headed across the field. When I was still 200 yards or so from the little corner, birds began leaping into flight, scattering over the trees.

By the time I hunkered in the weeds at the edge of the field, a low wedge of clouds loomed on the horizon and grew closer by the minute. Suddenly, the flannel shirt and shooting vest that were my Indian-summer outfit made me feel uncomfortable and stupid. I wished I could head back to the truck, pull on a jacket.

I was shivering and thinking about how good the truck's heater would feel when the birds started returning. I banged away at incomers that seemed panicked by the weather, desperate to get to food. The shots came so frequently that I barely noticed the temperature plunging, the wind rising. Deliriously happy that my dove hunt was successful, I experienced the kind of shooting that earns the dove the distinction of having more shots fired in its direction than any other game bird. My lack of dove-shooting prowess was relentlessly exposed.

Even before the cold numbed my hands, I had a quick succession of crossing shots. As the birds flared, seeing me, jinking and rolling as they bored over the cut beans, the tubes of my 20-gauge brought no feathery bursts from the sky, no slanting falls like I expected. My confidence dwindled, had me wondering: *What the hell was I doing wrong?*

A lone single came winging by, like it was trying to catch up with the pack. I doubled my lead, the tubes swinging in front of the hurtling shape. Double *whams*. The bird didn't even vary its wingbeats.

I never claimed to be a great shot, but something was way out of whack here. This wasn't just a shooting slump; it was a crisis. I pictured the barrel, the way it had been swinging, solidly ahead of the birds . . . and it came to me then, a moment of truth. It was the damned sustained lead. *Swing ahead of the target and keep swinging.* Sounds great, but the system breaks down when you don't *keep swinging!* My sustained lead wasn't being sustained. It was going limp as a noodle.

When the next chance came, seconds later, I was ready. Four birds were whistling past, just like the others, streamlined missiles built for speed. This time I got the barrel tracking *behind* one bird, then pulled it through and past the speedster, mentally reciting as I did, *Butt . . . belly . . . beak . . . bang!*

And there it was, painted against the gray turbulence of sky: a tight circle of feathers, yards above a folded bird plummeting into the stubble. My newfound prowess inspired a jolt of confidence. As I scored on more incomers, I was congratulating myself.

The miracle of my self-coaching stayed with me. When the cold deepened and the wind kept knifing into the pocket, the birds kept coming. Not in spectacular numbers, but in dribs and drabs sufficient to keep my eyes on the sky. There were crossing shots, overhead testers, and every obtuse angle you can imagine. By the time I was about to slide the ChapStick tube into my barrel, eight doves made my shooting vest puffy. Barely halfway to my limit, but a good day for me and my frozen fingers. I headed for my truck a happy man. My thoughts were alive with the English shooting tip that had somehow crossed the ocean to Georgia. The sustained lead couldn't be sustained. Pull to and through the bird, and when you pull the trigger the barrel will be moving with the speed it needs.

On that cold, wooden-fingered afternoon, the system wasn't foolproof. Neither were the birds' crossing angles best for *butt . . . belly . . . beak . . . bang.* I missed plenty, and the pocketful of empties I carried from the field was a stern reminder that I wasn't a crack dove shot. Never had been. Never would be. The difference between now and when I was younger is that now I didn't give a damn. Dove hunting/shooting is too important to me to be marred by some unnecessary label identifying my skill level.

I had definitely outgrown an old mantra that had its roots back when I was a teenager.

In my avid reading of outdoor magazines, I came across this: "Good dove shooters bag a limit of birds with a box of shells."

That sounded like a reasonable challenge, and when I first read the expression, it hit me like a gauntlet flung into my face. Was I really a good dove shot?

Until then, I had opened boxes of shells and dumped them into my pockets without counting. Suddenly, I felt compelled to count every hull I ejected. Was I a good dove shot, batting twelve for twenty-five, or better? Or did I belong among the mediocre mob? Or worse, among the embarrassing head-shakers and excuse-makers who burned a lot of ammo to take home their limits?

Certainly, there was nothing shameful about being a rank-and-file dove shooter. But there I was, in that awkward, pimply-faced, voice-breaking clutch of teen years, eager to make my mark. A limit of birds—twelve or fifteen, depending upon your state—with twenty-five shots. My shooting coaches had called the play. I had to run it.

That's when a new mental shooting block reared its ugly head. When shooting was good, and lots of birds flying, I became a cherry-picker. Without even realizing it, I started passing up the toughest shots—the high overhead screamers, the birds slanting past at extreme range. And I avoided taking a chance on the birds shooters all over the field seemed to have a crack at. The typical "survivor" bird set off a war-like eruption of *pop, pop, pop* as it turned on the after-burners, creating as much amusement as it did frustration as it got out of Dodge.

My cherry-picking, however, was short-lived. Dove shoots, with changes aplenty, were few and far between. In my freelance dove hunting, I had to take every chance I could get.

As a card-carrying dove hunter, I worked as hard to get shots as any upland hunter out for quail, pheasant, rabbits, or other favorites. In the countryside I had permission to roam; I was on the hunt for dove activity in the first sweaty days of September, then back for more in December's frozen fields. Finding the places doves were using in shootable numbers took me to watering holes with clean open banks (doves will not walk through brush to get to water); shady nooks with dead branches overhead where doves passed mid-day lulls; terrain breaks, the woodline passes between fields, slicing like freeway exits through timbered bottomlands; fields where anything from the dove's menu might be found, including favorites like soybeans, corn, wheat, sunflower seeds, and sorghum, to name some favorites; and, perhaps the greatest mother lode of them all, places where doves like to sit on telephone lines, with cover and fields nearby. These were the places that formed my treasure map that guided me throughout the seasons.

Even in its finest hours, freelance dove hunting cannot match the gun-blazing, action-packed excitement of dove shoots. Compared to the big shoots, my freelance dove hunting is a gentle, slow-paced affair, occasionally yielding a limit, sometimes five or six, sometimes none. Still, it's what I have, and I treasure its bounty even though I've been lucky enough to get in one big-shoot affair from time to time.

If you've never had a crack at a big shoot, you may not realize that a lot of what happens that afternoon will be out of your control. First, your host might designate a certain stand he wants you to take. Or perhaps other shooters, veterans on that ground, will suggest a spot. As you cast your dove-hunter's gaze over the terrain, certain spots may gleam like diamonds, but you'll probably end up where you're told to go, or someplace you manage to set up after the experienced shooters have raced off to grab their favorite spots.

If you haven't heard it before, you soon will: Dove-shoot stands are not created equal. At any shoot there are places doves cross repeatedly, as if drawn by magnets. I'm convinced that doves use certain landmarks like beacons, crossing and recrossing them in their daily travels between food, water, and rest. Sometimes these hotspots are created by a single tree, rising above the surrounding fields. Fence row junctions form another spot, where cropland boundaries meet. Doves, like gold, are where you find them. And, as Havilah Babcock pointed out about quail, "They can be in a lot of other places too."

If you end up swapping stands with a lucky shooter who has limited out, you won't be the first. Being a social gathering, at a dove shoot your smoothbore prowess, or lack of it, will be on full display. When the day ends with a picnic in the field, with doves simmering and cold beer flowing, you'll have plenty of company in describing hits and misses, and everything else that happened.

The Southern, barbecue, good-buddy afternoon shootfest is a tradition that holds us hard. When an interviewer told Nobel Prize winner William Faulkner, icon of Mississippi and Southern literature, that New Jersey had classified mourning doves as songbirds and closed down hunting, Faulkner, in a very disturbed voice, said, "My God, son! What do they do in September?"

The barbecue-and-doves frolics of September may have their roots in the South, but I have also enjoyed them in such diverse locations as Maryland, Pennsylvania, and Arizona. You don't have to have a Southern accent to pull together a group for a memorable afternoon of September action. You need the land and the doves.

While it's unlikely I'll ever turn down an invitation to a dove shoot, I remain a lifetime freelance dove hunter. The occasions when I can find doves on my own, hitting the spots I've scouted, form the core of my dove-hunting season.

I am pulled through the off-season months with thoughts as vivid as paintings:

A blurry-looking wad of birds headed my way . . . I hunker, watching . . . Yes, they're still coming . . . The wad becomes a clear, tight group . . . Six birds are streaking broadside over the stubble, the late-evening sun rosy on their breasts . . . A chance for a double . . . But no, the swing isn't fast enough . . . The first shot is a wild poke, causing jinks and twists with nothing falling . . . Then the second shot is like a parting salute.

I shake my head as I stuff the empty hulls into the growing pile. Even if I bag a limit today, it won't be with twenty-five shells.

All right, I'm not a very good dove shot. I take what I can get. I eat what I take. And the thing I want most is the chance to do it all over again.

3

That Twenty-Five-Pound Gobbler

by Archibald Rutledge

This editor has always looked upon the works of Archibald Rutledge (1883–1973) with great awe. His prose and poetry set in the South Carolina Lowcountry call out the life I spent as a youth in southeast Georgia. My days afield could not match the great Archibald Rutledge adventures from Hampton and the Santee River area, but I found much reading that bonded me with Mr. Rutledge. Poet laureate of South Carolina and author of so many stories and books too lengthy to mention in the limited space here, Rutledge was a man who led two lives. In one life he grew up on Hampton Plantation and returned there for lengthy Christmas vacations every year. His other life was as an English professor at Mercersburg Academy in Pennsylvania.

I SUPPOSE THAT THERE ARE OTHER THINGS WHICH MAKE A HUNTER uneasy, but of one thing I am very sure: that is to locate and to begin to stalk a deer or a turkey, only to find that another hunter is doing precisely the same thing at the same time. The feeling I had was worse than uneasy. It is, in fact, as inaccurate as if a man should say, after listening to a comrade swearing roundly, "Bill is expressing himself uneasily."

To be frank, I was jealous; and all the more so because I knew that Dade Saunders was just as good a turkey-hunter as I am—and maybe a good deal better. At any rate, both of us got after the same whopping gobbler. We knew this turkey and we knew each other; and I am positive that the wise old bird knew both of us far better than we knew him.

But we hunters have ways of improving our acquaintance with creatures that are over-wild and shy. Both Dade and I saw him, I suppose, a dozen times; and twice Dade shot at him. I had never fired at him, for I did not want to cripple, but to kill; and he never came within a hundred yards of me. Yet I felt that the gobbler ought to be mine; and for the simple reason that Dade Saunders was a shameless poacher and a hunter-out-of-season.

I have in mind the day when I came upon him in the pine-lands in mid-July, when he had in his wagon five bucks in the velvet, all killed that morning. Now, this isn't a fiction story; this is fact. And after I have told you of those bucks, I think you'll want me to beat Dade to the great American bird.

This wild turkey had the oddest range that you could imagine. You hear of turkeys ranging "original forests," "timbered wilds," and the like. Make up your mind that if wild turkeys have a chance they are going to come near civilization. The closer they are to man, the farther they are away from their other enemies. Near civilization they at least have (but for the likes of Dade Saunders) the protection of the law. But in the wilds what protection do they have from wildcats, from eagles, from weasels (I am thinking of young turkeys as well as old), and from all their other predatory persecutors?

Well, as I say, time and again I have known wild turkeys to come, and to seem to enjoy coming, close to houses. I have stood on the porch of my plantation home and have watched a wild flock feeding under the great live-oaks there. I have repeatedly flushed wild turkeys in an autumn cornfield. I have shot them in rice stubble.

Of course they do not come for sentiment. They are after grain. And if there is any better wild game than a rice-field wild turkey, stuffed with peanuts, circled with browned sweet potatoes, and fragrant with a rich gravy that plantation cooks know how to make, I'll follow you to it.

The gobbler I was after was a haunter of the edges of civilization. He didn't seem to like the wild woods. I think he got hungry there. But on the margins of fields that had been planted he could get all he wanted to eat of the things he most enjoyed. He particularly liked the edges of cultivated fields that bordered either on the pinewoods or else on the marshy rice-lands.

One day I spent three hours in the gaunt chimney of a burned rice-mill, watching this gobbler feeding on such edges. Although I was sure that sooner or later he would pass the mouth of the chimney, giving me a chance for a shot, he kept just that distance between us that makes a gun a vain thing in a man's hands. But though he did not give me my chance, he let me watch him all I pleased. This I did through certain dusty crevices between the bricks of the old chimney.

If I had been taking a post-graduate course in caution, this wise old bird would have been my teacher. Whatever he happened to be doing, his eyes and his ears were wide with vigilance. I saw him first standing beside a fallen pine log on the brow of a little hill where peanuts had been planted. I made the shelter of the chimney before he recognized me. But he must have seen the move I made.

I have hunted turkeys long enough to be thoroughly rid of the idea that a human being can make a motion that a wild turkey cannot see. One of my woodsman friends said to me, "Why, a gobbler can see any-thing. He can see a jaybird turn a somersault on the verge of the horizon." He was right.

Watching from my cover I saw this gobbler scratching for peanuts. He was very deliberate about this. Often he would draw back one huge handful (or footful) of viney soil, only to leave it there while he looked and listened. I have seen a turkey do the same thing while scratching in leaves. Now, a buck while feeding will alternately keep his head up and down; but a turkey gobbler keeps his down very little. That bright black eye of his, set in that sharp bluish head, is keeping its vision on every object on the landscape.

My gobbler (I called him mine from the first time I saw him) found many peanuts, and he relished them. From that feast he walked over into a patch of autumn-dried crabgrass. The long pendulous heads of this grass, full of seeds, he stripped skillfully. When satisfied with this food, he dusted himself beside an old stump. It was interesting to watch this; and while he was doing it I wondered if it was not my chance to leave the chimney, make a detour, and come up behind the stump. But of course just as I decided to do this, he got up, shook a small cloud of dust from his feathers, stepped off into the open, and there began to preen himself.

A short while thereafter he went down to a marshy edge, there finding a warm sandy hole on the sunny side of a briar patch, where he continued his dusting and loafing. I believe that he knew the stump, which shut off his view of what was behind it, was no place to choose for a midday rest.

All this time I waited patiently; interested, to be sure, but I would have been vastly more so if the lordly old fellow had turned my way. This I expected him to do when he got tired of loafing. Instead, he deliberately walked into the tall ranks of the marsh, which extended riverward for half a mile. At that I hurried forward, hoping to flush him on the margin; but he had vanished for that day. But though he had escaped me, the sight of him had made me keen to follow him until he expressed a willingness to accompany me home.

Just as I was turning away from the marsh I heard a turkey call from the shelter of a big live-oak beside the old chimney. I knew that it was Dade Saunders, and that he was after my gobbler. I walked over to where he was making his box-call plead. He expressed no surprise on seeing me. We greeted each other as two hunters, who are not over-friendly, greet when they find themselves after the same game.

"I seen his tracks," said Dade. "I believe he limps in the one foot since I shot him last Sunday will be a week."

"He must be a big bird," I said; "you were lucky to have a shot."

Dade's eyes grew hungrily bright.

"He's the biggest in these woods, and I'll git him yet. You jest watch me."

"I suppose you will, Dade. You are the best turkey-hunter of these parts."

I hoped to make him overconfident; and praise is a great corrupter of mankind. It is not unlikely to make a hunter miss a shot. I remember that a friend of mine once said laughingly: "If a man tells me I am a good shot, I will miss my next chance, as sure as guns; but if he cusses me and tells me I'm not worth a darn, then watch me shoot!"

Dade and I parted for the time. I went off toward the marsh, whistling an old song. I wanted to have the gobbler put a little more distance between himself and the poacher. Besides, I felt that it was right of me to do this: for while I was on my own land, my visitor was trespassing. I hung around in the scrub–oak thickets for awhile; but no gun spoke out, I knew that the old gobbler's intelligence plus my whistling game had "foiled the relentless" Dade. It was a week later that the three of us met again.

Not far from the peanut field there is a plantation corner. Now, most plantation corners are graveyards; that is, cemeteries of the old days.

Such a place is a wilderness for sure. Here grow towering pines, mournful and moss-draped. Here are hollies, canopied with jasmine-vines; here are thickets of myrtle, sweet gum, and young pines. If a covey of quail goes into such a place, you might as well whistle your dog off and go after another lot of birds.

Here deer love to come in the summer, where they can hide from the heat and the gauze-winged flies. Here in the winter is a haunt for woodcock, a good range (for great live-oaks drop their sweet acorns) for wild turkeys, and a harbor for foxes. In those great pines and oaks turkeys love to roost. It was on the borders of just such a corner that I roosted the splendid gobbler.

It was a glowing December sunset. I had left the house an hour before to stroll the plantation roads, counting (as I always do) the number of deer and turkey tracks that had recently been made in the soft damp sand. Coming near the dense corner, I sat against the bole of a monster pine. I love to be a mere watcher in woodlands as well as a hunter.

About two hundred yards away there was a little sunny hill, grown to scrub-oaks. They stood sparsely; that enabled me to see well what I now saw. Into my vision, with the rays of the sinking sun gleaming softly on the bronze of his neck and shoulders, the great gobbler stepped with superb beauty. Though he deigned to scratch once or twice in the leaves, and peck indifferently at what he thus uncovered, I knew he was bent on roosting; for not only was it nearly his bedtime, but he seemed to be examining with critical judgment every tall tree in his neighborhood.

He remained in my sight ten minutes; then he stepped into a patch of gallberries. I sat where I was. I tried my best to be as silent and as motionless as the bodies lying in the ancient graves behind me. The big fellow kept me on the anxious bench for five minutes. Then he shot his great bulk into the air, beating his ponderous way into the huge pine that seemed to sentry that whole wild tract of woodland.

I marked him when he came to his limb. He sailed up to it and alighted with much scraping of bark with his No. 10 shoes. There was my gobbler poised against the warm red sky of that winter twilight. It was hard to take my sight from him; but I did so in order to get my bearings in relation to his position. His flight had brought him nearer to me than he had been on the ground. But he was still far out of gun-range.

There was no use for me to look into the graveyard, for a man cannot see a foot into such a place. I glanced down the dim pinewood road. A moving object along its edge attracted my attention. It skulked. It seemed to flit like a ghostly thing from pine to pine. But, though I was near a cemetery, I knew I was looking at no "haunt." It was Dade Saunders.

He had roosted the gobbler, and he was trying to get up to him. Moreover, he was at least fifty yards closer to him than I was. I felt like shouting to him to get off my land; but then a better thought came. I pulled out my turkey call.

The first note was good, as was intended. But after that there came some heart-stilling squeaks and shrills. In the dusk I noted two things; I saw Dade make a furious gesture, and at almost the same instant the old gobbler launched out from the pine, winging a lordly way far across the graveyard thicket. I walked down slowly and peeringly to meet Dade.

"Your call's broke," he announced.

"What makes you think so?" I asked.

"Sounds awful funny to me," he said; "more than likely it might scare a turkey. Seen him lately?" he asked.

"You are better at seeing that old bird than I am, Dade."

Thus, I put him off; and shortly thereafter we parted. He was sure that I had not seen the gobbler; and that suited me all right.

Then came the day of days. I was up at dawn, and when certain red lights between the stems of the pines announced daybreak, I was at the far southern end of the plantation, on a road on either side of which were good turkey woods. I just had a notion that my gobbler might be found there, as he had of late taken to roosting in a tupelo swamp near the river, and adjacent to these woodlands.

Where some lumbermen had cut away the big timber, sawing the huge short-leaf pines close to the ground, I took my stand (or my seat) on one of these big stumps. Before me was a tangle of undergrowth; but it was not very thick or high. It gave me the screen I wanted; but if my turkey came out through it, I could see to shoot.

It was just before sunrise that I began to call. It was a little early in the year (then the end of February) to lure a solitary gobbler by a call; but otherwise the chance looked good. And I am vain enough to say that my willow box was not broken that morning. Yet it was not I but two Cooper's hawks that got the old wily rascal excited.

They were circling high and crying shrilly over a certain stretch of deep woodland; and the gobbler, undoubtedly irritated by the sounds, or at least not to be outdone by two mere marauders on a domain which he felt to be his own, would gobble fiercely every time one of the hawks would cry. The hawks had their eye on a building site; wherefore their excited maneuvering and shrilling continued; and as long as they kept up their screaming, so long did the wild gobbler answer in rivalry or provoked superiority, until his wattles must have been fiery red and near to bursting.

I had an idea that the hawks were directing some of their crying at the turkey, in which case the performance was a genuine scolding match of the wilderness. And before it was over, several gray squirrels had added to the already raucous debate their impatient coughing barks. This business lasted nearly an hour, until the sun had begun to make the thickets "smoke off" their shining burden of morning dew.

I had let up on my calling for awhile; but when the hawks had at last been silenced by the distance, I began once more to plead. Had I had a gobbler-call, the now enraged turkey would have come to me as straight as a surveyor runs a line. But I did my best with the one I had. I had answered by one short gobble, then by silence.

I laid down my call on the stump and took up my gun. It was in such a position that I could shoot quickly without much further motion. It is a genuine feat to shoot a turkey on the ground after he has made you out. I felt that a great moment was coming.

But you know how hunter's luck sometimes turns. Just as I thought it was about time for him to be in the pine thicket ahead of me, when, indeed, I thought I had heard his heavy but cautious step, from across the road, where lay the companion tract of turkey-woods to the one I was in, came a delicately pleading call from a hen turkey. The thing was irresistible to the gobbler; but I knew it to be Dade Saunders. What should I do?

At such a time a man has to use all the headwork he has. And in hunting I had long since learned that that often means not to do a darn thing but to sit tight. All I did was to put my gun to my face. If the gobbler was going to Dade, he might pass me. I had started him coming; if Dade kept him going, he might run within hailing distance. Dade was farther back in the woods than I was. I waited.

No step was heard. No twig was snapped. But suddenly, fifty yards ahead of me, the great bird emerged from the thicket of pines. For an instant the sun gleamed on his royal plumage. My gun was on him, but the glint of the sun along the barrel dazzled me. I stayed my finger on the trigger. At that instant he made me out. What he did was smart. He made himself so small that I believed it to be a second turkey. Then he ran crouching through the vines and huckleberry bushes.

Four times I thought I had my gun on him, but his dodging was that of an expert. He was getting away; moreover, he was making straight for Dade. There was a small gap in the bushes sixty yards from me, off to my left. He had not yet crossed that. I threw my gun in the opening. In a moment he flashed into it, running like a racehorse. I let him have it. And I saw him go down.

Five minutes later, when I had hung him on a scrub-oak, and was admiring the entire beauty of him, a knowing, cat-like step sounded behind me.

"Well, sir," said Dade, a generous admiration for the beauty of the great bird overcoming other less kindly emotions, "so you beat me to him."

There was nothing for me to do but to agree. I then asked Dade to walk home with me so that we might weigh him. He carried the scales well down at the 25-pound mark. An extraordinary feature of his manly equipment was the presence of three separate beards, one beneath the other, no two connected. And his spurs were respectable rapiers.

"Dade," I said, "what am I going to do with this gobbler? I am alone here on the plantation."

The pineland poacher did not solve my problem for me.

"I tell you," said I, trying to forget the matter of the five velveted bucks, "some of the boys from down the river are going to come up on Sunday to see how he tastes. Will you join us?"

You know Dade Saunders' answer; for when a hunter refuses an invitation to help eat a wild turkey, he can be sold to a circus.

4

On Seeing Whitetails

by Stewart Edward White

In this excerpt from his book The Mountains, *Stewart Edward White (1873–1946) shows us the prose skills that produced thirty-nine books, fiction and nonfiction, on outdoor adventures and travel. He was both prolific and popular during his time, turning many of his real episodes of outdoor life into nonfiction accounts of what actually happened.*

ONCE I HAPPENED TO BE SITTING OUT A DANCE WITH A TACTFUL YOUNG girl of tender disposition who thought she should adapt her conversation to the one with whom she happened to be talking. Therefore she asked questions concerning out-of-doors. She knew nothing whatever about it, but she gave a very good imitation of one interested. For some occult reason people never seem to expect me to own evening clothes, or to know how to dance, or to be able to talk about anything civilized; in fact, most of them appear disappointed that I do not pull off a war-jig in the middle of the drawing-room.

This young girl selected deer as her topic. She mentioned liquid eyes, beautiful form, slender ears; she said "cute," and "darlings," and "perfect dears." Then she shuddered prettily.

"And I don't see how you can ever BEAR to shoot them, Mr. White," she concluded.

"You quarter the onions and slice them very thin," said I dreamily. "Then you take a little bacon fat you had left over from the flap-jacks and put it in the frying-pan. The frying-pan should be very hot. While the onions are frying, you must keep turning them over with a fork. It's rather difficult to get them all browned without burning some. I should broil the meat. A broiler is handy, but two willows, peeled and charred a little so the willow taste won't penetrate the meat, will do. Have the steak fairly thick. Pepper and salt it thoroughly. Sear it well at first in order to keep the juices in; then cook rather slowly. When it is done, put it on a hot plate and pour the browned onions, bacon fat and all, over it."

"What ARE you talking about?" she interrupted.

"I'm telling you why I can bear to shoot deer," said I.

"But I don't see—" said she.

"Don't you?" said I. "Well; suppose you've been climbing a mountain late in the afternoon when the sun is on the other side of it. It is a mountain of big boulders, loose little stones, thorny bushes. The slightest misstep would send pebbles rattling, brush rustling; but you have gone all the way without making that misstep. This is quite a feat. It means that you've known all about every footstep you've taken. That would be business enough for most people, wouldn't it? But in addition you've managed to see EVERYTHING on that side of the mountain—especially patches of brown. You've seen lots of patches of brown, and you've examined each one of them. Besides that, you've heard lots of little rustlings, and you've identified each one of them. To do all these things well keys your nerves to a high tension, doesn't it? And then near the top you look up from your last noiseless step to see in the brush a very dim patch of brown. If you hadn't been looking so hard, you surely wouldn't have made it out. Perhaps, if you're not humble-minded, you may reflect that most people wouldn't have seen it at all. You whistle once sharply. The patch of brown defines itself. Your heart gives one big jump. You know that you have but the briefest moment, the tiniest fraction of time, to hold the white bead of your rifle motionless and to press the trigger. It has to be done VERY steadily, at that distance,—and you out of breath, with your nerves keyed high in the tension of such caution."

"NOW what are you talking about?" she broke in helplessly.

"Oh, didn't I mention it?" I asked, surprised. "I was telling you why I could bear to shoot deer."

"Yes, but—" she began.

"Of course not," I reassured her. "After all, it's very simple. The reason I can bear to kill deer is because, to kill deer, you must accomplish a skillful elimination of the obvious."

My young lady was evidently afraid of being considered stupid; and also convinced of her inability to understand what I was driving at. So she temporized in the manner of society.

"I see," she said, with an air of complete enlightenment.

Now of course she did not see. Nobody could see the force of that last remark without the grace of further explanation, and yet in the elimination of the obvious rests the whole secret of seeing deer in the woods.

In traveling the trail you will notice two things: that a tenderfoot will habitually contemplate the horn of his saddle or the trail a few yards ahead of his horse's nose, with occasionally a look about at the landscape; and the old-timer will be constantly searching the prospect with keen understanding eyes. Now in the occasional glances the tenderfoot takes, his perceptions have room for just so many impressions. When the number is filled out he sees nothing more. Naturally the obvious features of the landscape supply the basis for these impressions. He sees the configuration of the mountains, the nature of their covering, the course of their ravines, first of all. Then if he looks more closely, there catches his eye an odd-shaped rock, a burned black stub, a flowering bush, or some such matter. Anything less striking in its appeal to the attention actually has not room for its recognition. In other words, supposing that a man has the natural ability to receive x visual impressions, the tenderfoot fills out his full capacity with the striking features of his surroundings. To be able to see anything more obscure in form or color, he must naturally put aside from his attention some one or another of these obvious features. He can, for example, look for a particular kind of flower on a side hill only by refusing to see other kinds.

If this is plain, then, go one step further in the logic of that reasoning. Put yourself in the mental attitude of a man looking for deer. His eye sweeps rapidly over a side hill; so rapidly that you cannot understand how he can have gathered the main features of that hill, let alone concentrate and refine his attention to the seeing of an animal under a bush. As a matter of fact he pays no attention to the main features. He has trained his eye, not so much to see things, as to leave things out. The odd-shaped rock, the charred stub, the bright flowering bush do not exist for him. His eye passes over them as unseeing as yours over the patch of brown or gray that represents his quarry. His attention stops on the unusual, just as does yours; only in his case the unusual is not the obvious. He has succeeded by long training in eliminating that. Therefore he sees deer where you do not. As soon as you can forget the naturally obvious and construct an artificially obvious, then you too will see deer.

These animals are strangely invisible to the untrained eye even when they are standing "in plain sight." You can look straight at them, and not see them at all. Then some old woodsman lets you sight over his finger exactly to the spot. At once the figure of the deer fairly leaps into vision. I know of no more perfect example of the instantaneous than this. You are filled with astonishment that you could for a moment have avoided seeing it. And yet next time you will in all probability repeat just this "puzzle picture" experience.

The Tenderfoot tried for six weeks before he caught sight of one. He wanted to very much. Time and again one or the other of us would hiss back, "See the deer! over there by the yellow bush!" but before he could bring the deliberation of his scrutiny to the point of identification, the deer would be gone. Once a fawn jumped fairly within ten feet of the pack-horses and went bounding away through the bushes, and that fawn he could not help seeing. We tried conscientiously enough to get him a shot; but the Tenderfoot was unable to move through the brush less majestically than a Pullman car, so we had ended by becoming apathetic on the subject.

Finally, while descending a very abrupt mountain-side I made out a buck lying down perhaps three hundred feet directly below us. The buck was not looking our way, so I had time to call the Tenderfoot. He came. With difficulty and by using my rifle-barrel as a pointer I managed to show him the animal. Immediately he began to pant as though at the finish of a mile race, and his rifle, when he leveled it, covered a good half acre of ground. This would never do.

"Hold on!" I interrupted sharply.

He lowered his weapon to stare at me wild-eyed.

"What is it?" he gasped.

"Stop a minute!" I commanded. "Now take three deep breaths."
He did so.

"Now shoot," I advised, "and aim at his knees."

The deer was now on his feet and facing us, so the Tenderfoot had the entire length of the animal to allow for lineal variation. He fired. The deer dropped. The Tenderfoot thrust his hat over one eye, rested hand on hip in a manner cocky to behold.

"Simply slaughter!" he proffered with lofty scorn.

We descended. The bullet had broken the deer's back—about six inches from the tail. The Tenderfoot had overshot by at least three feet.

You will see many deer thus from the trail—in fact, we kept up our meat supply from the saddle, as one might say—but to enjoy the finer savor of seeing deer, you should start out definitely with that object in view. Thus you have opportunity for the display of a certain finer wood-craft. You must know where the objects of your search are likely to be found, and that depends on the time of year, the time of days their age, their sex, a hundred little things. When the bucks carry antlers in the velvet, they frequent the inaccessibilities of the highest rocky peaks, so their tender horns may not be torn in the brush, but nevertheless so that the advantage of a lofty viewpoint may compensate for the loss of cover. Later you will find them in the open slopes of a lower altitude, fully exposed to the sun, that there the heat may harden the antlers. Later still, the heads in fine condition and tough to withstand scratches, they plunge into the dense thickets. But in the mean time the fertile does have sought a lower country with patches of small brush interspersed with open passages. There they can feed with their fawns, completely concealed, but able, by merely raising the head, to survey the entire landscape for the threatening of danger. The barren does, on the other hand, you will find through the timber and brush, for they are careless of all responsibilities either to offspring or headgear. These are but a few of the considerations you will take into account, a very few of the many which lend the deer countries strange thrills of delight over new knowledge gained, over crafty expedients invented or well utilized, over the satisfactory matching of your reason, your instinct, your subtlety and skill against the reason, instinct, subtlety, and skill of one of the wariest of large wild animals.

Perversely enough the times when you did NOT see deer are more apt to remain vivid in your memory than the times when you did. I can still see distinctly sundry wide jump-marks where the animal I was tracking had evidently caught sight of me and lit out before I came up to him. Equally, sundry little thin disappearing clouds of dust; cracklings of brush, growing ever more distant; the tops of bushes waving to the steady passage of something remaining persistently concealed,—these are the chief ingredients often repeated which make up deer-stalking memory. When I think of seeing deer, these things automatically rise.

A few of the deer actually seen do, however, stand out clearly from the many. When I was a very small boy possessed of a 32-20 rifle and large ambitions, I followed the advantage my father's footsteps made me in the deep snow of an unused logging-road. His attention was focused on some very interesting fresh tracks. I, being a small boy, cared not at all for tracks, and so saw a big doe emerge from the bushes not ten yards away, lope leisurely across the road, and disappear, wagging earnestly her tail. When I had recovered my breath I vehemently demanded the sense of fooling with tracks when there were real live deer to be had. My father examined me.

"Well, why didn't you shoot her?" he inquired dryly.

I hadn't thought of that.

In the spring of 1900 I was at the head of the Piant River waiting for the log-drive to start. One morning, happening to walk over a slashing of many years before in which had grown a strong thicket of white popples, I jumped a band of nine deer. I shall never forget the bewildering impression made by the glancing, dodging, bouncing white of those nine snowy tails and rumps.

But most wonderful of all was a great buck, of I should be afraid to say how many points, that stood silhouetted on the extreme end of a ridge high above our camp. The time was just after twilight, and as we watched, the sky lightened behind him in prophecy of the moon.

5

"Yonder They Are!"

by Lamar Underwood

The first article I ever sold to a magazine was about quail hunting in my native Georgia. Hugh Grey, editor of Field & Stream, *liked it so much he assigned a photographer to meet me in Georgia and improve my rather weak selection of photographs to accompany the story. Dade Thornton took the photos, and the article appeared in* Field & Stream *in the September 1959 edition. Today, I still find myself with an urge to write about quail hunting. "'Yonder They Are!'" is my latest.*

THERE ARE WORDS THAT STRIKE A QUAIL HUNTER'S EARS LIKE CLAPS OF thunder, promising the end of a parching drought.

"Duke's acting birdy . . . Lots of scent . . . They've been here . . . Careful now."

The heartbeat leaps, pulling nerve ends taunt. Legs that were feeling tired become sprightly with new bursts of energy. The hands on the double gun caress the familiar shapes of walnut and steel with anticipation.

Then comes the cry: "Point!"

When that single word rings out in bobwhite quail country, in pinelands or tawny sedge patches or brush-tangled field edges, the stage is set for the bird hunter's ultimate reward. The pointer or setter is locked in a trance-like staunch pose. As he steps ahead of the dog, the hunter walks like he's afraid he's about to step on a land mine. He trembles when one boot snags on a briar, then breaks free. The other boot crunches on dry weeds, a sound too loud. His grip on the gun tightens. There's a wobbly feeling in his knees.

This is it!

This is the reason why he owns a bird dog; or why he dreamed of this hunt over countless hours of planning and research and bleary-eyed surfing on the internet; or even why he bought an airline ticket.

"Live in the moment." Where had he first heard that? he wonders as he creeps ahead. Anyway, it was true. He knew that. And the moment is now!

The explosion that follows is a feathery eruption of brownish hurtling bodies, startling fast as they vault toward the stubby black-jack oaks at the edge of the field. As the gun comes to his shoulder, the hunter sees the birds are already among the oaks, twisting into narrow corridors. He pokes the barrel toward one image. No time to aim, swing the gun. Just stab at it. *Wham!* He sees bark and twigs scattering. The oaks are swallowing the birds. There's a final fleeting image. Another stab. *Wham!* Suddenly the oaks are empty; the double gun is empty; the dog is scouring the grass for dead birds in vain.

Not every scenario that begins with the shout "Point!" turns out as described here. For openers, the birds might run ahead of the dog's initial point. (That's exactly the reason savvy hunters do not take off their safety until birds are in the air. They might trip or stumble as they move ahead of the dog for running birds.) The "Point!" may not be for a covey at all, but a single bird, hunted after a covey has been scattered. The covey rise itself may vary in intensity, depending on the size of the covey and whether or not these are wild birds or pen-raised for preserve hunting. Once you have put up a covey of wild birds, you'll never again wonder if there's a difference between wild and pen-raised.

For this aging tramper of stubble and tangles, the issue—wild or pen-raised—isn't worth worrying about. My boots are laced; my briar-guarded trousers are cut a little short at the ankles to clear the weeds. My 20-guage side-by-side is an old friend, and the game pocket of my shooting vest still has feathers from the day of my last hunt. I'm going quail hunting. I'll hunt where I can, when I can, with the vision of staunch and gallant dogs and whirring wings leading me on like a kid at Christmas.

The boy who first hunted bobwhite quail in Georgia pinelands in the late 1940s is still very much alive inside me, calling for me to find another covey, to experience yet again the classic upland scene that is bobwhite quail hunting.

I use the word "Point!" with a touch of hesitation. For while "Point!" resounded from the magazine and book pages of my youth—and still does today—the elders who took this lad quail hunting used a simpler and more colorful expression to announce that Mack, or Lily, or Queen had locked up on birds. The exalted cry that rang through the crisp air was, "Yonder they are!" For me, there is pure magic in that phrase. So much so that I still use it today. Even though the years have carried me far from my Southern accent, the heritage is still there. And when we're in the field together, on a preserve or one of those elusive and almost-rare wild-bird hunts, you'll be happier than a pig in slop when you hear my voice ring out, "Yonder they are!"

If our dog can remain a statue, as expected and trained, and if the birds hold tight as quail-hunting literature and legend suggest, our "Yonder" is about to turn into a rush of excitement few bird-hunting episodes can equal. The good covey rise is indeed quail hunting's moment of truth, an event conjured in dreams, relived in the paintings of talented artists, and sought by folks like us who appreciate dog work and a game bird with the qualities of bobwhite quail. When things are right, they come in coveys; they offer single-bird shots that are like flushing small ruffed grouse in tight cover; and they're so good on the table that they inspire culinary artistry in enough ways to fill a cookbook.

The two equally challenging acts of traditional bobwhite hunting—covey rises then prying loose single birds—have lost some of their distinct differences in today's released-bird shooting. In preserve opportunities at their lovingly managed best, covey rises come in spurts of six or eight birds at best. Of course, there are exceptions. In a superb moment you might see a dozen birds bouncing from the sedge grass.

The sudden vision of multiple targets over your gun barrels is so unusual that it's startling. The confidence and cool reflexes of a crack shot are lost in a heartbeat. *Pick a bird! Stay with it!* The commands whip through your thoughts, but the sight of so many birds in the air at once is overwhelming, your dream come alive. Breaking that vision down to one bird, staying with it, is hard to do. Without you even realizing it, your head is lifting slightly as you peer down the gun barrel in elation. Your timing is shattered. Your gun is slow—glacier-slow it seems—obeying the commands your reflexes dictate.

Three seconds! That's all you have. *Mississippi One . . . Mississippi Two . . .* By *Mississippi Three* your smooth swing has degenerated into a panicked throw shot—a stab, a poke, a desperate jab at a disappearing brownish blur.

For sure, covey rises take some getting used to. For openers, take the fact that most of the great quail paintings you've admired over the years show the covey leaping from almost right under the dogs' noses. Sometimes they do. But often they can be fifteen or even twenty yards in front of the point. Wild birds particularly. You're behind from the git-go with the need of speed.

Perhaps the "covey" you're expecting turns out to be four or five birds. A paltry bunch if you were expecting an honest-to-God covey. Good dog work and shooting action, yes. But not the covey rise of twelve or fifteen birds of quail hunting's halcyon days. Back then, coveys of five or six birds were left for seed; the singles were not pursued. Now the average shooting preserve party tries to hunt down every escaping single, like they're dollar bills getting away. Which, of course, they are.

Thinking about what used to be isn't good for the quail hunter's morale. Better instead to loosen up and do yourself the favor of enjoying whatever turns you on in the great outdoors. If the fish aren't hitting top-water—a passion for all anglers—you'll go deep. Lures, baits, rigs—whatever the hell will make fish strike. If a K-Mart is standing where your grand-dad once kept his hunting coat puffy with Bobs, you'll press on to find new grounds to rekindle the flame.

Of course quail hunting was better when Nash Buckingham was tramping behind his setters and pointers. Truth is, not many people who lived back then were able to get in on the fun. Except for a few lucky farmers, tending the fields, quail hunting has never come easy. The inspirations that drive us to the sport—the dog work, the game bird itself, the pastoral surroundings where quail are found—these visions must be nourished with effort and money. What we seek is irresistible. It can't be replaced by golf or football games or even fishing. We can enjoy those things if we like them, but the love of following pointing dogs in treks toward whirring wings is a force like no other.

We yield, we respond, doing whatever it takes to keep alive a certain part of our guarded world of dreams and memories we refuse to allow to wither away. If you are a bird hunter to the core, no matter what you have loved and lost over the years, that part of you never dies.

So we're out there, tramping again. As noted bobwhite storyteller Havilah Babcock so wisely wrote, "Birds, like gold, are where you find them. They can be a lot of other places too."

Sometimes those "other places" seem beyond the radar noses of our canine companions. Whether working in "Hunt Close" sweeps, or bending out to promising horizons, they simply can't find the birds. Indeed, boots are made for walking, and ours get in some overtime while doubt creeps into our minds about the ground we're hunting, the vagaries of scenting conditions, and the mysterious movements of bobwhite coveys. At such times it pays to be persistent, but also patient.

Aboard in the uplands (is there anywhere else you'd rather be?), enjoying the good dog work, no matter how fruitless, we become part of a setting where things might happen that we will remember the rest of our lives. The air has the tawny sharpness we missed all summer; the sun is warm on our bird vests; winter visitors like mallards flash past, and we hear the jabbering of familiar crows. Sometimes we look over the treetops ahead and see a hawk floating in circles, a sight that immediately triggers the frightening notion that the winged hunter has found and spooked our birds.

Finding the mother lodes of birds on land we can hunt rests on a game plan with two critical elements: the choke-bore noses of pointing dogs and our tactics in using them.

Bird dogs are not created equal. Some seem to have an uncanny ability. Their noses are radar-sharp. They work the terrain with careful, methodical sweeps, bending back or off to the sides to check out birdy-looking copses. They do not plunge into tangles of briars and field-edge bushes; nor do they ignore them. They circle such thick spots, probing all sides for precious scent.

It is more likely on my hunts that such a dog was trained—"broke" to use that terrible word—on a farm or in a suburban backyard where a copy of the late Dick Wolter's mellow *Gun Dog* book was on hand, than on the prairies of Saskatchewan or Alberta frequented by professional trainers. Big-going field trial dogs, trained by pros and destined to hunt leased land and plantations, get in many weeks of work with sharp-tail grouse long before open quail season dawns in places like in Texas or Georgia.

While there is something undeniably exciting about the vision of a pointer or setter slamming into a wall of scent at full gallop, such events are often a speck on the horizon, a jeep or horseback ride away. Our "Gun Dog" pointer or setter, plodding along, will be working where our legs can take us, within sensible range. We won't be walking past many coveys without contacting them. We hope.

Sometimes, even with the best dogs money can buy or we can train, we bobwhite hunters are up against a stacked deck. Take a morning when you open the dog box over iron-hard ground with a stinging wind out of the northeast. Scenting conditions will be somewhere between nil and none. Rain is another deal-breaker. Although a little moisture is good for scent, days when the world around you is like one vast soaked sponge will not be fun. Preserve shooting can be ridiculous in the rain, with the birds mobbing up in briar-choked nooks the dogs can't reach. When you do get these soaked fugitives up, their flight may be nothing more than a short hop, dangerously close to the dogs' noses. I'll take a pass on preserve birds in the rain, unless I'm gunning where the operator's birds are proven fliers, in all weathers.

Successful quail hunters have a mental map marking the home ranges of every covey. My own *Treasure Island* sketches of bobwhite heaven focus on Bob's predictable schedule: feeding somewhere in the morning; loafing, dusting, catching insects in some secluded spot in midday; feeding in the late afternoon; then roosting in some weedy field with no trees overhead.

A gleaner from the moment they are born, bobwhites possess tough gizzards and ample crops to enable them to snatch whatever tidbits they can find from the ground under their feet. Special treats like golden corn kernels and soybean and wheat seeds are backed up by a multitude of seed-bearing wild plants. Acorns are shattered and consumed eagerly. Bugs that fail to scamper from Bob's path are quickly pecked. The food chain in all seasons stretches through a landscape of brushy edges alongside crop fields, pinelands with broom sedge and gallberry patches, meadows and old fields lush with weeds. Swampy wall-like tangles where enemy predators thrive may be nearby, but where they choke out the open country, they doom Bob's chances.

Over most of the bird's natural range, wild bobwhite populations are devastated by crop fields cut clean as billiard tables and bordered by dense walls of brush and briars, heaven for predators. So clean do today's combines leave fields like corn and soybeans, "A chicken following behind one would starve to death," as one of my Georgia uncles puts it. Even the most efficient combines spill some grain—particularly where they make sharp turns—and Bobs risk a few moments of exposure in the fields for these treats. They fly—not walk as in bobwhite literature!—into the field from nearby cover, feed quickly (the big yellow corn kernels are their favorite), then fly back to safety. Of course, they are spooky as hawks out in the open,

In good quail country the croplands are bordered by the reaches of open pinelands with broom sedge, old fields of ragweed—cover a dog can hunt through. To make the picture perfect, add in patches of sunflowers, millet, or lespedeza. These Valhallas are maintained on plantations, shooting preserves, and private farms where the owners care about bobwhite coveys.

Perhaps it is on such a place that good luck smiles on us. Up ahead, pointer Mack's ground-eating strides have broken into a stalking, tiptoeing creep. Then he stops altogether, right at the field's edge, a figure as locked and solid as granite.

My heart surges. Hands tighten on the smoothbore. Then, from the Southern boy that will always live inside me, my call rings out, "Yonder they are!"

6

An Elk Hunt at Two-Ocean Pass

by Theodore Roosevelt

In his love of the strenuous, outdoor life as a hunter and naturalist, the twenty-sixth president of the United States was a man unlike any other at his level of influence and authority. And the man could write—and did! This old world is not likely to ever see another Theodore Roosevelt. Of Roosevelt's many volumes of hunting and exploration, my personal favorite is Ranch Life and the Hunting Trail. *Roosevelt based the book on his experiences after he moved to the West for three years to live the life of an ordinary rancher following the death of his young wife and his mother within twelve hours of each other in 1884. Roosevelt's ranch was in the Dakota Territory on the Little Missouri River. From there, he ranged far and wide in his hunting adventures. Despite his political achievements and his courage in battle, as exemplified by San Juan Hill, I'll always hold in my head an image of this remarkable man sitting by the campfire, the light playing off those thick eyeglasses, as he relives the day's experiences with his cowboy companions.*

In September, 1891, with my ranch-partner, Ferguson, I made an elk-hunt in northwestern Wyoming among the Shoshone Mountains, where they join the Hoodoo and Absoraka ranges. There is no more beautiful game-country in the United States. It is a park land, where glades, meadows, and high mountain pastures break the evergreen forest; a forest which is open compared to the tangled density of the woodland farther north. It is a high, cold region of many lakes and clear rushing streams. The steep mountains are generally of the rounded form so often seen in the ranges of the Cordilleras of the United States; but the Hoodoos, or Goblins, are carved in fantastic and extraordinary shapes; while the Tetons, a group of isolated rock-peaks, show a striking boldness in their lofty outlines.

This was one of the pleasantest hunts I ever made. As always in the mountains, save where the country is so rough and so densely wooded that one must go a-foot, we had a pack-train; and we took a more complete outfit than we had ever before taken on such a hunt, and so travelled in much comfort. Usually when in the mountains I have merely had one companion, or at most a couple, and two or three pack-ponies; each of us doing his share of the packing, cooking, fetching water, and pitching the small square of canvas which served as tent. In itself packing is both an art and a mystery, and a skilful professional packer, versed in the intricacies of the "diamond hitch," packs with a speed which no non-professional can hope to rival, and fixes the side packs and top packs with such scientific nicety, and adjusts the doubles and turns of the lash-rope so accurately, that everything stays in place under any but the most adverse conditions. Of course, like most hunters, I can myself in case of need throw the diamond hitch after a fashion, and pack on either the off or near side. Indeed, unless a man can pack it is not possible to make a really hard hunt in the mountains, if alone, or with only a single companion. The mere fair-weather hunter, who trusts entirely to the exertions of others, and does nothing more than ride or walk about under favorable circumstances, and shoot at what somebody else shows him, is a hunter in name only. Whoever would really deserve the title must be able at a pinch to shift for himself, to grapple with the difficulties and hardships of wilderness life unaided, and not only to hunt, but at times to travel for days, whether on foot or on horseback, alone. However, after one has passed one's novitiate, it is pleasant to be comfortable when the comfort does not interfere with the sport; and although a man sometimes likes to hunt alone, yet often it is well to be with some old mountain hunter, a master of woodcraft, who is a first-rate hand at finding game, creeping upon it, and tracking it when wounded. With such a companion one gets much more game, and learns many things by observation instead of by painful experience.

On this trip we had with us two hunters, Tazewell Woody and Elwood Hofer, a packer who acted as cook, and a boy to herd the horses. Of the latter, there were twenty; six saddle-animals and fourteen for the packs—two or three being spare horses, to be used later in carrying the elk-antlers, sheep-horns, and other trophies. Like most hunters' pack-animals, they were either half broken, or else broken down; tough, unkempt; jaded-looking beasts of every color—sorrel, buckskin, pinto, white, bay, roan. After the day's work was over, they were turned loose to shift for themselves; and about once a week they strayed, and all hands had to spend the better part of the day hunting for them. The worst ones for straying, curiously enough, were three broken-down old "bear-baits," which went by themselves, as is generally the case with the cast-off horses of a herd. There were two sleeping-tents, another for the provisions,—in which we ate during bad weather,—and a canvas tepee, which was put up with lodge-poles, Indian fashion, like a wigwam. A tepee is more difficult to put up than an ordinary tent; but it is very convenient when there is rain or snow. A small fire kindled in the middle keeps it warm, the smoke escaping through the open top—that is, when it escapes at all; strings are passed from one pole to another, on which to hang wet clothes and shoes, and the beds are made around the edges. As an offset to the warmth and shelter, the smoke often renders it impossible even to sit upright. We had a very good camp-kit, including plenty of cooking- and eating-utensils; and among our provisions were some canned goods and sweetmeats, to give a relish to our meals of meat and bread. We had fur coats and warm clothes—which are chiefly needed at night—and plenty of bedding, including water-proof canvas sheeting and a couple of caribou-hide sleeping-bags, procured from the survivors of a party of arctic explorers. Except on rainy days I used my buckskin hunting-shirt or tunic; in dry weather I deem it, because of its color, texture, and durability, the best possible garb for the still-hunter, especially in the woods.

Starting a day's journey south of Heart Lake, we travelled and hunted on the eastern edge of the great basin, wooded and mountainous, wherein rise the head-waters of the mighty Snake River. There was not so much as a spotted line—that series of blazes made with the axe, man's first highway through the hoary forest,—but this we did not mind, as for most of the distance we followed well-worn elk-trails. The train travelled in Indian file. At the head, to pick the path, rode tall, silent old Woody, a true type of the fast-vanishing race of game hunters and Indian fighters, a man who had been one of the California forty-niners, and who ever since had lived the restless, reckless life of the wilderness. Then came Ferguson and myself; then the pack-animals, strung out in line; while from the rear rose the varied oaths of our three companions, whose miserable duty it was to urge forward the beasts of burden.

It is heart-breaking work to drive a pack-train through thick timber and over mountains, where there is either a dim trail or none. The animals have a perverse faculty for choosing the wrong turn at critical moments; and they are continually scraping under branches and squeezing between tree-trunks, to the jeopardy or destruction of their burdens. After having been laboriously driven up a very steep incline, at the cost of severe exertion both to them and to the men, the foolish creatures turn and run down to the bottom, so that all the work has to be done over again. Some travel too slow; others travel too fast. Yet one cannot but admire the toughness of the animals, and the surefootedness with which they pick their way along the sheer mountain sides, or among boulders and over fallen logs.

As our way was so rough, we found that we had to halt at least once every hour to fix the packs. Moreover, we at the head of the column were continually being appealed to for help by the unfortunates in the rear. First it would be "that white-eyed cayuse; one side of its pack's down!" then we would be notified that the saddle-blanket of the "lopeared Indian buckskin" had slipped back; then a shout "Look out for the pinto!" would be followed by that pleasing beast's appearance, bucking and squealing, smashing dead timber, and scattering its load to the four winds. It was no easy task to get the horses across some of the boggy places without miring; or to force them through the denser portions of the forest, where there was much down timber. Riding with a pack-train, day in and day out, becomes both monotonous and irritating, unless one is upheld by the hope of a game-country ahead, or by the delight of exploration of the unknown. Yet when buoyed by such a hope, there is pleasure in taking a train across so beautiful and wild a country as that which lay on the threshold of our hunting grounds in the Shoshones. We went over mountain passes, with ranges of scalped peaks on either hand; we skirted the edges of lovely lakes, and of streams with boulder-strewn beds; we plunged into depths of sombre woodland, broken by wet prairies. It was a picturesque sight to see the loaded pack-train stringing across one of these high mountain meadows, the motley colored line of ponies winding round the marshy spots through the bright green grass, while beyond rose the dark line of frowning forest, with lofty peaks towering in the background. Some of the meadows were beautiful with many flowers—goldenrod, purple aster, bluebells, white immortelles, and here and there masses of blood-red Indian pinks. In the park-country, on the edges of the evergreen forest, were groves of delicate quaking-aspen, the trees often growing to quite a height; their tremulous leaves were already changing to bright green and yellow, occasionally with a reddish blush. In the Rocky Mountains the aspens are almost the only deciduous trees, their foliage offering a pleasant relief to the eye after the monotony of the unending pine and spruce woods, which afford so striking a contrast to the hardwood forest east of the Mississippi.

For two days our journey was uneventful, save that we came on the camp of a man—one Beaver Dick, an old mountain hunter, living in a skin tepee. He had quite a herd of horses, many of them mares and colts; they had evidently been well treated, and came up to us fearlessly.

The morning of the third day of our journey was gray and lowering. Gusts of rain blew in my face as I rode at the head of the train. It still lacked an hour of noon, as we were plodding up a valley beside a rapid brook running through narrow willow-flats, the dark forest crowding down on either hand from the low foot-hills of the mountains. Suddenly the call of a bull elk came echoing down through the wet woodland on our right, beyond the brook, seemingly less than half a mile off; and was answered by a faint, far-off call from a rival on the mountain beyond. Instantly halting the train, Woody and I slipped off our horses, crossed the brook, and started to still-hunt the first bull.

In this place the forest was composed of the western tamarack; the large, tall trees stood well apart, and there was much down timber, but the ground was covered with deep wet moss, over which we trod silently. The elk was travelling up-wind, but slowly, stopping continually to paw the ground and thresh the bushes with his antlers. He was very noisy, challenging every minute or two, being doubtless much excited by the neighborhood of his rival on the mountain. We followed, Woody leading, guided by the incessant calling.

It was very exciting as we crept toward the great bull, and the challenge sounded nearer and nearer. While we were still at some distance the pealing notes were like those of a bugle, delivered in two bars, first rising, then abruptly falling; as we drew nearer they took on a harsh squealing sound. Each call made our veins thrill; it sounded like the cry of some huge beast of prey. At last we heard the roar of the challenge not eighty yards off. Stealing forward three or four yards, I saw the tips of the horns through a mass of dead timber and young growth, and I slipped to one side to get a clean shot. Seeing us, but not making out what we were, and full of fierce and insolent excitement, the wapiti bull stepped boldly toward us with a stately swinging gait. Then he stood motionless, facing us, barely fifty yards away, his handsome twelve-tined antlers tossed aloft, as he held his head with the lordly grace of his kind. I fired into his chest, and as he turned I raced forward and shot him in the flank; but the second bullet was not needed, for the first wound was mortal, and he fell before going fifty yards.

The dead elk lay among the young evergreens. The huge, shapely body was set on legs that were as strong as steel rods, and yet slender, clean, and smooth; they were in color a beautiful dark brown, contrasting well with the yellowish of the body. The neck and throat were garnished with a mane of long hair; the symmetry of the great horns set off the fine, delicate lines of the noble head. He had been wallowing, as elk are fond of doing, and the dried mud clung in patches to his flank; a stab in the haunch showed that he had been overcome in battle by some master bull who had turned him out of the herd.

We cut off the head, and bore it down to the train. The horses crowded together, snorting, with their ears pricked forward, as they smelt the blood. We also took the loins with us, as we were out of meat, though bull elk in the rutting season is not very good. The rain had changed to a steady downpour when we again got under way. Two or three miles farther we pitched camp, in a clump of pines on a hillock in the bottom of the valley, starting hot fires of pitchy stumps before the tents, to dry our wet things.

Next day opened with fog and cold rain. The drenched pack-animals, when driven into camp, stood mopingly, with drooping heads and arched backs; they groaned and grunted as the loads were placed on their backs and the cinches tightened, the packers bracing one foot against the pack to get a purchase as they hauled in on the lash-rope. A stormy morning is a trial to temper; the packs are wet and heavy, and the cold makes the work even more than usually hard on the hands. By ten we broke camp. It needs between two and three hours to break camp and get such a train properly packed; once started, our day's journey was six to eight hours, making no halt. We started up a steep, pine-clad mountain side, broken by cliffs. My hunting-shoes, though comfortable, were old and thin, and let the water through like a sieve. On the top of the first plateau, where black spruce groves were strewn across the grassy surface, we saw a band of elk, cows and calves, trotting off through the rain. Then we plunged down into a deep valley, and, crossing it, a hard climb took us to the top of a great bare table-land, bleak and wind-swept. We passed little alpine lakes, fringed with scattering dwarf evergreens. Snow lay in drifts on the north sides of the gullies; a cutting wind blew the icy rain in our faces. For two or three hours we travelled toward the farther edge of the table-land. In one place a spike bull elk stood half a mile off, in the open; he travelled to and fro, watching us.

As we neared the edge the storm lulled, and pale, watery sunshine gleamed through the rifts in the low-scudding clouds. At last our horses stood on the brink of a bold cliff. Deep down beneath our feet lay the wild and lonely valley of Two-Ocean Pass, walled in on either hand by rugged mountain chains, their flanks scarred and gashed by precipice and chasm. Beyond, in a wilderness of jagged and barren peaks, stretched the Shoshones. At the middle point of the pass, two streams welled down from either side. At first each flowed in but one bed, but soon divided into two; each of the twin branches then joined the like branch of the brook opposite, and swept one to the east and one to the west, on their long journey to the two great oceans. They ran as rapid brooks, through wet meadows and willow-flats, the eastern to the Yellowstone, the western to the Snake. The dark pine forests swept down from the flanks and lower ridges of the mountains to the edges of the marshy valley. Above them jutted gray rock peaks, snow-drifts lying in the rents that seamed their northern faces. Far below us, from a great basin at the foot of the cliff, filled with the pine forest, rose the musical challenge of a bull elk; and we saw a band of cows and calves looking like mice as they ran among the trees.

It was getting late, and after some search we failed to find any trail leading down; so at last we plunged over the brink at a venture. It was very rough scrambling, dropping from bench to bench, and in places it was not only difficult but dangerous for the loaded pack-animals. Here and there we were helped by well-beaten elk-trails, which we could follow for several hundred yards at a time. On one narrow pine-clad ledge, we met a spike bull face to face; and in scrambling down a very steep, bare, rock-strewn shoulder the loose stones started by the horses' hoofs, bounding in great leaps to the forest below, dislodged two cows.

As evening fell, we reached the bottom, and pitched camp in a beautiful point of open pine forest, thrust out into the meadow. There was good shelter, and plenty of wood, water, and grass; we built a huge fire and put up our tents, scattering them in likely places among the pines, which grew far apart and without undergrowth. We dried our steaming clothes, and ate a hearty supper of elk-meat; then we turned into our beds, warm and dry, and slept soundly under the canvas, while all night long the storm roared without. Next morning it still stormed fitfully; the high peaks and ridges round about were all capped with snow. Woody and I started on foot for an all-day tramp; the amount of game seen the day before showed that we were in a good elk-country, where the elk had been so little disturbed that they were travelling, feeding, and whistling in daylight. For three hours we walked across the forest-clad spurs of the foot-hills. We roused a small band of elk in thick timber; but they rushed off before we saw them, with much smashing of dead branches. Then we climbed to the summit of the range. The wind was light and baffling; it blew from all points, veering every few minutes. There were occasional rain-squalls; our feet and legs were well soaked; and we became chilled through whenever we sat down to listen. We caught a glimpse of a big bull feeding up-hill, and followed him; it needed smart running to overtake him, for an elk, even while feeding, has a ground-covering gait. Finally we got within a hundred and twenty-five yards, but in very thick timber, and all I could see plainly was the hip and the after-part of the flank. I waited for a chance at the shoulder, but the bull got my wind and was off before I could pull trigger. It was just one of those occasions when there are two courses to pursue, neither very good, and when one is apt to regret whichever decision is made.

At noon we came to the edge of a deep and wide gorge, and sat down shivering to await what might turn up, our fingers numb, and our wet feet icy. Suddenly the love-challenge of an elk came pealing across the gorge, through the fine, cold rain, from the heart of the forest opposite. An hour's stiff climb, down and up, brought us nearly to him; but the wind forced us to advance from below through a series of open glades. He was lying on a point of the cliff-shoulder, surrounded by his cows; and he saw us and made off. An hour afterward, as we were trudging up a steep hill-side dotted with groves of fir and spruce, a young bull of ten points, roused from his day-bed by our approach, galloped across us some sixty yards off. We were in need of better venison than can be furnished by an old rutting bull; so I instantly took a shot at the fat and tender young ten-pointer. I aimed well ahead and pulled trigger just as he came to a small gully; and he fell into it in a heap with a resounding crash. This was on the birthday of my eldest small son; so I took him home the horns, "for his very own." On the way back that afternoon I shot off the heads of two blue grouse, as they perched in the pines.

That evening the storm broke, and the weather became clear and very cold, so that the snow made the frosty mountains gleam like silver. The moon was full, and in the flood of light the wild scenery round our camp was very beautiful. As always where we camped for several days, we had fixed long tables and settles, and were most comfortable; and when we came in at nightfall, or sometimes long afterward, cold, tired, and hungry, it was sheer physical delight to get warm before the roaring fire of pitchy stumps, and then to feast ravenously on bread and beans, on stewed or roasted elk venison, on grouse and sometimes trout, and flapjacks with maple syrup.

Next morning dawned clear and cold, the sky a glorious blue. Woody and I started to hunt over the great table-land, and led our stout horses up the mountain-side, by elk-trails so bad that they had to climb like goats. All these elk-trails have one striking peculiarity. They lead through thick timber, but every now and then send off short, well-worn branches to some cliff-edge or jutting crag, commanding a view far and wide over the country beneath. Elk love to stand on these lookout points, and scan the valleys and mountains round about.

Blue grouse rose from beside our path; Clarke's crows flew past us, with a hollow, flapping sound, or lit in the pine-tops, calling and flirting their tails; the gray-clad whisky-jacks, with multitudinous cries, hopped and fluttered near us. Snow-shoe rabbits scuttled away, the big furry feet which give them their name already turning white. At last we came out on the great plateau, seamed with deep, narrow ravines. Reaches of pasture alternated with groves and open forests of varying size. Almost immediately we heard the bugle of a bull elk, and saw a big band of cows and calves on the other side of a valley. There were three bulls with them, one very large, and we tried to creep up on them; but the wind was baffling and spoiled our stalk. So we returned to our horses, mounted them, and rode a mile farther, toward a large open wood on a hill-side. When within two hundred yards we heard directly ahead the bugle of a bull, and pulled up short. In a moment I saw him walking through an open glade; he had not seen us. The slight breeze brought us down his scent. Elk have a strong characteristic smell; it is usually sweet, like that of a herd of Alderney cows; but in old bulls, while rutting, it is rank, pungent, and lasting. We stood motionless till the bull was out of sight, then stole to the wood, tied our horses, and trotted after him. He was travelling fast, occasionally calling; whereupon others in the neighborhood would answer. Evidently he had been driven out of some herd by the master bull.

He went faster than we did, and while we were vainly trying to overtake him we heard another very loud and sonorous challenge to our left. It came from a ridge-crest at the edge of the woods, among some scattered clumps of the northern nut-pine or pinyon—a queer conifer, growing very high on the mountains, its multiforked trunk and wide-spreading branches giving it the rounded top, and, at a distance, the general look of an oak rather than a pine. We at once walked toward the ridge, up-wind. In a minute or two, to our chagrin, we stumbled on an outlying spike bull, evidently kept on the outskirts of the herd by the master bull. I thought he would alarm all the rest; but, as we stood motionless, he could not see clearly what we were. He stood, ran, stood again, gazed at us, and trotted slowly off. We hurried forward as fast as we dared, and with too little care; for we suddenly came in view of two cows. As they raised their heads to look, Woody squatted down where he was, to keep their attention fixed, while I cautiously tried to slip off to one side unobserved. Favored by the neutral tint of my buckskin hunting-shirt, with which my shoes, leggings, and soft hat matched, I succeeded. As soon as I was out of sight I ran hard and came up to a hillock crested with pinyons, behind which I judged I should find the herd. As I approached the crest, their strong, sweet smell smote my nostrils. In another moment I saw the tips of a pair of mighty antlers, and I peered over the crest with my rifle at the ready. Thirty yards off, behind a clump of pinyons, stood a huge bull, his head thrown back as he rubbed his shoulders with his horns. There were several cows around him, and one saw me immediately, and took alarm. I fired into the bull's shoulder, inflicting a mortal wound; but he went off, and I raced after him at top speed, firing twice into his flank; then he stopped, very sick, and I broke his neck with a fourth bullet. An elk often hesitates in the first moments of surprise and fright, and does not get really under way for two or three hundred yards; but, when once fairly started, he may go several miles, even though mortally wounded; therefore, the hunter, after his first shot, should run forward as fast as he can, and shoot again and again until the quarry drops. In this way many animals that would otherwise be lost are obtained, especially by the man who has a repeating-rifle. Nevertheless the hunter should beware of being led astray by the ease with which he can fire half a dozen shots from his repeater; and he should aim as carefully with each shot as if it were his last. No possible rapidity of fire can atone for habitual carelessness of aim with the first shot.

The elk I thus slew was a giant. His body was the size of a steer's, and his antlers, though not unusually long, were very massive and heavy. He lay in a glade, on the edge of a great cliff. Standing on its brink we overlooked a most beautiful country, the home of all homes for the elk: a wilderness of mountains, the immense evergreen forest broken by park and glade, by meadow and pasture, by bare hill-side and barren table-land. Some five miles off lay the sheet of water known to the old hunters as Spotted Lake; two or three shallow, sedgy places, and spots of geyser formation, made pale green blotches on its wind-rippled surface. Far to the southwest, in daring beauty and majesty, the grand domes and lofty spires of the Tetons shot into the blue sky. Too sheer for the snow to rest on their sides, it yet filled the rents in their rough flanks, and lay deep between the towering pinnacles of dark rock.

That night, as on more than one night afterward, a bull elk came down whistling to within two or three hundred yards of the tents, and tried to join the horse herd. The moon had set, so I could not go after it. Elk are very restless and active throughout the night in the rutting season; but where undisturbed they feed freely in the daytime, resting for two or three hours about noon.

Next day, which was rainy, we spent in getting in the antlers and meat of the two dead elk; and I shot off the heads of two or three blue grouse on the way home. The following day I killed another bull elk, following him by the strong, not unpleasing, smell, and hitting him twice as he ran, at about eighty yards. So far I had had good luck, killing everything I had shot at; but now the luck changed, through no fault of mine, as far as I could see, and Ferguson had his innings. The day after I killed this bull he shot two fine mountain rams; and during the remainder of our hunt he killed five elk,—one cow, for meat, and four good bulls. The two rams were with three others, all old and with fine horns; Ferguson peeped over a lofty precipice and saw them coming up it only fifty yards below him. His two first and finest bulls were obtained by hard running and good shooting; the herds were on the move at the time, and only his speed of foot and soundness of wind enabled him to get near enough for a shot. One herd started before he got close, and he killed the master bull by a shot right through the heart, as it trotted past, a hundred and fifty yards distant.

As for me, during the next ten days I killed nothing save one cow for meat; and this though I hunted hard every day from morning till night, no matter what the weather. It was stormy, with hail and snow almost every day; and after working hard from dawn until nightfall, laboriously climbing the slippery mountain-sides, walking through the wet woods, and struggling across the bare plateaus and cliff-shoulders, while the violent blasts of wind drove the frozen rain in our faces, we would come in after dusk wet through and chilled to the marrow. Even when it rained in the valleys it snowed on the mountaintops, and there was no use trying to keep our feet dry. I got three shots at bull elk, two being very hurried snap-shots at animals running in thick timber, the other a running-shot in the open, at over two hundred yards; and I missed all three. On most days I saw no bull worth shooting; the two or three I did see or hear we failed to stalk, the light, shifty wind baffling us, or else an outlying cow which we had not seen giving the alarm. There were many blue and a few ruffed grouse in the woods, and I occasionally shot off the heads of a couple on my way homeward in the evening. In racing after one elk, I leaped across a gully and so bruised and twisted my heel on a rock that, for the remainder of my stay in the mountains, I had to walk on the fore part of that foot. This did not interfere much with my walking, however, except in going down-hill.

Our ill success was in part due to sheer bad luck; but the chief element therein was the presence of a great hunting-party of Shoshone Indians. Split into bands of eight or ten each, they scoured the whole country on their tough, sure-footed ponies. They always hunted on horseback, and followed the elk at full speed wherever they went. Their method of hunting was to organize great drives, the riders strung in lines far apart; they signalled to one another by means of willow whistles, with which they also imitated the calling of the bull elk, thus tolling the animals to them, or making them betray their whereabouts. As they slew whatever they could, but by preference cows and calves, and as they were very persevering, but also very excitable and generally poor shots, so that they wasted much powder, they not only wrought havoc among the elk, but also scared the survivors out of all the country over which they hunted.

Day in and day out we plodded on. In a hunting-trip the days of long monotony in getting to the ground, and the days of unrequited toil after it has been reached, always far outnumber the red-letter days of success. But it is just these times of failure that really test the hunter. In the long run, common-sense and dogged perseverance avail him more than any other qualities. The man who does not give up, but hunts steadily and resolutely through the spells of bad luck until the luck turns, is the man who wins success in the end.

After a week at Two-Ocean Pass, we gathered our pack-animals one frosty morning, and again set off across the mountains. A two-days' jaunt took us to the summit of Wolverine Pass, near Pinyon Peak, beside a little mountain tarn; each morning we found its surface skimmed with black ice, for the nights were cold. After three or four days, we shifted camp to the mouth of Wolverine Creek, to get off the hunting grounds of the Indians. We had used up our last elk-meat that morning, and when we were within a couple of hours' journey of our intended halting-place, Woody and I struck off on foot for a hunt. Just before sunset we came on three or four elk; a spike bull stood for a moment behind some thick evergreens a hundred yards off. Guessing at his shoulder, I fired, and he fell dead after running a few rods. I had broken the luck, after ten days of ill success.

Next morning Woody and I, with the packer, rode to where this elk lay. We loaded the meat on a pack-horse, and let the packer take both the loaded animal and our own saddle-horses back to camp, while we made a hunt on foot. We went up the steep, forest-clad mountain-side, and before we had walked an hour heard two elk whistling ahead of us. The woods were open, and quite free from undergrowth, and we were able to advance noiselessly; there was no wind, for the weather was still, clear, and cold. Both of the elk were evidently very much excited, answering each other continually; they had probably been master bulls, but had become so exhausted that their rivals had driven them from the herds, forcing them to remain in seclusion until they regained their lost strength. As we crept stealthily forward, the calling grew louder and louder, until we could hear the grunting sounds with which the challenge of the nearest ended. He was in a large wallow, which was also a lick. When we were still sixty yards off, he heard us, and rushed out, but wheeled and stood a moment to gaze, puzzled by my buckskin suit. I fired into his throat, breaking his neck, and down he went in a heap. Rushing in and turning, I called to Woody, "He's a twelve-pointer, but the horns are small!" As I spoke I heard the roar of the challenge of the other bull not two hundred yards ahead, as if in defiant answer to my shot.

Running quietly forward, I speedily caught a glimpse of his body. He was behind some fir-trees about seventy yards off, and I could not see which way he was standing, and so fired into the patch of flank which was visible, aiming high, to break the back. My aim was true, and the huge beast crashed down-hill through the evergreens, pulling himself on his fore legs for fifteen or twenty rods, his hind quarters trailing. Racing forward, I broke his neck. His antlers were the finest I ever got. A couple of whisky-jacks appeared at the first crack of the rifle with their customary astonishing familiarity and heedlessness of the hunter; they followed the wounded bull as he dragged his great carcass down the hill, and pounced with ghoulish blood-thirstiness on the gouts of blood that were sprinkled over the green herbage.

These two bulls lay only a couple of hundred yards apart, on a broad game-trail, which was as well beaten as a good bridle-path. We began to skin out the heads; and as we were finishing we heard another bull challenging far up the mountain. He came nearer and nearer, and as soon as we had ended our work we grasped our rifles and trotted toward him along the game-trail. He was very noisy, uttering his loud, singing challenge every minute or two. The trail was so broad and firm that we walked in perfect silence. After going only five or six hundred yards, we got very close indeed, and stole forward on tiptoe, listening to the roaring music. The sound came from a steep, narrow ravine, to one side of the trail, and I walked toward it with my rifle at the ready. A slight puff gave the elk my wind, and he dashed out of the ravine like a deer; but he was only thirty yards off, and my bullet went into his shoulder as he passed behind a clump of young spruce. I plunged into the ravine, scrambled out of it, and raced after him. In a minute I saw him standing with drooping head, and two more shots finished him. He also bore fine antlers. It was a great piece of luck to get three such fine bulls at the cost of half a day's light work; but we had fairly earned them, having worked hard for ten days, through rain, cold, hunger, and fatigue, to no purpose. That evening my home-coming to camp, with three elk-tongues and a brace of ruffed grouse hung at my belt, was most happy.

Next day it snowed, but we brought a pack-pony to where the three great bulls lay, and took their heads to camp; the flesh was far too strong to be worth taking, for it was just the height of the rut.

This was the end of my hunt; and a day later Hofer and I, with two pack-ponies, made a rapid push for the Upper Geyser Basin. We travelled fast. The first day was gray and overcast, a cold wind blowing strong in our faces. Toward evening we came on a bull elk in a willow thicket; he was on his knees in a hollow, thrashing and beating the willows with his antlers. At dusk we halted and went into camp, by some small pools on the summit of the pass north of Red Mountain. The elk were calling all around us. We pitched our cozy tent, dragged great stumps for the fire, cut evergreen boughs for our beds, watered the horses, tethered them to improvised picket-pins in a grassy glade, and then set about getting supper ready. The wind had gone down, and snow was falling thick in large, soft flakes; we were evidently at the beginning of a heavy snowstorm. All night we slept soundly in our snug tent. When we arose at dawn there was a foot and a half of snow on the ground, and the flakes were falling as fast as ever. There is no more tedious work than striking camp in bad weather; and it was over two hours from the time we rose to the time we started. It is sheer misery to untangle picket-lines and to pack animals when the ropes are frozen; and by the time we had loaded the two shivering, wincing pack-ponies, and had bridled and saddled our own riding-animals, our hands and feet were numb and stiff with cold, though we were really hampered by our warm clothing. My horse was a wild, nervous roan, and as I swung carelessly into the saddle, he suddenly began to buck before I got my right leg over, and threw me off. My thumb was put out of joint. I pulled it in again, and speedily caught my horse in the dead timber. Then I treated him as what the cowboys call a "mean horse," and mounted him carefully, so as not to let him either buck or go over backward. However, his preliminary success had inspirited him, and a dozen times that day he began to buck, usually choosing a down grade, where the snow was deep, and there was much fallen timber.

All day long we pushed steadily through the cold, blinding snow-storm. Neither squirrels nor rabbits were abroad; and a few Clarke's crows, whisky-jacks, and chickadees were the only living things we saw. At nightfall, chilled through, we reached the Upper Geyser Basin. Here I met a party of railroad surveyors and engineers, coming in from their summer's field-work. One of them lent me a saddle-horse and a pack-pony, and we went on together, breaking our way through the snow-choked roads to the Mammoth Hot Springs, while Hofer took my own horses back to Ferguson.

I have described this hunt at length because, though I enjoyed it particularly on account of the comfort in which we travelled and the beauty of the land, yet, in point of success in finding and killing game, in value of trophies procured, and in its alternations of good and bad luck, it may fairly stand as the type of a dozen such hunts I have made. Twice I have been much more successful; the difference being due to sheer luck, as I hunted equally hard in all three instances. Thus on this trip I killed and saw nothing but elk; yet the other members of the party either saw, or saw fresh signs of, not only blacktail deer, but sheep, bear, bison, moose, cougar, and wolf. Now in 1889 I hunted over almost precisely similar country, only farther to the northwest, on the boundary between Idaho and Montana, and, with the exception of sheep, I stumbled on all the animals mentioned, and white goat in addition, so that my bag of twelve head actually included eight species—much the best bag I ever made, and the only one that could really be called out of the common. In 1884, on a trip to the Bighorn Mountains, I killed three bear, six elk and six deer. In laying in the winter stock of meat for my ranch I often far excelled these figures as far as mere numbers went; but on no other regular hunting trip, where the quality and not the quantity of the game was the prime consideration, have I ever equalled them; and on several where I worked hardest I hardly averaged a head a week. The occasional days or weeks of phenomenal luck, are more than earned by the many others where no luck whatever follows the very hardest work. Yet, if a man hunts with steady resolution he is apt to strike enough lucky days amply to repay him.

On this Shoshone trip I fired fifty-eight shots. In preference to using the knife I generally break the neck of an elk which is still struggling; and I fire at one as long as it can stand, preferring to waste a few extra bullets, rather than see an occasional head of game escape. In consequence of these two traits the nine elk I got (two running at sixty and eighty yards, the others standing, at from thirty to a hundred) cost me twenty-three bullets; and I missed three shots—all three, it is but fair to say, difficult ones. I also cut off the heads of seventeen grouse, with twenty-two shots; and killed two ducks with ten shots—fifty-eight in all. On the Bighorn trip I used a hundred and two cartridges. On no other trip did I use fifty.

To me still-hunting elk in the mountains, when they are calling, is one of the most attractive of sports, not only because of the size and stately beauty of the quarry and the grand nature of the trophy, but because of the magnificence of the scenery, and the stirring, manly, exciting nature of the chase itself. It yields more vigorous enjoyment than does lurking stealthily through the grand but gloomy monotony of the marshy woodland where dwells the moose. The climbing among the steep forest-clad and glade-strewn mountains is just difficult enough thoroughly to test soundness in wind and limb, while without the heart-breaking fatigue of white goat hunting. The actual grapple with an angry grisly is of course far more full of strong, eager pleasure; but bear hunting is the most uncertain, and usually the least productive, of sports.

As regards strenuous, vigorous work, and pleasurable excitement the chase of the bighorn alone stands higher. But the bighorn, grand beast of the chase though he be, is surpassed in size, both of body and of horns, by certain of the giant sheep of Central Asia; whereas the wapiti is not only the most stately and beautiful of American game—far more so than the bison and moose, his only rivals in size—but is also the noblest of the stag kind throughout the world. Whoever kills him has killed the chief of his race; for he stands far above his brethren of Asia and Europe.

7

The Man-Eaters of Tsavo

by Lt. Col. J. H. Patterson, DSO

When assigned to help supervise the building of a Uganda Railroad bridge over the Tsavo River in east Africa in March 1898, Lt. Col. J. H. Patterson, DSO, had little idea of the magnitude of the adventure upon which he was embarking. The site of the bridge, which is today a part of Kenya, became the scene of savage attacks by man-eating lions preying on the workers. Colonel Patterson's stirring book, The Man-Eaters of Tsavo, *remains in print to this day. The drama was also captured quite well in the film* The Ghost and the Darkness, *starring Val Kilmer and Michael Douglas.*

THE FIRST APPEARANCE OF THE MAN-EATERS

UNFORTUNATELY THIS HAPPY STATE OF AFFAIRS DID NOT CONTINUE FOR long, and our work was soon interrupted in a rude and startling manner. Two most voracious and insatiable man-eating lions appeared upon the scene, and for over nine months waged an intermittent warfare against the railway and all those connected with it in the vicinity of Tsavo. This culminated in a perfect reign of terror in December, 1898, when they actually succeeded in bringing the railway works to a complete standstill for about three weeks. At first they were not always successful in their efforts to carry off a victim, but as time went on they stopped at nothing and indeed braved any danger in order to obtain their favourite food. Their methods then became so uncanny, and their man-stalking so well-timed and so certain of success, that the workmen firmly believed that they were not real animals at all, but devils in lions' shape. Many a time the coolies solemnly assured me that it was absolutely useless to attempt to shoot them. They were quite convinced that the angry spirits of two departed native chiefs had taken this form in order to protect against a railway being made through their country, and by stopping its progress to avenge the insult thus shown to them.

I had only been a few days at Tsavo when I first heard that these brutes had been seen in the neighbourhood. Shortly afterwards one or two coolies mysteriously disappeared, and I was told that they had been carried off by night from their tents and devoured by lions. At the time I did not credit this story, and was more inclined to believe that the unfortunate men had been the victims of foul play at the hands of some of their comrades. They were, as it happened, very good workmen, and had each saved a fair number of rupees, so I thought it quite likely that some scoundrels from the gangs had murdered them for the sake of their money. This suspicion, however, was very soon dispelled. About three weeks after my arrival, I was roused one morning about daybreak and told that one of my jemadars, a fine powerful Sikh named Ungan Singh, had been seized in his tent during the night, and dragged off and eaten.

Naturally I lost no time in making an examination of the place, and was soon convinced that the man had indeed been carried off by a lion, and its "pug" marks were plainly visible in the sand, while the furrows made by the heels of the victim showed the direction in which he had been dragged away. Moreover, the jemadar shared his tent with half a dozen other workmen, and one of his bedfellows had actually witnessed the occurrence. He graphically described how, at about midnight, the lion suddenly put its head in at the open tent door and seized Ungan Singh—who happened to be nearest the opening—by the throat. The unfortunate fellow cried out "Choro" ("Let go"), and threw his arms up round the lion's neck. The next moment he was gone, and his panic-stricken companions lay helpless, forced to listen to the terrible struggle which took place outside. Poor Ungan Singh must have died hard; but what chance had he? As a coolie gravely remarked, "Was he not fighting with a lion?"

On hearing this dreadful story I at once set out to try to track the animal, and was accompanied by Captain Haslem, who happened to be staying at Tsavo at the time, and who, poor fellow, himself met with a tragic fate very shortly afterwards. We found it an easy matter to follow the route taken by the lion, as he appeared to have stopped several times before beginning his meal. Pools of blood marked these halting-places, where he doubtless indulged in the man-eaters' habit of licking the skin off so as to get at the fresh blood. (I have been led to believe that this is their custom from the appearance of two half-eaten bodies which I subsequently rescued: the skin was gone in places, and the flesh looked dry, as if it had been sucked.) On reaching the spot where the body had been devoured, a dreadful spectacle presented itself. The ground all round was covered with blood and morsels of flesh and bones, but the unfortunate jemadar's head had been left intact, save for the holes made by the lion's tusks on seizing him, and lay a short distance away from the other remains, the eyes staring wide open with a startled, horrified look in them. The place was considerably cut up, and on closer examination we found that two lions had been there and had probably struggled for possession of the body. It was the most gruesome sight I had ever seen. We collected the remains as well as we could and heaped stones on them, the head with its fixed, terrified stare seeming to watch us all the time, for it we did not bury, but took back to camp for identification before the Medical Officer.

Thus occurred my first experience of man-eating lions, and I vowed there and then that I would spare no pains to rid the neighbourhood of the brutes. I little knew the trouble that was in store for me, or how narrow were to be my own escapes from sharing poor Ungan Singh's fate.

That same night I sat up in a tree close to the late jemadar's tent, hoping that the lions would return to it for another victim. I was followed to my perch by a few of the more terrified coolies, who begged to be allowed to sit up in the tree with me; all the other workmen remained in their tents, but no more doors were left open. I had with me my .303 and 12-bore shot gun, one barrel loaded with ball and the other with slug. Shortly after settling down to my vigil, my hopes of bagging one of the brutes were raised by the sound of their ominous roaring coming closer and closer. Presently this ceased, and quiet reigned for an hour or two, as lions always stalk their prey in complete silence. All at once, however, we heard a great uproar and frenzied cries coming from another camp about half a mile away; we knew then that the lions had seized a victim there, and that we should see or hear nothing further of them that night.

Next morning I found that one of the brutes had broken into a tent at Railhead Camp—whence we had heard the commotion during the night—and had made off with a poor wretch who was lying there asleep. After a night's rest, therefore, I took up my position in a suitable tree near this tent. I did not at all like the idea of walking the half-mile to the place after dark, but all the same I felt fairly safe, as one of my men carried a bright lamp close behind me. He in his turn was followed by another leading a goat, which I tied under my tree in the hope that the lion might be tempted to seize it instead of a coolie. A steady drizzle commenced shortly after I had settled down to my night of watching, and I was soon thoroughly chilled and wet. I stuck to my uncomfortable post, however, hoping to get a shot, but I well remember the feeling of impotent disappointment I experienced when about midnight I heard screams and cries and a heartrending shriek, which told me that the man-eaters had again eluded me and had claimed another victim elsewhere.

At this time the various camps for the workmen were very scattered, so that the lions had a range of some eight miles on either side of Tsavo to work upon; and as their tactics seemed to be to break into a different camp each night, it was most difficult to forestall them. They almost appeared, too, to have an extraordinary and uncanny faculty of finding out our plans beforehand, so that no matter in how likely or how tempting a spot we lay in wait for them, they invariably avoided that particular place and seized their victim for the night from some other camp. Hunting them by day moreover, in such a dense wilderness as surrounded us, was an exceedingly tiring and really foolhardy undertaking. In a thick jungle of the kind round Tsavo the hunted animal has every chance against the hunter, as however careful the latter may be, a dead twig or something of the sort is sure to crackle just at the critical moment and so give the alarm. Still I never gave up hope of some day finding their lair, and accordingly continued to devote all my spare time to crawling about through the undergrowth. Many a time when attempting to force my way through this bewildering tangle I had to be released by my gun-bearer from the fast clutches of the "wait-a-bit"; and often with immense pains I succeeded in tracing the lions to the river after they had seized a victim, only to lose the trail from there onwards, owing to the rocky nature of the ground which they seemed to be careful to choose in retreating to their den.

At this early stage of the struggle, I am glad to say, the lions were not always successful in their efforts to capture a human being for their nightly meal, and one or two amusing incidents occurred to relieve the tension from which our nerves were beginning to suffer. On one occasion an enterprising bunniah (Indian trader) was riding along on his donkey late one night, when suddenly a lion sprang out on him knocking over both man and beast. The donkey was badly wounded, and the lion was just about to seize the trader, when in some way or other his claws became entangled in a rope by which two empty oil tins were strung across the donkey's neck. The rattle and clatter made by these as he dragged them after him gave him such a fright that he turned tail and bolted off into the jungle, to the intense relief of the terrified bunniah, who quickly made his way up the nearest tree and remained there, shivering with fear, for the rest of the night.

Shortly after this episode, a Greek contractor named Themistocles Pappadimitrini had an equally marvellous escape. He was sleeping peacefully in his tent one night, when a lion broke in, and seized and made off with the mattress on which he was lying. Though rudely awakened, the Greek was quite unhurt and suffered from nothing worse than a bad fright. This same man, however, met with a melancholy fate not long afterwards. He had been to the Kilima N'jaro district to buy cattle, and on the return journey attempted to take a short cut across country to the railway, but perished miserably of thirst on the way.

On another occasion fourteen coolies who slept together in a large tent were one night awakened by a lion suddenly jumping on to the tent and breaking through it. The brute landed with one claw on a coolie's shoulder, which was badly torn; but instead of seizing the man himself, in his hurry he grabbed a large bag of rice which happened to be lying in the tent, and made off with it, dropping it in disgust some little distance away when he realised his mistake.

These, however, were only the earlier efforts of the man-eaters. Later on, as will be seen, nothing flurried or frightened them in the least, and except as food they showed a complete contempt for human beings. Having once marked down a victim, they would allow nothing to deter them from securing him, whether he were protected by a thick fence, or inside a closed tent, or sitting round a brightly burning fire. Shots, shouting and firebrands they alike held in derision.

THE ATTACK ON THE GOODS-WAGON

All this time my own tent was pitched in an open clearing, unprotected by a fence of any kind round it. One night when the medical officer, Dr. Rose, was staying with me, we were awakened about midnight by hearing something tumbling about among the tent ropes, but on going out with a lantern we could discover nothing. Daylight, however, plainly revealed the "pug" marks of a lion, so that on that occasion I fancy one or other of us had a narrow escape. Warned by this experience, I at once arranged to move my quarters, and went to join forces with Dr. Brock, who had just arrived at Tsavo to take medical charge of the district. We shared a hut of palm leaves and boughs, which we had constructed on the eastern side of the river, close to the old caravan route leading to Uganda; and we had it surrounded by a circular boma, or thorn fence, about seventy yards in diameter, well made and thick and high. Our personal servants also lived within the enclosure, and a bright fire was always kept up throughout the night. For the sake of coolness, Brock and I used to sit out under the verandah of this hut in the evenings; but it was rather trying to our nerves to attempt to read or write there, as we never knew when a lion might spring over the boma, and be on us before we were aware. We therefore kept our rifles within easy reach, and cast many an anxious glance out into the inky darkness beyond the circle of the firelight. On one or two occasions, we found in the morning that the lions had come quite close to the fence; but fortunately they never succeeded in getting through.

By this time, too, the camps of the workmen had also been surrounded by thorn fences; nevertheless the lions managed to jump over or to break through some one or other of these, and regularly every few nights a man was carried off, the reports of the disappearance of this or that workman coming in to me with painful frequency. So long, however, as Railhead Camp—with its two or three thousand men, scattered over a wide area—remained at Tsavo, the coolies appeared not to take much notice of the dreadful deaths of their comrades. Each man felt, I suppose, that as the man-eaters had such a large number of victims to choose from, the chances of their selecting him in particular were very small. But when the large camp moved ahead with the railway, matters altered considerably. I was then left with only some few hundred men to complete the permanent works; and as all the remaining workmen were naturally camped together the attentions of the lions became more apparent and made a deeper impression. A regular panic consequently ensued, and it required all my powers of persuasion to induce the men to stay on. In fact, I succeeded in doing so only by allowing them to knock off all regular work until they had built exceptionally thick and high bomas round each camp. Within these enclosures fires were kept burning all night, and it was also the duty of the night-watchman to keep clattering half a dozen empty oil tins suspended from a convenient tree. These he manipulated by means of a long rope, while sitting in the hopes of terrifying away the man-eaters. In spite of all these precautions, however, the lions would not be denied, and men continued to disappear.

When the railhead workmen moved on, their hospital camp was left behind. It stood rather apart from the other camps, in a clearing about three-quarters of a mile from my hut, but was protected by a good thick fence and to all appearance was quite secure. It seemed, however, as if barriers were of no avail against the "demons", for before very long one of them found a weak spot in the boma and broke through. On this occasion the Hospital Assistant had a marvellous escape. Hearing a noise outside, he opened the door of his tent and was horrified to see a great lion standing a few yards away looking at him. The beast made a spring towards him, which gave the Assistant such a fright that he jumped backwards, and in doing so luckily upset a box containing medical stores. This crashed down with such a loud clatter of breaking glass that the lion was startled for the moment and made off to another part of the

75

enclosure. Here, unfortunately, he was more successful, as he jumped on to and broke through a tent in which eight patients were lying. Two of them were badly wounded by his spring, while a third poor wretch was seized and dragged off through the thorn fence. The two wounded coolies were left where they lay; a piece of torn tent having fallen over them; and in this position the doctor and I found them on our arrival soon after dawn next morning. We at once decided to move the hospital closer to the main camp; a fresh site was prepared, a stout hedge built round the enclosure, and all the patients were moved in before nightfall.

As I had heard that lions generally visit recently deserted camps, I decided to sit up all night in the vacated boma in the hope of getting an opportunity of bagging one of them; but in the middle of my lonely vigil I had the mortification of hearing shrieks and cries coming from the direction of the new hospital, telling me only too plainly that our dreaded foes had once more eluded me. Hurrying to the place at daylight I found that one of the lions had jumped over the newly erected fence and had carried off the hospital bhisti (water-carrier), and that several other coolies had been unwilling witnesses of the terrible scene which took place within the circle of light given by the big camp fire. The bhisti, it appears, had been lying on the floor, with his head towards the centre of the tent and his feet nearly touching the side. The lion managed to get its head in below the canvas, seized him by the foot and pulled him out. In desperation the unfortunate water-carrier clutched hold of a heavy box in a vain attempt to prevent himself being carried off, and dragged it with him until he was forced to let go by its being stopped by the side of the tent. He then caught hold of a tent rope, and clung tightly to it until it broke. As soon as the lion managed to get him clear of the tent, he sprang at his throat and after a few vicious shakes the poor bhisti's agonising cries were silenced for ever. The brute then seized him in his mouth, like a huge cat with a mouse, and ran up and down the boma looking for a weak spot to break through. This he presently found and plunged into, dragging his victim with him and leaving shreds of torn cloth and flesh as ghastly evidences of his passage through the thorns. Dr. Brock and I were easily able to follow his track, and soon found the remains about four hundred yards away in the bush. There was the usual horrible sight. Very little was left of the unfortunate bhisti—only the skull, the jaws, a few of the larger bones and a portion of the palm with one or two fingers attached. On one of these was a silver ring, and this, with the teeth (a relic much prized by certain castes), was sent to the man's widow in India.

Again it was decided to move the hospital; and again, before night-fall, the work was completed, including a still stronger and thicker boma. When the patients had been moved, I had a covered goods-wagon placed in a favourable position on a siding which ran close to the site which had just been abandoned, and in this Brock and I arranged to sit up that night. We left a couple of tents still standing within the enclosure, and also tied up a few cattle in it as bait for the lions, who had been seen in no less than three different places in the neighbourhood during the afternoon (April 23). Four miles from Tsavo they had attempted to seize a coolie who was walking along the line. Fortunately, however, he had just time to escape up a tree, where he remained, more dead than alive, until he was rescued by the Traffic Manager, who caught sight of him from a passing train. They next appeared close to Tsavo Station, and a couple of hours later some workmen saw one of the lions stalking Dr. Brock as he was returning about dusk from the hospital.

In accordance with our plan, the doctor and I set out after dinner for the goods-wagon, which was about a mile away from our hut. In the light of subsequent events, we did a very foolish thing in taking up our position so late; nevertheless, we reached our destination in safety, and settled down to our watch about ten o'clock. We had the lower half of the door of the wagon closed, while the upper half was left wide open for observation: and we faced, of course, in the direction of the abandoned boma, which, however, we were unable to see in the inky darkness. For an hour or two everything was quiet, and the deadly silence was becoming very monotonous and oppressive, when suddenly, to our right, a dry twig snapped, and we knew that an animal of some sort was about. Soon afterwards we heard a dull thud, as if some heavy body had jumped over the boma. The cattle, too, became very uneasy, and we could hear them moving about restlessly. Then again came dead silence. At this juncture I proposed to my companion that I should get out of the wagon and lie on the ground close to it, as I could see better in that position should

77

the lion come in our direction with his prey. Brock, however, persuaded me to remain where I was; and a few seconds afterwards I was heartily glad that I had taken his advice, for at that very moment one of the man-eaters—although we did not know it—was quietly stalking us, and was even then almost within springing distance. Orders had been given for the entrance to the boma to be blocked up, and accordingly we were listening in the expectation of hearing the lion force his way out through the bushes with his prey. As a matter of fact, however, the doorway had not been properly closed, and while we were wondering what the lion could be doing inside the boma for so long, he was outside all the time, silently reconnoitring our position.

Presently I fancied I saw something coming very stealthily towards us. I feared however, to trust to my eyes, which by that time were strained by prolonged staring through the darkness, so under my breath I asked Brock whether he saw anything, at the same time covering the dark object as well as I could with my rifle. Brock did not answer; he told me afterwards that he, too, thought he had seen something move, but was afraid to say so lest I should fire and it turn out to be nothing after all. After this there was intense silence again for a second or two, then with a sudden bound a huge body sprang at us. "The lion!" I shouted, and we both fired almost simultaneously—not a moment too soon, for in another second the brute would assuredly have landed inside the wagon. As it was, he must have swerved off in his spring, probably blinded by the flash and frightened by the noise of the double report which was increased a hundredfold by the reverberation of the hollow iron roof of the truck. Had we not been very much on the alert, he would undoubtedly have got one of us, and we realised that we had had a very lucky and very narrow escape. The next morning we found Brock's bullet embedded in the sand close to a footprint; it could not have missed the lion by more than an inch or two. Mine was nowhere to be found.

Thus ended my first direct encounter with one of the man-eaters.

The Reign of Terror
The lions seemed to have got a bad fright the night Brock and I sat up in wait for them in the goods-wagon, for they kept away from Tsavo and

did not molest us in any way for some considerable time—not, in fact, until long after Brock had left me and gone on safari (a caravan journey) to Uganda. In this breathing space which they vouchsafed us, it occurred to me that should they renew their attacks, a trap would perhaps offer the best chance of getting at them, and that if I could construct one in which a couple of coolies might be used as bait without being subjected to any danger, the lions would be quite daring enough to enter it in search of them and thus be caught. I accordingly set to work at once, and in a short time managed to make a sufficiently strong trap out of wooden sleepers, tram-rails, pieces of telegraph wire, and a length of heavy chain. It was divided into two compartments—one for the men and one for the lion. A sliding door at one end admitted the former, and once inside this compartment they were perfectly safe, as between them and the lion, if he entered the other, ran a cross wall of iron rails only three inches apart, and embedded both top and bottom in heavy wooden sleepers. The door which was to admit the lion was, of course, at the opposite end of the structure, but otherwise the whole thing was very much on the principle of the ordinary rat-trap, except that it was not necessary for the lion to seize the bait in order to send the door clattering down. This part of the contrivance was arranged in the following manner. A heavy chain was secured along the top part of the lion's doorway, the ends hanging down to the ground on either side of the opening; and to these were fastened, strongly secured by stout wire, short lengths of rails placed about six inches apart. This made a sort of flexible door which could be packed into a small space when not in use, and which abutted against the top of the doorway when lifted up. The door was held in this position by a lever made of a piece of rail, which in turn was kept in its place by a wire fastened to one end and passing down to a spring concealed in the ground inside the cage. As soon as the lion entered sufficiently far into the trap, he would be bound to tread on the spring; his weight on this would release the wire, and in an instant down would come the door behind him; and he could not push it out in any way, as it fell into a groove between two rails firmly embedded in the ground.

In making this trap, which cost us a lot of work, we were rather at a loss for want of tools to bore holes in the rails for the doorway, so as to enable them to be fastened by the wire to the chain. It occurred to me, however, that a hard-nosed bullet from my .303 would penetrate the iron, and on making the experiment I was glad to find that a hole was made as cleanly as if it had been punched out.

When the trap was ready I pitched a tent over it in order further to deceive the lions, and built an exceedingly strong boma round it. One small entrance was made at the back of the enclosure for the men, which they were to close on going in by pulling a bush after them; and another entrance just in front of the door of the cage was left open for the lions. The wiseacres to whom I showed my invention were generally of the opinion that the man-eaters would be too cunning to walk into my parlour; but, as will be seen later, their predictions proved false. For the first few nights I baited the trap myself, but nothing happened except that I had a very sleepless and uncomfortable time, and was badly bitten by mosquitoes.

As a matter of fact, it was some months before the lions attacked us again, though from time to time we heard of their depredations in other quarters. Not long after our night in the goods-wagon, two men were carried off from railhead, while another was taken from a place called Engomani, about ten miles away. Within a very short time, this latter place was again visited by the brutes, two more men being seized, one of whom was killed and eaten, and the other so badly mauled that he died within a few days. As I have said, however, we at Tsavo enjoyed complete immunity from attack, and the coolies, believing that their dreaded foes had permanently deserted the district, resumed all their usual habits and occupations, and life in the camps returned to its normal routine.

At last we were suddenly startled out of this feeling of security. One dark night the familiar terror-stricken cries and screams awoke the camps, and we knew that the "demons" had returned and had commenced a new list of victims. On this occasion a number of men had been sleeping outside their tents for the sake of coolness, thinking, of course, that the lions had gone for good, when suddenly in the middle of the night one of the brutes was discovered forcing its way through the boma. The alarm was at once given, and sticks, stones and firebrands were hurled in the direction of the intruder. All was of no avail, however, for the lion burst into the midst of the terrified group, seized an unfortunate wretch amid the cries and shrieks of his companions, and dragged him off through the thick thorn fence. He was joined outside by the second lion, and so daring had the two brutes become that they did not trouble to carry their victim any further away, but devoured him within thirty yards of the tent where he had been seized. Although several shots were fired in their direction by the jemadar of the gang to which the coolie belonged, they took no notice of these and did not attempt to move until their horrible meal was finished. The few scattered fragments that remained of the body I would not allow to be buried at once, hoping that the lions would return to the spot the following night; and on the chance of this I took up my station at nightfall in a convenient tree. Nothing occurred to break the monotony of my watch, however, except that I had a visit from a hyena, and the next morning I learned that the lions had attacked another camp about two miles from Tsavo—for by this time the camps were again scattered, as I had works in progress all up and down the line. There the man-eaters had been successful in obtaining a victim, whom, as in the previous instance, they devoured quite close to the camp. How they forced their way through the bomas without making a noise was, and still is, a mystery to me; I should have thought that it was next to impossible for an animal to get through at all. Yet they continually did so, and without a sound being heard.

After this occurrence, I sat up every night for over a week near likely camps, but all in vain. Either the lions saw me and then went elsewhere, or else I was unlucky, for they took man after man from different places without ever once giving me a chance of a shot at them. This constant night watching was most dreary and fatiguing work, but I felt that it was a duty that had to be undertaken, as the men naturally looked to me for protection. In the whole of my life I have never experienced anything more nerve-shaking than to hear the deep roars of these dreadful monsters growing gradually nearer and nearer, and to know that some one or other of us was doomed to be their victim before morning dawned. Once they reached the vicinity of the camps, the roars completely ceased, and we knew that they were stalking for their prey. Shouts would then pass from camp to camp, "Khabar dar, bhaieon, shaitan ata" ("Beware, brothers, the devil is coming"), but the warning cries would prove of no avail, and sooner or later agonising shrieks would break the silence and another man would be missing from roll-call next morning.

I was naturally very disheartened at being foiled in this way night after night, and was soon at my wits' end to know what to do; it seemed as if the lions were really "devils" after all and bore a charmed life. As I have said before, tracking them through the jungle was a hopeless task; but as something had to be done to keep up the men's spirits, I spent many a wry day crawling on my hands and knees through the dense undergrowth of the exasperating wilderness around us. As a matter of fact, if I had come up with the lions on any of these expeditions, it was much more likely that they would have added me to their list of victims than that I should have succeeded in killing either of them, as everything would have been in their favour. About this time, too, I had many helpers, and several officers—civil, naval and military—came to Tsavo from the coast and sat up night after night in order to get a shot at our daring foes. All of us, however, met with the same lack of success, and the lions always seemed capable of avoiding the watchers, while succeeding at the same time in obtaining a victim.

I have a very vivid recollection of one particular night when the brutes seized a man from the railway station and brought him close to my camp to devour. I could plainly hear them crunching the bones, and the sound of their dreadful purring filled the air and rang in my ears for days afterwards. The terrible thing was to feel so helpless; it was useless to attempt to go out, as of course the poor fellow was dead, and in addition it was so pitch dark as to make it impossible to see anything. Some half a dozen workmen, who lived in a small enclosure close to mine, became so terrified on hearing the lions at their meal that they shouted and implored me to allow them to come inside my boma. This I willingly did, but soon afterwards I remembered that one man had been lying ill in their camp, and on making enquiry I found that they had callously left him behind alone. I immediately took some men with me to bring him to my boma, but on entering his tent I saw by the light of the lantern that the poor fellow was beyond need of safety. He had died of shock at being deserted by his companions.

From this time matters gradually became worse and worse. Hitherto, as a rule, only one of the man-eaters had made the attack and had done the foraging, while the other waited outside in the bush; but now they began to change their tactics, entering the bomas together and each seizing a victim. In this way two Swahili porters were killed during the last week of November, one being immediately carried off and devoured. The other was heard moaning for a long time, and when his terrified companions at last summoned up sufficient courage to go to his assistance, they found him stuck fast in the bushes of the boma through which for once the lion had apparently been unable to drag him. He was still alive when I saw him next morning, but so terribly mauled that he died before he could be got to the hospital.

Within a few days of this the two brutes made a most ferocious attack on the largest camp in the section, which for safety's sake was situated within a stone's throw of Tsavo Station and close to a Permanent Way Inspector's iron hut. Suddenly in the dead of night the two man-eaters burst in among the terrified workmen, and even from my boma, some distance away, I could plainly hear the panic-stricken shrieking of the coolies. Then followed cries of "They've taken him; they've taken him," as the brutes carried off their unfortunate victim and began their horrible feast close beside the camp. The Inspector, Mr. Dalgairns, fired over fifty shots in the direction in which he heard the lions, but they were not to be frightened and calmly lay there until their meal was finished. After examining the spot in the morning, we at once set out to follow the brutes, Mr. Dalgairns feeling confident that he had wounded one of them, as there was a trail on the sand like that of the toes of a broken limb. After some careful stalking, we suddenly found ourselves in the vicinity of the lions, and were greeted with ominous growlings. Cautiously advancing and pushing the bushes aside, we saw in the gloom what we at first took to be a lion cub; closer inspection, however, showed it to be the remains of the unfortunate coolie, which the man-eaters had evidently abandoned at our approach. The legs, one arm and half the body had been eaten, and it was the stiff fingers of the other arm trailing along the sand which had left the marks we had taken to be the trail of a wounded lion. By this time the beasts had retired far into the thick jungle where it was impossible to follow them, so we had the remains of the coolie buried and once more returned home disappointed.

Now the bravest men in the world, much less the ordinary Indian coolie, will not stand constant terrors of this sort indefinitely. The whole district was by this time thoroughly panic-stricken, and I was not at all surprised, therefore, to find on my return to camp that same afternoon (December 1) that the men had all struck work and were waiting to speak to me. When I sent for them, they flocked to my boma in a body and stated that they would not remain at Tsavo any longer for anything or anybody; they had come from India on an agreement to work for the government, not to supply food for either lions or "devils." No sooner had they delivered this ultimatum than a regular stampede took place. Some hundreds of them stopped the first passing train by throwing themselves on the rails in front of the engine, and then, swarming on to the trucks and throwing in their possessions anyhow, they fled from the accursed spot.

After this the railway works were completely stopped; and for the next three weeks practically nothing was done but build "lion-proof" huts for those workmen who had had sufficient courage to remain. It was a strange and amusing sight to see these shelters perched on the top of water-tanks, roofs and girders—anywhere for safety—while some even went so far as to dig pits inside their tents, into which they descended at night, covering the top over with heavy logs of wood. Every good-sized tree in the camp had as many beds lashed on to it as its branches would bear—and sometimes more. I remember that one night when the camp was attacked, so many men swarmed on to one particular tree that down it came with a crash, hurling its terror-stricken load of shrieking coolies close to the very lions they were trying to avoid. Fortunately for them, a victim had already been secured, and the brutes were too busy devouring him to pay attention to anything else.

THE DISTRICT OFFICER'S NARROW ESCAPE

Some little time before the flight of the workmen, I had written to Mr. Whitehead, the District Officer, asking him to come up and assist me in my campaign against the lions, and to bring with him any of his askaris (native soldiers) that he could spare. He replied accepting the invitation, and told me to expect him about dinner-time on December 2, which turned out to be the day after the exodus. His train was due at Tsavo about six o'clock in the evening, so I sent my "boy" up to the station to meet him and to help in carrying his baggage to the camp. In a very short time, however, the "boy" rushed back trembling with terror, and informed me that there was no sign of the train or of the railway staff, but that an enormous lion was standing on the station platform. This extraordinary story I did not believe in the least, as by this time the coolies—never remarkable for bravery—were in such a state of fright that if they caught sight of a hyena, or a baboon, or even a dog, in the bush, they were sure to imagine it was a lion; but I found out next day that it was an actual fact, and that both stationmaster and signalman had been obliged to take refuge from one of the man-eaters by locking themselves in the station building.

I waited some little time for Mr. Whitehead, but eventually, as he did not put in an appearance, I concluded that he must have postponed his journey until the next day, and so had my dinner in my customary solitary state. During the meal I heard a couple of shots, but paid no attention to them, as rifles were constantly being fired off in the neighbourhood of the camp. Later in the evening, I went out as usual to watch for our elusive foes, and took up my position in a crib made of sleepers which I had built on a big girder close to a camp which I thought was likely to be attacked. Soon after settling down at my post, I was surprised to hear the man-eaters growling and purring and crunching up bones about seventy yards from the crib. I could not understand what they had found to eat, as I had heard no commotion in the camps, and I knew by bitter experience that every meal the brutes obtained from us was announced by shrieks and uproar. The only conclusion I could come to was that they had pounced upon some poor unsuspecting native traveller. After a time I was able to make out their eyes glowing in the darkness, and I took as careful aim as was possible in the circumstances and fired; but the only notice they paid to the shot was to carry off whatever they were devouring and to retire quietly over a slight rise, which prevented me from seeing them. There they finished their meal at their ease.

85

As soon as it was daylight, I got out of my crib and went towards the place where I had last heard them. On the way, whom should I meet but my missing guest, Mr. Whitehead, looking very pale and ill, and generally dishevelled.

"Where on earth have you come from?" I exclaimed. "Why didn't you turn up to dinner last night?"

"A nice reception you give a fellow when you invite him to dinner," was his only reply.

"Why, what's up?" I asked.

"That infernal lion of yours nearly did for me last night," said Whitehead.

"Nonsense, you must have dreamed it!" I cried in astonishment.

For answer he turned round and showed me his back. "That's not much of a dream, is it?" he asked.

His clothing was rent by one huge tear from the nape of the neck downwards, and on the flesh there were four great claw marks, showing red and angry through the torn cloth. Without further parley, I hurried him off to my tent, and bathed and dressed his wounds; and when I had made him considerably more comfortable, I got from him the whole story of the events of the night.

It appeared that his train was very late, so that it was quite dark when he arrived at Tsavo Station, from which the track to my camp lay through a small cutting. He was accompanied by Abdullah, his sergeant of askaris, who walked close behind him carrying a lighted lamp. All went well until they were about half-way through the gloomy cutting, when one of the lions suddenly jumped down upon them from the high bank, knocking Whitehead over like a ninepin, and tearing his back in the manner I had seen. Fortunately, however, he had his carbine with him, and instantly fired. The flash and the loud report must have dazed the lion for a second or two, enabling Whitehead to disengage himself; but the next instant the brute pounced like lightning on the unfortunate Abdullah, with whom he at once made off. All that the poor fellow could say was: "Eh, Bwana, simba" ("Oh, Master, a lion"). As the lion was dragging him over the bank, Whitehead fired again, but without effect, and the brute quickly disappeared into the darkness with his prey. It was, of course, this unfortunate man whom I had heard the lions devouring during the night. Whitehead himself had a marvellous escape; his wounds were happily not very deep, and caused him little or no inconvenience afterwards.

On the same day, December 3, the forces arrayed against the lions were further strengthened. Mr. Farquhar, the Superintendent of Police, arrived from the coast with a score of sepoys to assist in hunting down the man-eaters, whose fame had by this time spread far and wide, and the most elaborate precautions were taken, his men being posted on the most convenient trees near every camp. Several other officials had also come up on leave to join in the chase, and each of these guarded a likely spot in the same way, Mr. Whitehead sharing my post inside the crib on the girder. Further, in spite of some chaff, my lion trap was put in thorough working order, and two of the sepoys were installed as bait.

Our preparations were quite complete by nightfall, and we all took up our appointed positions. Nothing happened until about nine o'clock, when to my great satisfaction the intense stillness was suddenly broken by the noise of the door of the trap clattering down. "At last," I thought, "one at least of the brutes is done for." But the sequel was an ignominious one.

The bait-sepoys had a lamp burning inside their part of the cage, and were each armed with a Martini rifle, with plenty of ammunition. They had also been given strict orders to shoot at once if a lion should enter the trap. Instead of doing so, however, they were so terrified when he rushed in and began to lash himself madly against the bars of the cage, that they completely lost their heads and were actually too unnerved to fire. Not for some minutes—not, indeed, until Mr. Farquhar, whose post was close by, shouted at them and cheered them on—did they at all recover themselves. Then when at last they did begin to fire, they fired with a vengeance—anywhere, anyhow. Whitehead and I were at right angles to the direction in which they should have shot, and yet their bullets came whizzing all round us. Altogether they fired over a score of shots, and in the end succeeded only in blowing away one of the bars of the door, thus allowing our prize to make good his escape. How they failed to kill him several times over is, and always will be, a complete mystery to me, as they could have put the muzzles of their rifles absolutely touching his body. There was, indeed, some blood scattered about the trap, but it was small consolation to know that the brute, whose capture and death seemed so certain, had only been slightly wounded.

Still we were not unduly dejected, and when morning came, a hunt was at once arranged. Accordingly we spent the greater part of the day on our hands and knees following the lions through the dense thickets of thorny jungle, but though we heard their growls from time to time, we never succeeded in actually coming up with them. Of the whole party, only Farquhar managed to catch a momentary glimpse of one as it bounded over a bush. Two days more were spent in the same manner, and with equal unsuccess; and then Farquhar and his sepoys were obliged to return to the coast. Mr. Whitehead also departed for his district, and once again I was left alone with the man-eaters.

The Death of the First Man-Eater

A day or two after the departure of my allies, as I was leaving my boma soon after dawn on December 9, I saw a Swahili running excitedly towards me, shouting out "Simba! Simba!" ("Lion! Lion!"), and every now and again looking behind him as he ran. On questioning him I found that the lions had tried to snatch a man from the camp by the river, but being foiled in this had seized and killed one of the donkeys, and were at that moment busy devouring it not far off. Now was my chance.

I rushed for the heavy rifle which Farquhar had kindly left with me for use in case an opportunity such as this should arise, and, led by the Swahili, I started most carefully to stalk the lions, who, I devoutly hoped, were confining their attention strictly to their meal. I was getting on splendidly, and could just make out the outline of one of them through the dense bush, when unfortunately my guide snapped a rotten branch. The wily beast heard the noise, growled his defiance, and disappeared in a moment into a patch of even thicker jungle close by. In desperation at the thought of his escaping me once again, I crept hurriedly back to the camp, summoned the available workmen and told them to bring all the tom-toms, tin cans and other noisy instruments of any kind that could be found. As quickly as possible I posted them in a half-circle round the thicket, and gave the head jemadar instructions to start a simultaneous beating of the tom-toms and cans as soon as he judged that I had had time to get round to the other side. I then crept round by myself and soon found a good position and one which the lion was most likely to retreat past, as it was in the middle of a broad animal path leading straight from the place where he was concealed. I lay down behind a small ant hill, and waited expectantly. Very soon I heard a tremendous din being raised by the advancing line of coolies, and almost immediately, to my intense joy, out into the open path stepped a huge maneless lion. It was the first occasion during all these trying months upon which I had had a fair chance at one of these brutes, and my satisfaction at the prospect of bagging him was unbounded.

Slowly he advanced along the path, stopping every few seconds to look round. I was only partially concealed from view, and if his attention had not been so fully occupied by the noise behind him, he must have observed me. As he was oblivious to my presence, however, I let him approach to within about fifteen yards of me, and then covered him with my rifle. The moment I moved to do this, he caught sight of me, and seemed much astonished at my sudden appearance, for he stuck his fore-feet into the ground, threw himself back on his haunches and growled savagely. As I covered his brain with my rifle, I felt that at last I had him absolutely at my mercy, but . . . never trust an untried weapon! I pulled the trigger, and to my horror heard the dull snap that tells of a misfire.

Worse was to follow. I was so taken aback and disconcerted by this untoward accident that I entirely forgot to fire the left barrel, and lowered the rifle from my shoulder with the intention of reloading—if I should be given time. Fortunately for me, the lion was so distracted by the terrific din and uproar of the coolies behind him that instead of springing on me, as might have been expected, he bounded aside into the jungle again. By this time I had collected my wits, and just as he jumped I let him have the left barrel. An answering angry growl told me that he had been hit; but nevertheless he succeeded once more in getting clear away, for although I tracked him for some little distance, I eventually lost his trail in a rocky patch of ground.

Bitterly did I anathematise the hour in which I had relied on a borrowed weapon, and in my disappointment and vexation I abused owner, maker, and rifle with fine impartiality. On extracting the unexploded cartridge, I found that the needle had not struck home, the cap being only slightly dented; so that the whole fault did indeed lie with the rifle, which I later returned to Farquhar with polite compliments. Seriously, however, my continued ill-luck was most exasperating; and the result was that the Indians were more than ever confirmed in their belief that the lions were really evil spirits, proof against mortal weapons. Certainly, they did seem to bear charmed lives.

After this dismal failure there was, of course, nothing to do but to return to camp. Before doing so, however, I proceeded to view the dead donkey, which I found to have been only slightly devoured at the quarters. It is a curious fact that lions always begin at the tail of their prey and eat upwards towards the head. As their meal had thus been interrupted evidently at the very beginning, I felt pretty sure that one or other of the brutes would return to the carcase at nightfall. Accordingly, as there was no tree of any kind close at hand, I had a staging erected some ten feet away from the body. This machan was about twelve feet high and was composed of four poles stuck into the ground and inclined toward each other at the top, where a plank was lashed to serve as a seat. Further, as the nights were still pitch dark, I had the donkey's carcase secured by strong wires to a neighbouring stump, so that the lions might not be able to drag it away before I could get a shot at them.

At sundown, therefore, I took up my position on my airy perch, and much to the disgust of my gun-bearer, Mahina, I decided to go alone. I would gladly have taken him with me, indeed, but he had a bad cough, and I was afraid lest he should make any involuntary noise or movement which might spoil all. Darkness fell almost immediately, and everything became extraordinarily still. The silence of an African jungle on a dark night needs to be experienced to be realised; it is most impressive, especially when one is absolutely alone and isolated from one's fellow creatures, as I was then. The solitude and stillness, and the purpose of my vigil, all had their effect on me, and from a condition of strained expectancy I gradually fell into a dreamy mood which harmonised well with my surroundings. Suddenly I was startled out of my reverie by the snapping of a twig; and, straining my ears for a further sound, I fancied I could hear the rustling of a large body forcing its way through the bush. "The man-eater," I thought to myself; "surely to-night my luck will change and I shall bag one of the brutes." Profound silence again succeeded; I sat on my eyrie like a statue, every nerve tense with excitement. Very soon, however, all doubts as to the presence of the lion was dispelled. A deep long-drawn sigh—sure sign of hunger—came up from the bushes, and the rustling commenced again as he cautiously advanced. In a moment or two a sudden stop, followed by an angry growl, told me that my presence had been noticed; and I began to fear that disappointment awaited me once more.

But no; matters quickly took an unexpected turn. The hunter became the hunted; and instead of either making off or coming for the bait prepared for him, the lion began stealthily to stalk me! For about two hours he horrified me by slowly creeping round and round my crazy structure, gradually edging his way nearer and nearer. Every moment I expected him to rush it; and the staging had not been constructed with an eye to such a possibility. If one of the rather flimsy poles should break, or if the lion could spring the twelve feet which separated me from the ground . . . the thought was scarcely a pleasant one. I began to feel distinctly "creepy," and heartily repented my folly in having placed myself in such a dangerous position. I kept perfectly still, however, hardly daring even to blink my eyes: but the long continued strain was telling on my nerves, and my feelings may be better imagined than described when about midnight suddenly something came flop and struck me on the back of the head. For a moment I was so terrified that I nearly fell off the plank, as I thought that the lion had sprung on me from behind. Regaining my senses in a second or two, I realised that I had been hit by nothing more formidable than an owl, which had doubtless mistaken me for the branch of a tree—not a very alarming thing to happen in ordinary circumstances, I admit, but coming at the time it did, it almost paralysed me. The involuntary start which I could not help giving was immediately answered by a sinister growl from below.

After this I again kept as still as I could, though absolutely trembling with excitement; and in a short while I heard the lion begin to creep stealthily towards me. I could barely make out his form as he crouched among the whitish undergrowth; but I saw enough for my purpose and before he could come any nearer, I took careful aim and pulled the trigger. The sound of the shot was at once followed by a most terrific roar, and then I could hear him leaping about in all directions. I was no longer able to see him, however, as his first bound had taken him into the thick bush; but to make assurance doubly sure, I kept blazing away in the direction in which I heard him plunging about. At length came a series of mighty groans, gradually subsiding into deep sighs, and finally ceasing altogether; and I felt convinced that one of the "devils" who had so long harried us would trouble us no more.

As soon as I ceased firing, a tumult of inquiring voices was borne across the dark jungle from the men in camp about a quarter of a mile away. I shouted back that I was safe and sound, and that one of the lions was dead: whereupon such a mighty cheer went up from all the camps as must have astonished the denizens of the jungle for miles around. Shortly I saw scores of lights twinkling through the bushes: every man in camp turned out, and with tom-toms beating and horns blowing came running to the scene. They surrounded my eyrie, and to my amazement prostrated themselves on the ground before me, saluting me with cries of "Mabarak! Mabarak!" which I believe means "blessed one" or "saviour." All the same, I refused to allow any search to be made that night for the body of the lion, in case his companion might be close by; besides, it was possible that he might be still alive, and capable of making a last spring. Accordingly we all returned in triumph to the camp, where great rejoicings were kept up for the remainder of the night, the Swahili and other African natives celebrating the occasion by an especially wild and savage dance.

For my part, I anxiously awaited the dawn; and even before it was thoroughly light I was on my way to the eventful spot, as I could not completely persuade myself that even yet the "devil" might not have eluded me in some uncanny and mysterious way. Happily my fears proved groundless, and I was relieved to find that my luck—after playing me so many exasperating tricks—had really turned at last. I had scarcely traced the blood for more than a few paces when, on rounding a bush, I was startled to see a huge lion right in front of me, seemingly alive and crouching for a spring. On looking closer, however, I satisfied myself that he was really and truly stone-dead, whereupon my followers crowded round, laughed and danced and shouted with joy like children, and bore me in triumph shoulder-high round the dead body. These thanksgiving ceremonies being over, I examined the body and found that two bullets had taken effect—one close behind the left shoulder, evidently penetrating the heart, and the other in the off hind leg. The prize was indeed one to be proud of; his length from tip of nose to tip of tail was nine feet eight inches, he stood three feet nine inches high, and it took eight men to carry him back to camp. The only blemish was that the skin was much scored by the boma thorns through which he had so often forced his way in carrying off his victims.

The news of the death of one of the notorious man-eaters soon spread far and wide over the country: telegrams of congratulations came pouring in, and scores of people flocked from up and down the railway to see the skin for themselves.

THE DEATH OF THE SECOND MAN-EATER

It must not be imagined that with the death of this lion our troubles at Tsavo were at an end; his companion was still at large, and very soon began to make us unpleasantly aware of the fact. Only a few nights elapsed before he made an attempt to get at the Permanent Way Inspector, climbing up the steps of his bungalow and prowling round the verandah. The Inspector, hearing the noise and thinking it was a drunken coolie, shouted angrily "Go away!" but, fortunately for him, did not attempt to come out or to open the door. Thus disappointed in his attempt to obtain a meal of human flesh, the lion seized a couple of the Inspector's goats and devoured them there and then.

On hearing of this occurrence, I determined to sit up the next night near the Inspector's bungalow. Fortunately there was a vacant iron shanty close at hand, with a convenient loophole in it for firing from; and outside this I placed three full-grown goats as bait, tying them to a half-length of rail, weighing about 250 lbs. The night passed uneventfully until just before daybreak, when at last the lion turned up, pounced on one of the goats and made off with it, at the same time dragging away the others, rail and all. I fired several shots in his direction, but it was pitch dark and quite impossible to see anything, so I only succeeded in hitting one of the goats. I often longed for a flashlight on such occasions.

Next morning I started off in pursuit and was joined by some others from the camp. I found that the trail of the goats and rail was easily followed, and we soon came up, about a quarter of a mile away, to where the lion was still busy at his meal. He was concealed in some thick bush and growled angrily on hearing our approach; finally, as we got closer, he suddenly made a charge, rushing through the bushes at a great pace. In an instant, every man of the party scrambled hastily up the nearest tree, with the exception of one of my assistants, Mr. Winkler, who stood steadily by me throughout. The brute, however, did not press his charge home: and on throwing stones into the bushes where we had last seen him, we guessed by the silence that he had slunk off. We therefore advanced cautiously, and on getting up to the place discovered that he had indeed escaped us, leaving two of the goats scarcely touched.

Thinking that in all probability the lion would return as usual to finish his meal, I had a very strong scaffolding put up a few feet away from the dead goats, and took up my position on it before dark. On this occasion I brought my gun-bearer, Mahina, to take a turn at watching, as I was by this time worn out for want of sleep, having spent so many nights on the look-out. I was just dozing off comfortably when suddenly I felt my arm seized, and on looking up saw Mahina pointing in the direction of the goats. "Sher!" ("Lion!") was all he whispered. I grasped my double smooth-bore, which I had charged with slug, and waited patiently. In a few moments I was rewarded, for as I watched the spot where I expected the lion to appear, there was a rustling among the bushes and I saw him stealthily emerge into the open and pass almost directly beneath us. I fired both barrels practically together into his shoulder, and to my joy could see him go down under the force of the blow. Quickly I reached for the magazine rifle, but before I could use it, he was out of sight among the bushes, and I had to fire after him quite at random. Nevertheless I was confident of getting him in the morning, and accordingly set out as soon as it was light. For over a mile there was no difficulty in following the blood-trail, and as he had rested several times I felt sure that he had been badly wounded. In the end, however, my hunt proved fruitless, for after a time the traces of blood ceased and the surface of the ground became rocky, so that I was no longer able to follow the spoor.

About this time Sir Guilford Molesworth, K. C. I. E., late Consulting Engineer to the Government of India for State Railways, passed through Tsavo on a tour of inspection on behalf of the Foreign Office. After examining the bridge and other works and expressing his satisfaction, he took a number of photographs, one or two of which he has kindly allowed me to reproduce in this book. He thoroughly sympathised with us in all the trials we had endured from the man-eaters, and was delighted that one at least was dead. When he asked me if I expected to get the second lion soon, I well remember his half-doubting smile as I rather too confidently asserted that I hoped to bag him also in the course of a few days.

As it happened, there was no sign of our enemy for about ten days after this, and we began to hope that he had died of his wounds in the bush. All the same we still took every precaution at night, and it was fortunate that we did so, as otherwise at least one more victim would have been added to the list. For on the night of December 27, I was suddenly aroused by terrified shouts from my trolley men, who slept in a tree close outside my boma to the effect that a lion was trying to get at them. It would have been madness to have gone out, as the moon was hidden by dense clouds and it was absolutely impossible to see anything more than a yard in front of one; so all I could do was to fire off a few rounds just to frighten the brute away. This apparently had the desired effect, for the men were not further molested that night; but the man-eater had evidently prowled about for some time, for we found in the morning that he had gone right into every one of their tents, and round the tree was a regular ring of his footmarks.

The following evening I took up my position in this same tree, in the hope that he would make another attempt. The night began badly, as while climbing up to my perch I very nearly put my hand on a venomous snake which was lying coiled round one of the branches. As may be imagined, I came down again very quickly, but one of my men managed to despatch it with a long pole. Fortunately the night was clear and cloudless, and the moon made every thing almost as bright as day. I kept watch until about 2 a.m., when I roused Mahina to take his turn. For about an hour I slept peacefully with my back to the tree, and then woke suddenly with an uncanny feeling that something was wrong. Mahina, however, was on the alert, and had seen nothing; and although I looked carefully round us on all sides, I too could discover nothing unusual. Only half satisfied, I was about to lie back again, when I fancied I saw something move a little way off among the low bushes. On gazing intently at the spot for a few seconds, I found I was not mistaken. It was the man-eater, cautiously stalking us.

The ground was fairly open round our tree, with only a small bush every here and there; and from our position it was a most fascinating sight to watch this great brute stealing stealthily round us, taking advantage of every bit of cover as he came. His skill showed that he was an old hand at the terrible game of man-hunting: so I determined to run no undue risk of losing him this time. I accordingly waited until he got quite close—about twenty yards away—and then fired my .303 at his chest. I heard the bullet strike him, but unfortunately it had no knockdown effect, for with a fierce growl he turned and made off with great long bounds. Before he disappeared from sight, however, I managed to have three more shots at him from the magazine rifle, and another growl told me that the last of these had also taken effect.

We awaited daylight with impatience, and at the first glimmer of dawn we set out to hunt him down. I took a native tracker with me, so that I was free to keep a good look-out, while Mahina followed immediately behind with a Martini carbine. Splashes of blood being plentiful, we were able to get along quickly; and we had not proceeded more than a quarter of a mile through the jungle when suddenly a fierce warning growl was heard right in front of us. Looking cautiously through the bushes, I could see the man-eater glaring out in our direction, and showing his tusks in an angry snarl. I at once took careful aim and fired. Instantly he sprang out and made a most determined charge down on us. I fired again and knocked him over; but in a second he was up once more and coming for me as fast as he could in his crippled condition. A third shot had no apparent effect, so I put out my hand for the Martini, hoping to stop him with it. To my dismay, however, it was not there. The terror of the sudden charge had proved too much for Mahina, and both he and the carbine were by this time well on their way up a tree. In the circumstances there was nothing to do but follow suit, which I did without loss of time: and but for the fact that one of my shots had broken a hind leg, the brute would most certainly have had me. Even as it was, I had barely time to swing myself up out of his reach before he arrived at the foot of the tree.

When the lion found he was too late, he started to limp back to the thicket; but by this time I had seized the carbine from Mahina, and the first shot I fired from it seemed to give him his quietus, for he fell over and lay motionless. Rather foolishly, I at once scrambled down from the tree and walked up towards him. To my surprise and no little alarm he jumped up and attempted another charge. This time, however, a Martini bullet in the chest and another in the head finished him for good and all; he dropped in his tracks not five yards away from me, and died gamely, biting savagely at a branch which had fallen to the ground.

By this time all the workmen in camp, attracted by the sound of the firing, had arrived on the scene, and so great was their resentment against the brute who had killed such numbers of their comrades that it was only with the greatest difficulty that I could restrain them from tearing the dead body to pieces. Eventually, amid the wild rejoicings of the natives and coolies, I had the lion carried to my boma, which was close at hand. On examination we found no less than six bullet holes in the body, and embedded only a little way in the flesh of the back was the slug which I had fired into him from the scaffolding about ten days previously. He measured nine feet six inches from tip of nose to tip of tail, and stood three feet eleven and a half inches high; but, as in the case of his companion, the skin was disfigured by being deeply scored all over by the boma thorns.

The news of the death of the second "devil" soon spread far and wide over the country, and natives actually travelled from up and down the line to have a look at my trophies and at the "devil-killer," as they called me. Best of all, the coolies who had absconded came flocking back to Tsavo, and much to my relief work was resumed and we were never again troubled by man-eaters. It was amusing, indeed, to notice the change which took place in the attitude of the workmen towards me after I had killed the two lions. Instead of wishing to murder me, as they once did, they could not now do enough for me, and as a token of their gratitude they presented me with a beautiful silver bowl, as well as with a long poem written in Hindustani describing all our trials and my ultimate victory. As the poem relates our troubles in somewhat quaint and biblical language, I have given a translation of it in the appendix. The bowl I shall always consider my most highly prized and hardest won trophy. The inscription on it reads as follows:—

Sir,—We, your Overseer, Timekeepers, Mistaris and Workmen, present you with this bowl as a token of our gratitude to you for your bravery in killing two man-eating lions at great risk to your own life, thereby saving us from the fate of being devoured by these terrible monsters who nightly broke into our tents and took our fellow-workers from our side. In presenting you with this bowl, we all add our prayers for your long life, happiness and prosperity. We shall ever remain, Sir, Your grateful servants,

Baboo Purshotam Hurjee Purmar, Overseer and Clerk of the Works, on behalf of your Workmen.

Dated at Tsavo, January 30, 1899.

Before I leave the subject of "The Man-Eaters of Tsavo," it may be of interest to mention that these two lions possess the distinction, probably unique among wild animals, of having been specifically referred to in the House of Lords by the Prime Minister of the day. Speaking of the difficulties which had been encountered in the construction of the Uganda Railway, the late Lord Salisbury said:—

The whole of the works were put a stop to for three weeks because a party of man-eating lions appeared in the locality and conceived a most unfortunate taste for our porters. At last the labourers entirely declined to go on unless they were guarded by an iron entrenchment. Of course it is difficult to work a railway under these conditions, and until we found an enthusiastic sportsman to get rid of these lions, our enterprise was seriously hindered.

Also, *The Spectator* of March 3, 1900, had an article entitled "The Lions that Stopped the Railway," from which the following extracts are taken:—

The parallel to the story of the lions which stopped the rebuilding of Samaria must occur to everyone, and if the Samaritans had quarter as good cause for their fears as had the railway coolies, their wish to propitiate the local deities is easily understood. If the whole body of lion anecdote, from the days of the Assyrian Kings till the last year of the nineteenth century, were collated and brought together, it would not equal in tragedy or atrocity, in savageness or in sheer insolent contempt for man, armed or unarmed, white or black, the story of these two beasts. . . .

"To what a distance the whole story carries us back, and how impossible it becomes to account for the survival of primitive man against this kind of foe! For fire—which has hitherto been regarded as his main safeguard against the carnivora—these cared nothing. It is curious that the Tsavo lions were not killed by poison, for strychnine is easily used, and with effect.* Poison may have been used early in the history of man, for its powers are employed with strange skill by the men in the tropical forest, both in American and West Central Africa. But there is no evidence that the old inhabitants of Europe, or if Assyria or Asia Minor, ever killed lions or wolves by this means. They looked to the King or chief, or some champion, to kill these monsters for them. It was not the sport but the duty of Kings, and was in itself a title to be a ruler of men. Theseus, who cleared the roads of beasts and robbers; Hercules, the lion killer; St. George, the dragon-slayer, and all the rest of their class owed to this their everlasting fame. From the story of the Tsavo River we can appreciate their services to man

even at this distance of time. When the jungle twinkled with hundreds of lamps, as the shout went on from camp to camp that the first lion was dead, as the hurrying crowds fell prostrate in the midnight forest, laying their heads on his feet, and the Africans danced savage and cere-monial dances of thanksgiving, Mr. Patterson must have realised in no common way what it was to have been a hero and deliverer in the days when man was not yet undisputed lord of the creation, and might pass at any moment under the savage dominion of the beasts."

(*I may mention that poison was tried, but without effect. The poisoned carcases of transport animals which had died from the bite of the tsetse fly were placed in likely spots, but the wily man-eaters would not touch them, and much preferred live men to dead donkeys.)

Well had the two man-eaters earned all this fame; they had devoured between them no less than twenty-eight Indian coolies, in addition to scores of unfortunate African natives of whom no official record was kept.

8

The Plural of Moose Is Mise

by Irvin S. Cobb

This moose-hunting story first appeared in Field & Stream *in 1927. Born in Kentucky, Irvin S. Cobb (1876–1944) was a humorist, author, and editor who could make writing on any subject interesting. He published more than sixty books and three hundred short stories.*

AT THE OUTSET, WHEN OUR EXPEDITION WAS STILL IN THE PREPARAtory stages, we collectively knew a few sketchy details regarding the general architectural plan and outward aspect of the moose. One of us had once upon a time, years and years before, shot at or into—this point being debatable—a moose up in Maine. Another professed that in his youth he had seriously annoyed a moose with buckshot somewhere in Quebec. The rest of us had met the moose only in zoos with iron bars between us and him or in dining halls, where his head, projecting in a stuffed and mounted condition from the wall, gave one the feeling of dining with somebody out of the Old Testament. Speaking with regard to his family history, we understood he was closely allied to the European elk—the Unabridged told us that—and we gathered that, viewed at a distance, he rather suggested a large black mule with a pronounced Roman nose and a rustic hatrack sprouted out between his ears. Also, through our reading upon the subject, we knew that next to the buffalo he was the largest vegetarian in North America and, next to a man who believes in the forecast of a campaign manager on the eve of an election, the stupidest native mammal that we have. By hearsay we had been made aware that he possessed a magnificent sense of smell and a perfectly wonderful sense of hearing, but was woefully shy on the faculty of thought, the result being that while by the aid of his nose and his ear he might all day elude you, if then perchance you did succeed in getting within gunning range of him he was prone to remain right where he was, peering blandly at you and accommodatingly shifting his position so as to bring his shape broadside on, thereby offering a better target until you, mastering the tremors of eagerness, succeeded in implanting a leaden slug in one of his vital areas.

But, offhand, we couldn't decide what the plural of him was. Still if the plural of goose were geese and the plural of mouse were mice it seemed reasonable to assume that the plural of moose should be mise. Besides, we figured that when we had returned and met friends and told them about our trip it would sound more impressive, in fact more plural, to say that we had slain mise rather than that we had slaughtered moose. In the common acceptance of the term as now used, moose might mean one moose or a herd of them, but mise would mean at least a bag of two of these mighty creatures and from two on up to any imaginable number.

One mentally framed the conversation:

"Well, I hear you've been up in Canada moose hunting." This is the other fellow speaking. "Kill any moose?"

"Kill any moose? Huh, we did better than that—we killed mise."

So by agreement we arranged that mise it should be. This being settled we went ahead with plans for outfitting ourselves against our foray into the game country. We equipped ourselves with high-powered rifles, with patent bedding rolls, with fanciful conceits in high boots and blanket overcoats. We bought everything that the clerk in the shop, who probably had never ventured north of the Bronx in all the days of his sheltered life, thought we should buy, including wicked-looking sheath knives and hand axes to be carried in the belt, tomahawk fashion, and pocket compasses. Personally, I have never been able to figure out the exact value of a compass to a man adrift in a strange country. What is the use of knowing where north is if you don't know where you are? Nevertheless, I was prevailed upon to purchase a compass, along with upward of a great gross of other articles large and small which the clerk believed would be needful to one starting upon such an expedition as we contemplated.

On my account he did a deal of thinking. Not since the fall of 1917, when we were making the world safe for the sporting-goods dealers of America, could he have spent so busy and so happy an afternoon as the afternoon when I dropped in on him.

By past experience I should have known better than to permit myself to be swept off my feet by this tradesman's flood of suggestions and recommendations. Already I had an ample supply of khaki shirts that were endeared to me by associations of duck-hunting forays in North Carolina and chill evenings in an Adirondack camp and a memorable journey to Wyoming, where the sage hen abides. I treasured a pair of comfortable hunting boots that had gone twice to European battlefields and down into the Grand Canyon and up again and across the California desert, without ever breeding a blister or chafing a shin. Among my most valued possessions I counted an ancient shooting coat, wearing which I had missed quail in Kentucky, snipe on Long Island, grouse in Connecticut, doves in Georgia, and woodcock in New York State. Finally, had I but taken time for sober second consideration, I should have recalled that the guides I have from time to time known considered themselves properly accoutered for the chase when they put on the oldest suit of store clothes they owned and stuck an extra pair of wool socks in their pockets. But to the city-bred sportsman half the joy of going on a camping trip consists in getting ready for it. So eminent an authority as Emerson Hough is much given to warning the amateur sportsman against burdening himself with vain adornments, and yet I am reliably informed that the said Hough has a larger individual collection of pretty devices in canvas and leather than any person in this republic.

That clerk had a seductive way about him; he had a positive gift. Otherwise I suppose he would have been handling some line which practically sells itself, such as oil stocks or mining shares. Under the influence of his blandishments I invested in a sweater of a pattern which he assured me was being favored by the really prominent moose hunters in the current season, and a pair of corduroy hunting pants which, when walked in, gave off a pleasant swishing sound like a soft-shoe dancer starting to do a sand jig. I was particularly drawn to these latter garments as being the most vocal pants I had ever seen. As I said before, I bought ever and ever so many other things; I am merely mentioning some of the main items.

We assembled the most impassive group of guides in the whole Dominion—men who, filled with the spirit of the majestic wilds, had never been known publicly to laugh at the expense of a tender-footed stranger. They did not laugh at Harry Leon Wilson's conception of the proper equipment for a man starting upon such an excursion as this one. Wilson on being wired an invitation to go on a hunt for moose promptly telegraphed back that to the best of his recollection he had not lost any moose, but that if any of his friends had been so unfortunate or so careless as to mislay one he would gladly join in the quest for the missing. He brought along an electric flashlight, in case the search should be prolonged after nightfall, a trout rod and a camera. The guides did not laugh at Colonel Tillinghast Houston's unique notion of buying an expensive rifle and a hundred rounds of ammunition and then spending his days in camp sitting in a tent reading a history of the Maritime Provinces in two large volumes. They did not laugh at Colonel Bozeman Bulger's overseas puttees or at Damon Runyon's bowie knife, or at Major McGeehan's eight-pound cartridge belt—it weighed more than that when loaded; I am speaking of it, net—or at Frank Stevens' sleeping cap or at Bill Mac-Beth's going-away haircut—the handiwork of a barber who was a person looking with abhorrence upon the thought of leaving any hair upon the human neck when it is so easy to shave all exposed surfaces smooth and clean from a point drawn across the back of the head at the level of the tops of the ears on down as far as the rear collar button. He must have been a lover of the nude in necks, that barber.

The guides did not laugh even at my vociferous corduroys, which at every step I took, went hist, hist, as though entreating their wearer to be more quiet so they might the better be heard.

By a series of relay journeys we moved up across the line into Quebec, thence back again below the boundary and across the state of Maine, thence out of Maine into New Brunswick and to the thriving city of St. John, with its justly celebrated reversible falls which, by reason of the eccentricities of the tide, tumble upstream part of the time and downstream part of the time, thence by steamer across that temperamental body of water known as the Bay of Fundy, and so on into the interior of Nova Scotia. If anywhere on this continent there is a lovelier spot than the southern part of Nova Scotia in mid-fall I earnestly desire that, come next October, someone shall take me by the hand and lead me to it and let me rave. It used to be the land of Evangeline and the Acadians; now it is the land of the apple. You ran out of the finnan-haddie belt in and around Digby into the wonderful valley of the apples. On every hand are apples—on this side of the right-of-way, orchards stretching down to the blue waters of one of the most beautiful rivers in America, on that side, orchards climbing up the flanks of the rolling hills to where the combing of thick timber comes down and meets them; and everywhere, at roadside, on the verges of thickets, in pastures and old fields, are seedlings growing singly, in pairs and in clumps. They told us that the valley scenically considered is at its best in the spring after the bloom bursts out upon the trees and the whole countryside turns to one vast pink and white bridal bouquet, but hardly can one picture it revealing itself as a more delectable vision than when the first frosts have fallen and every bough of every tree is studded with red and green and yellow globes and the scent of the ripened fruit rises like an incense of spices and wine.

The transition from the pastoral to the wilderness is abrupt. You leave Annapolis Royal in a motor car—that is, you do if you follow in our footsteps—and almost immediately you strike into the big game country. Not that the big game does not lap over into the settlements and even into the larger towns on occasion, for it does. It is recorded that on a certain day a full-grown moose—and a full-grown moose is almost the largest full-grown thing you ever saw—strolled through one of the principal streets of St. John and sought to enter—this being in the old sinful times—a leading saloon. A prominent lawyer of the same city told me that some four weeks before our arrival a woman client of his, living some two miles from the corporate limits, called him on the telephone at his office to ask his professional advice as to how legally she might go about getting rid of a bull moose which insisted on frequenting her orchard and frightening her children when they went to gather pippins. She felt, she said, that a lawyer was the proper person to seek in the emergency that had arisen, seeing that the closed season for moose was still on and it would be unlawful to take a shot at the intruder, so what she particularly desired to know was whether she couldn't have him impounded for trespass or something of that nature.

But such things as these do not happen every day. Probably a man could spend months on end in St. John without seeing the first of the above-mentioned animals rambling down the sidewalk in the manner of a young moose-about-town and trying to drop into the place where the saloon used to be, only to back out again, with chagrin writ large upon his features, upon discovering that the establishment in question had been transformed into a hat store.

To meet the moose where frequently he is and not merely where occasionally he is, one must go beyond the outlying orchards and on into the vasty expanse of the real moose country—hundreds of hundreds of miles of virgin waste, trackless except for game trails and portages across the ridges between waterways. It is a country of tamaracks and hemlocks, of maples and beech and birch, of berries and flowering shrubs, of bogs and barrens and swampy swales, of great granite boulders left behind by the glaciers when the world was young and thawing, of countless lakes and brawling white rapids and deep blue pools where, in the spawning season, the speckled trout are so thick that the small trout have to travel on the backs of the larger ones to avoid being crushed in the jam. I did not see this last myself; my authority for the statement is my friend the veracious lawyer of St. John. But I saw all the rest of it—the woods wearing the flaunting war-paint colors of the wonderful Canadian Indian summer—crimson of huckleberry, tawny of tamarack, yellow of birch, scarlet of maple; the ruffed grouse strutting, unafraid as barnyard fowl and, thanks be to a three-year period of protection, almost as numerous as sparrows in a city street; the signs of hoofed and padded creatures crossing and crisscrossing wherever the earth was soft enough to register the foot tracks of wild things.

And if you want to know how interior New Brunswick looked after Nova Scotia, you are respectfully requested to reread the foregoing paragraph, merely leaving out some of the lakes and most of the boulders.

On a flawless morning, in a motorboat we crossed a certain lake, and I wish I knew the language that might serve to describe the glory of the colors that ringed that lake around and were reflected to the last flame-tipped leaf and the last smooth white column of birchen trunk in its still waters, but I don't. I'll go further and say I can't believe Noah Webster had the words to form the picture, and he had more words than anybody up to the time William J. Bryan went actively into politics. As for myself, I can only say that these colors fairly crackled. There were hues and combinations of hues, shadings and contrasts such as no artist ever has painted and no artist will care to paint, either, for fear of being called a nature faker.

The scene shifts to our main camp. We have met our guides and have marveled at their ability to trot over steep up-and-down-hill portages carrying, each one of them, upon his back a load which no humane man would put on a mule, and have marveled still more when these men, having deposited their mountainous burdens at the farther end of the carry, go hurrying back across the ridge presently to reappear bearing upon their shoulders upturned canoes, their heads hidden inside the inverted interiors and yet by some magic gift peculiar to their craft, managing somehow to dodge the overhanging boughs of trees and without losing speed or changing gait to skip along from one slick round-topped boulder top to another.

Now we are in the deep woods, fifty miles from a railroad and thirty miles from a farmhouse. We sleep at night in canvas lean-tos, with log fires at our feet; we wash our faces and hands in the lake and make high resolves—which we never carry out—to take dips in that same frosty water; we breakfast at sun-up and sup at dusk in a log shanty set behind the cluster of tents, and between breakfast and supper we seek, under guidance, for fresh meat and dining-room trophies.

We have come too late for the calling season, it seems. In the calling season Mr. Moose desires female society, and by all accounts desires it mightily. So the guide takes a mean advantage of his social cravings. Generally afoot, but sometimes in a canoe, he escorts the gunner to a likely feeding ground or a drinking place and through a scroll of birch bark rolled up in a megaphone shape, he delivers a creditable imitation of the call of the flirtatious cow moose. There are guides who can sound the love note through their cupped hands, but most of the fraternity favor the birchen cornucopia. The sound—part lonely bleat, part plaintive bellow—travels across the silent reaches for an incredible distance. Once when the wind was right there is record of a moose call having been heard six miles away from where it was uttered, but in this case the instrumentalist was Louis Harlowe, a Micmac Indian, the champion moose caller of Nova Scotia and perhaps of the world.

In the bog where he is lying, or on the edge of the barren where he is feeding, the bull hears the pleading entreaty and thereby is most grossly deceived. Forgetting the caution which guides his course at other times, he hurries to where the deceiver awaits him, in his haste smashing down saplings, clattering his great horns against the tree boles, splashing through the brooks. And then when he bursts forth into the open, snorting and puffing and grunting, the hunter beholds before him a target which in that setting and with that background must loom up like a grain elevator. Yet at a distance of twenty yards or thirty, he has been known to miss the mark clean and to keep on missing it, while the vast creature stands there, its dull brain filled with wonder that the expected cow should not be where he had had every vocal assurance that she would be, and seemingly only mildly disturbed by the crashing voice of the repeater and by the unseen, mysterious things which pass whistling over his back or under his belly as the gun quivers in the uncertain grasp of the overanxious or mayhap the buckague-stricken sportsman.

Once though he has made up his sluggish mind that all is not well for him in that immediate vicinity, he vanishes into deep cover as silently as smoke and as suddenly as a wink.

The mating time comes in mid-September and lasts about a month, more or less; and since the open season does not begin until October the first, it behooves the hunter who wishes to bag his moose with the least amount of physical exertion to be in camp during the first two weeks of October, for after that the bull moose is reverting to bachelorhood again. He may answer the call, but the chances are that he will not.

A little later on, after the snows have come, one may trail him with comparative ease. Besides, he is browsing more liberally then and consequently is moving pretty consistently. But between the time when the leaves begin to fall and the time when the snow begins to fly he is much given to staying in the densest coverts he can find and doing the bulk of his grazing by night.

So he must be still-hunted, as the saying goes, and it was still-hunting that we were called upon to do. The guide takes his birch-bark horn along each morning when he starts out, carrying it under one arm and an axe under the other, and upon his back a pouch containing the ingredients for a midday lunch and the inevitable fire-blackened teapot, which he calls by the affectionate name of "kittle." He never speaks of stopping for lunch. When the sun stands overhead and your foreshort-ened shadow has snuggled up close beneath your feet like a friendly black puppy, he suggests the advisability of "biling a kittle," by which he means building a fire and making tea. So the pack between his shoulders is nec-essary but the moose call is largely ornamental; it is habit for him to tote it and tote it he does; but mainly he depends upon his eyes and his ears and his uncanny knowledge of the ways of the thing we aim to destroy.

Yes, they call it still-hunting and still-hunting it truly is so far as Louis Harlowe, or Sam Glode, a Micmac, or Charley Charlton, the head guide, is concerned, as he goes worming his way through the undergrowth in his soft-soled moccasins, instinctively avoiding the rotted twig, the loose bit of stone and the swishy bough. But the pair of us, following in his footsteps, in our hard-bottomed, hobnailed boots, our creaky leather gear and our noisy waterproofed nether garments, cannot, by the wildest latitude in descriptive terminology, be called still-hunters. Carrying small avalanches with us, we slide down rocky slopes which the guide on ahead of us negotiated in pussyfooted style; and we blunder into undergrowth; and we trip over logs and we flounder into bogs and out of them again with loud, churning sounds. Going into second on a hillside we pant like switch engines. I was two weeks behind with my panting when I came out of Canada and at odd times now I still pant briskly, trying to catch up.

Reaching level ground we reverse gears and halt to blow. Toward mid-afternoon, on the homebound hike, our weary legs creak audibly at the joints and our tired feet blunder and fumble among the dried leaves. We create all the racket which, without recourse to bass drums or slide trombones, it is humanly possible for a brace of overdressed, city-softened sojourners to create in deep woods. And still our guide—that person so utterly lacking in a sense of humor—speaks of our endeavor as still-hunting. If an ethical Nova Scotian guide—and all professional guides everywhere, so far as I have observed, are most ethical—were hired to chaperon Sousa's band on a still-hunt through the wilderness and on the way Mr. Sousa should think up a new march full of oom-pahs and everything, and the band should practice it while cruising from bog to barren, the guide, returning to the settlements after the outing, would undoubtedly refer to it as a still-hunt.

In our own case, I trust that our eagerness in some measure compensated for our awkwardness. At least, we worked hard—worked until muscles that we never knew before we had achingly forced themselves upon our attention. Yes, if for the first day or two our exertion brought us no reward in the shape of antlered frontlets or great black pelts drying on the rocks at the canoe landing or savory moose steaks in the frying pan; if it seemed that after all we would have to content ourselves with taking home a stuffed guide's head or so; if twilight found us reuniting at the supper table each with tales of endless miles of tramping to our credit but no game, nevertheless and notwithstanding, the labor we spent was not without its plenteous compensations.

To begin with, there was ever the hope that beyond the next thicket or across the next swale old Mr. Sixty Inch Spread would be browsing about waiting for us to come stealing upon him with all the stealthy approach of a runaway moving van and blow him over. There was the joy of watching our guide trailing, he reading the woods as a scholar reads a book and seeing there plain as print what we never would have seen—the impress of a great splayed hoof in the yellowed moss, the freshly gnawed twigs of the moose wood, the scarred bark high up on a maple to show that here a bull had whetted his horns, the scuffed earth where a bear had been digging for grubs, the wallow a buck deer had made at a crossing. And when he told us that the moose had passed this way, trotting, less than an hour before, but that the deer's bed was at least two nights old, while the bear's scratching dated back for days, we knew that he knew. Real efficiency in any line carries its own credentials and needs no bolstering affidavits. There may be better eyes in some human head than the pair Louis Harlowe owns or than that equally keen pair belonging to Harry Allen, the dean of New Brunswick guides, but I have yet to see their owner, and I am quite sure that for woodcraft there are no better equipped men anywhere than the two I have named.

We couldn't decide which was the finer—the supper at night with a great log fire chasing back the dense shadows, and the baked beans and the talk and the crisp bacon and the innocent lies passing back and forth or the midday lunch out in the tangy, painted forest, miles and miles away from anywhere at all, with the chickadees and the snowbirds and the robins flittering about, waiting their chance to gather the crumbs they knew we would leave behind for them, and with the moose birds informally dropping in on us before ever the kettle had begun to sing.

Naturalists know the moose bird, I believe, as the Canada jay and over the line in the States they call him the venison hawk, but by any name he is a handsome, saucy chap, as smart as Satan and as impudent as they make 'em. The first thin wisp of your fire, rising above the undergrowth, is his signal. For some of the denizens of the wilderness it may be just twelve o'clock, but to him it's feeding time. Here he comes in his swooping flight, a graceful, slate-blue figure with his snowy bib and tucker like a trencherman prepared. And there, following close behind him, are other members of his tribe. There always is one in the flock more daring than the rest. If you sit quietly, this fellow will flit closer and closer, his head cocked on one side, uttering half-doubtful, half-confident cheeps until he is snatching up provender right under your feet or even out of your hand. His preference is for meat—raw meat for choice, but his taste is catholic; he'll eat anything. Small morsels he swallows on the spot, larger tidbits he takes in his bill and flies away with to hide in a nearby tree crotch. His friends watch him, and by the time he has returned for another helping they have stolen his cache, so that chiefly what he gets out of the burden of his thriftful industry is the exercise. I do not know whether this should teach us that it is better to strive to lay something against a rainy day and take a chance on the honesty of the neighbors or to seize our pleasure when and where we find it and forget the morrow. Aesop might be able to figure it out, but, being no Aesop, I must continue to register uncertainty.

Campfire suppers and high noon barbecues and glorious sunrises and shooting the rapids in the rivers and paddling across the blue lake, scaring up the black duck and the loons from before us, and all the rest of it, was fine enough in its way, but it was not killing the bull moose. So we hunted and we hunted. We dragged our reluctant feet through moose bogs—beaver meadows these are in the Adirondacks—and we ranged the high ground and the low. Cow moose we encountered frequently and calves aplenty. But the adult male was what we sought.

We had several close calls, or perhaps I should say he did. One of our outfit—nameless here because I have no desire to heap shame upon an otherwise well-meaning and always dependable companion—had been cruising through thick timber all day without seeing anything to fire at. Emerging into an open glade on a ridge above Little Red Lake, he was moved to try his new and virgin automatic at a target. So he loosed off at one of the big black crows of the North that was perched, like a disconsolate undertaker, with bunched shoulders and drooping head, on a dead tamarack fifty yards away. He did not hit Brother Corbie but he tore the top out of the tamarack snag. And then when he and the guide had rounded the shoulder of the little hill and descended to a swamp below they read in certain telltale signs a story which came near to moving the marksman to tears.

Moving up the slope from the other side the guide had been calling, a bull moose—and a whaling big one, to judge by his hoof marks—had been stirred to inquire into the circumstances. He had quitted the swamp and had ambled up the hill to within a hundred yards of the crest when—as the guide deduced it—the sound of the shot just above caused him to halt and swing about and depart from that neighborhood at his very best gait. But for that unlucky rifle report he probably would have walked right into the enemy. My friend does not now feel toward crows as he formerly felt. He thinks they should be abolished.

An experience of mine was likewise fraught with the germs of a tragic disappointment. In a densely thicketed district, my guide, with a view to getting a view of the surrounding terrain above the tops of the saplings, scaled the steep side of a boulder that was as big as an icehouse and then beckoned to me to follow.

But as a scaler I am not a conspicuous success. By main strength and awkwardness I managed to clamber up. Just as I reached the top and put my rifle down so that I might fan breath into myself with both hands, my boot soles slipped off the uncertain surface and I slid off my perch into space. Wildly I threw out both arms in a general direction. My clutching fingers closed on a limb of a maple which overshadowed the rock and I swung out into the air twelve feet or so above the inhospitable earth, utterly unable to reach with my convulsively groping feet the nearermost juts of granite. For an agonized moment it seemed probable that the only thing that might break my fall would be myself. But I kept my presence of mind. I flatter myself that in emergencies I am a quick thinker. As I dangled there an expedient came to me. I let go gradually.

And then as I plumped with a dull sickening thud into the herbage below and lay there weaponless, windless and jarred I saw, vanishing into the scrub not a hundred feet away, the black shape of a big and startled moose. I caught one fleeting glimpse of an enormous head, of a profile which might have belonged to one of the major prophets, of a set of horns outspreading even as the fronded palm outspreads itself, of a switching tail and a slab-sided rump, and then the shielding bushes closed and the apparition was gone, and gone for keeps. For my part there was nothing to do but to sit there for a spell and cherish regrets. Under the circumstances, trailing a frightened bull moose would have been about as satisfactory as trailing a comet, and probably not a bit more successful as to results.

For the majority of the members of our troupe the duration of the hunt had a time limit. On the afternoon of the last day in camp two of the party strolled into the immediate presence of a fair-sized bull and, firing together, one of them put a slug of lead in a twitching ear which he turned toward them. It must have been his deaf ear, else he would have been aware of their approach long before. But one moose was singular and the achievement of the plural number was our ambition. So four of us crossed back into New Brunswick, where, according to all native New Brunswickers, the moose grow larger than they do in the sister province,

Nova Scotians taking the opposing side and being willing to argue it at all times.

With unabated determination the gallant quartet of us hunted and hunted. Three big deer died to make holiday for us but the moose displayed a coyness and diffidence which might be accounted for only on the ground that they heard we were coming. Indeed they could not very well help hearing it.

Each morning under the influence of the frost the flaming frost colors showed a dimming hue. Day before yesterday they had been like burning brands, yesterday there were dulled embers, today smoldering coals; and tomorrow they would be as dead ashes. Each night the sun went down in a nimbus of cold gray clouds. There was a taste and a smell as of snow in the air. The last tardy robin packed up and went south; the swarms of juncos grew thicker; wedge-shaped flights of coot and black duck passed overhead, their bills all pointing toward the Gulf of Mexico. Then on the last day there fell a rain which turned to sleet and the sleet to snow—four inches of it—and in the snow on that last day the reward which comes—sometimes—to the persevering was ours.

To know the climactic sensation which filled the triumphant amateur you must first of all care for the outdoors and for big-game shooting, and in the second place you must have known the feeling of hope deferred, and in the third place you must have reached the eleventh hour, so to speak, of your stay in these parts with the anticipation you had been nurturing for all these weeks since the trip was first proposed still unrealized in your soul.

You and your camp mate and your guide were on the last lap of the journey back to camp; the sun was slipping down the western wall of the horizon; the shadows were deepening under the spruces; you rounded the shoulder of a ridge and stood for a moment at your guide's back looking across a fire-burned barren. He stiffened like a pointer on a warm scent and pointed straight ahead. Your eye followed where his finger aimed, and two hundred yards away you saw a dark blot against a background of faded tamarack—a bull standing head-on. You shot together, you and your companion. Apparently the animal swung himself about and started moving at the seemingly languid lope of the moose, which really is a faster gait than you would suppose until you measure the length of his stride. You kept on firing, both of you, as rapidly almost as you could pull the triggers of your automatics. Twice he shook himself and humped his hindquarters as though stung, but he did not check his speed. You emptied your magazine, five shots. Your mate's fifth shell jammed in the chamber, putting him out of the running for the moment. In desperate haste you fumbled one more shell into your rifle, and just as the fugitive topped a little rise before disappearing for good into the shrouding second growth you got your sight full on the mark and sent a farewell bullet whistling on its way. The black hulk vanished magically.

"That'll do," said your guide, grinning broadly. "You got 'im. But load up again before we go down there. He's down and down for keeps, I think, judgin' by the way he flopped, but he might get up again."

But he didn't get up again. You came on him where he lay, still feebly twitching, with two flesh wounds in his flanks and a third hole right through him behind the shoulders—a thousand pounds of meat, a head worth saving and mounting and bragging about in the years to come, a pelt as big as a double blanket and at last the accomplished plural of moose was mise.

So then you did what man generally does when language fails to express what he feels. You harked back sundry thousands of years and you did as your remote ancestors, the cave dweller, did when he slew the sabretoothed whatyoumaycallhim. About the carcass of your kill you executed a war dance; at least you did if you chambered the emotions which filled the present writer to the choking point.

And then the next day, back in the settlements, when you reunited with the two remaining members of the outfit who had been in camp eight miles away from the camp where you stayed, and when you learned that now there was a total tally of three deceased beasties, the war dance was repeated, only this time it was a four-handed movement instead of a solo number.

9

Whitetail Hunting

by Theodore Roosevelt

Theodore Roosevelt's literary output was prodigious, a staggering forty-two volumes, plus countless articles. He came to love hunting as part of the outdoor life he embraced on his own initiative, striving as a youngster to overcome a plethora of illnesses, such as asthma. His hunting articles and books shared experiences and observations that are timeless.

THE WHITETAIL DEER IS NOW, AS IT ALWAYS HAS BEEN, THE MOST PLENtiful and most widely distributed of American big game. It holds its own in the land better than any other species, because it is by choice a dweller in the thick forests and swamps, the places around which the tide of civilization flows, leaving them as islets of refuge for the wild creatures which formerly haunted all the country. The range of the whitetail is from the Atlantic to the Pacific, and from the Canadian to the Mexican borders, and somewhat to the north and far to the south of these limits. The animal shows a wide variability, both individually and locally, within these confines; from the hunter's standpoint it is not necessary to try to determine exactly the weight that attaches to these local variations.

There is also a very considerable variation in habits. As compared with the mule-deer, the whitetail is not a lover of the mountains. As compared with the prongbuck, it is not a lover of the treeless plains. Yet in the Alleghanies and the Adirondacks, at certain seasons especially, and in some places at all seasons, it dwells high among the densely wooded mountains, wandering over their crests and sheer sides, and through the deep ravines; while in the old days there were parts of Texas and the Indian Territory where it was found in great herds far out on the prairie. Moreover, the peculiar nature of its chosen habitat, while generally enabling it to resist the onslaught of man longer than any of its fellows, sometimes exposes it to speedy extermination. To the westward of the rich bottom-lands and low prairies of the Mississippi Valley proper, when the dry plains country is reached, the natural conditions are much less favorable for whitetail than for other big game. The black bear, which in the East has almost precisely the same habitat as the whitetail, disappears entirely on the great plains, and reappears in the Rockies in regions which the whitetail does not reach. All over the great plains, into the foothills of the Rockies, the whitetail is found, but only in the thick timber of the river bottoms. Throughout the regions of the Upper Missouri and Upper Platte, the Big Horn, Powder, Yellowstone, and Cheyenne, over all of which I have hunted, the whitetail lives among the cottonwood groves and dense brush growth that fringe the river beds and here and there extend some distance up the mouths of the large creeks. In these places the whitetail and the mule-deer may exist in close proximity; but normally neither invades the haunts of the other.

Along the ordinary plains river, such as the Little Missouri, where I ranched for many years, there are three entirely different types of country through which a man passes as he travels away from the bed of the river. There is first the alluvial river bottom covered with cottonwood and box-elder, together with thick brush. These bottoms may be a mile or two across, or they may shrink to but a few score yards. After the extermination of the wapiti, which roamed everywhere, the only big game animal found in them was the whitetail deer. Beyond this level alluvial bottom the ground changes abruptly to bare, rugged hills or fantastically carved and shaped Bad Lands rising on either side of the river, the ravines, coulees, creeks, and canyons twisting through them in every direction. Here there are patches of ash, cedar, pine, and occasionally other trees, but the country is very rugged, and the cover very scanty. This is the home of the mule-deer, and, in the roughest and wildest parts, of the bighorn. The absolutely clear and sharply defined line of demarkation between this rough, hilly country, flanking the river, and the alluvial river bottom, serves as an equally clearly marked line of demarkation between the ranges of the whitetail and the mule-deer. This belt of broken country may be only a few hundred yards in width; or it may extend for a score of miles before it changes into the open prairies, the high plains proper. As soon as these are reached, the prongbuck's domain begins.

As the plains country is passed, and the vast stretches of mountainous region entered, the river bottoms become narrower, and the plains on which the prongbuck is found become of very limited extent, shrinking to high valleys and plateaus, while the mass of rugged foothills and mountains add immensely to the area of the mule-deer's habitat.

Given equal areas of country, of the three different types alluded to above, that in which the mule-deer is found offers the greatest chance of success to the rifle-bearing hunter, because there is enough cover to shield him and not enough to allow his quarry to escape by stealth and hiding. On the other hand, the thick river bottoms offer him the greatest difficulty. In consequence, where the areas of distribution of the different game animals are about equal, the mule-deer disappears first before the hunter, the prongbuck next, while the whitetail holds out the best of all. I saw this frequently on the Yellowstone, the Powder, and the Little Missouri. When the ranchmen first came into this country the mule-deer swarmed, and yielded a far more certain harvest to the hunter than did either the prongbuck or the whitetail. They were the first to be thinned out, the prongbuck lasting much better. The cowboys and small ranchmen, most of whom did not at the time have hounds, then followed the prongbuck; and this, in its turn, was killed out before the whitetail. But in other places a slight change in the conditions completely reversed the order of destruction. In parts of Wyoming and Montana the mountainous region where the mule-deer dwelt was of such vast extent, and the few river bottoms on which the whitetail were found were so easily hunted, that the whitetail was completely exterminated throughout large districts where the mule-deer continued to abound. Moreover, in these regions the table-lands and plains upon which the prongbuck was found were limited in extent, and although the prongbuck outlasted the whitetail, it vanished long before the herds of the mule-deer had been destroyed from among the neighboring mountains.

The whitetail was originally far less common in the forests of northern New England than was the moose, for in the deep snows the moose had a much better chance to escape from its brute foes and to withstand cold and starvation. But when man appeared upon the scene he followed the moose so much more eagerly than he followed the deer that the conditions were reversed and the moose was killed out. The moose thus vanished entirely from the Adirondacks, and almost entirely from Maine; but the excellent game laws of the latter State, and the honesty and efficiency with which they have been executed during the last twenty years, have resulted in an increase of moose during that time. During the same period the whitetail deer has increased to an even greater extent. It is doubtless now more plentiful in New York and New England than it was a quarter of a century ago. Stragglers are found in Connecticut, and, what is still more extraordinary, even occasionally come into wild parts of densely populated little Rhode Island—my authority for the last statement being Mr. C. Grant La Farge. Of all our wild game, the whitetail responds most quickly to the efforts for its protection, and except the wapiti, it thrives best in semi-domestication; in consequence, it has proved easy to preserve it, even in such places as Cape Cod in Massachusetts and Long Island in New York; while it has increased greatly in Vermont, New Hampshire, and Maine, and has more than held its own in the Adirondacks. Mr. James R. Sheffield, of New York City, in the summer of 1899, spent several weeks on a fishing trip through northern Maine. He kept count of the moose and deer he saw, and came across no less than thirty-five of the former and over five hundred and sixty of the latter. In the most lonely parts of the forest deer were found by the score, feeding in broad daylight on the edges of the ponds. Deer are still plentiful in many parts of the Alleghany Mountains, from Pennsylvania southward, and also in the swamps and canebrakes of the South Atlantic and Gulf States.

Where the differences in habitat and climate are so great there are many changes of habits, and some of them of a noteworthy kind. Mr. John A. McIlhenny, of Avery's Island, Louisiana, formerly a lieutenant

in my regiment, lives in what is still a fine game country. His plantation is in the delta of the Mississippi, among the vast marshes, north of
which lie the wooded swamps. Both the marshes and the swamps were
formerly literally thronged with whitetail deer, and the animals are still
plentiful in them. Mr. McIlhenny has done much deer-hunting, always
using hounds. He informs me that the breeding times are unexpectedly
different from those of the northern deer. In the North, in different
localities, the rut takes place in October or November, and the fawns
are dropped in May or June. In the Louisiana marshes around Avery's
Island the rut begins early in July and the fawns are dropped in February.
In the swamps immediately north of these marshes the dates are fully a
month later. The marshes are covered with tall reeds and grass and broken
by bayous, while there are scattered over them what are called "islands"
of firmer ground overgrown with timber. In this locality the deer live in
the same neighborhood all the year round, just as, for instance, they do
on Long Island. So on the Little Missouri, in the neighborhood of my
ranch, they lived in exactly the same localities throughout the entire year.
Occasionally they would shift from one river bottom to another, or go a
few miles up or down stream because of scarcity of food. But there was
no general shifting.

On the Little Missouri, in one place where they were not molested,
I knew a particular doe and fawn with whose habits I became quite inti-
mately acquainted. When the moon was full they fed chiefly by night,
and spent most of the day lying in the thick brush. When there was little
or no moon they would begin to feed early in the morning, then take a
siesta, and then—what struck me as most curious of all—would go to a
little willow-bordered pool about noon to drink, feeding for some time
both before and after drinking. After another siesta they would come out
late in the afternoon and feed until dark.

In the Adirondacks the deer often completely alter their habits at
different seasons. Soon after the fawns are born they come down to the
water's edge, preferring the neighborhood of the lakes, but also haunting
the stream banks. The next three months, during the hot weather, they
keep very close to the water, and get a large proportion of their food by
wading in after the lilies and other aquatic plants. Where they are much

hunted, they only come to the water's edge after dark, but in regions where they are little disturbed they are quite as often diurnal in their habits. I have seen dozens feeding in the neighborhood of a lake, some of them two or three hundred yards out in shallow places, up to their bellies; and this after sunrise, or two or three hours before sunset. Before September the deer cease coming to the water, and go back among the dense forests and on the mountains. There is no genuine migration, as in the case of the mule-deer, from one big tract to another, and no entire desertion of any locality. But the food supply which drew the animals to the water's edge during the summer months shows signs of exhaustion toward fall; the delicate water-plants have vanished, the marsh-grass is dying, and the lilies are less succulent. An occasional deer still wanders along the shores or out into the lake, but most of them begin to roam the woods, eating the berries and the leaves and twig ends of the deciduous trees, and even of some of the conifers—although a whitetail is fond of grazing, especially upon the tips of the grass. I have seen moose feeding on the tough old lily stems and wading after them when the ice had skimmed the edges of the pool. But the whitetail has usually gone back into the woods long before freezing-time.

From Long Island south there is not enough snow to make the deer alter their habits in the winter. As soon as the rut is over, which in different localities may be from October to December, whitetail are apt to band together—more apt than at any other season, although even then they are often found singly or in small parties. While nursing, the does have been thin, and at the end of the rut the bucks are gaunt, with their necks swollen and distended. From that time on bucks and does alike put on flesh very rapidly in preparation for the winter. Where there is no snow, or not enough to interfere with their travelling, they continue to roam anywhere through the woods and across the natural pastures and meadows, eating twigs, buds, nuts, and the natural hay which is cured on the stalk.

In the Northern woods they form yards during the winter. These yards are generally found in a hardwood growth which offers a supply of winter food, and consist simply of a tangle of winding trails beaten out through the snow by the incessant passing and repassing of the animal.

The yard merely enables the deer to move along the various paths in order to obtain food. If there are many deer together, the yards may connect by interlacing paths, so that a deer can run a considerable distance through them. Often, however, each deer will yard by itself, as food is the prime consideration, and a given locality may only have enough to support a single animal. When the snows grow deep the deer is wholly unable to move, once the yard is left, and hence it is absolutely at the mercy of a man on snowshoes, or of a cougar or a wolf, if found at such times. The man on snowshoes can move very comfortably; and the cougar and the wolf, although hampered by the snow, are not rendered helpless like the deer. I have myself scared a deer out of a yard, and seen it flounder helplessly in a great drift before it had gone thirty rods. When I came up close it ploughed its way a very short distance through the drifts, making tremendous leaps. But as the snow was over six feet deep, so that the deer sank below the level of the surface at each jump, and yet could not get its feet on the solid ground, it became so exhausted that it fell over on its side and bleated in terror as I came up. After looking at it I passed on. Hide-hunters and frontier settlers sometimes go out after the deer on snowshoes when there is a crust, and hence this method of killing is called crusting. It is simple butchery, for the deer cannot, as the moose does, cause its pursuer a chase which may last days. No self-respecting man would follow this method of hunting save from the necessity of having meat.

In very wild localities deer sometimes yard on the ice along the edges of lakes, eating off all the twigs and branches, whether of hardwood trees or of conifers, which they can reach.

At the beginning of the rut the does flee from the bucks, which follow them by scent at full speed. The whitetail buck rarely tries to form a herd of does, though he will sometimes gather two or three. The mere fact that his tactics necessitate a long and arduous chase after each individual doe prevents his organizing herds as the wapiti bull does. Sometimes two or three bucks will be found strung out one behind the other, following the same doe. The bucks wage desperate battle among themselves during this season, coming together with a clash, and then pushing and straining for an hour or two at a time, with their mouths open, until the weakest gives way. As soon as one abandons the fight he flees with all possible speed, and usually escapes unscathed. While head to head there is no opportunity for a disabling thrust, but if, in the effort to retreat, the beaten buck gets caught, he may be killed. Owing to the character of the antlers, whitetail bucks are peculiarly apt to get them interlocked in such a fight, and if the efforts of the two beasts fail to disentangle them, both ultimately perish by starvation. I have several times come across a pair of skulls with interlocked antlers. The same thing occurs, though far less frequently, to the mule-deer and even the wapiti.

The whitetail is the most beautiful and graceful of all our game animals when in motion. I have never been able to agree with Judge Caton that the mule-deer is clumsy and awkward in his gait. I suppose all such terms are relative. Compared to the moose or caribou the mule-deer is light and quick in his movements, and to me there is something very attractive in the poise and power with which one of the great bucks bounds off, all four legs striking the earth together and shooting the body upward and forward as if they were steel springs. But there can be no question as to the infinitely superior grace and beauty of the whitetail when he either trots or runs. The mule-deer and blacktail bound, as already described. The prongbuck gallops with an even gait, and so does the bighorn, when it happens to be caught on a flat; but the whitetail moves with an indescribable spring and buoyancy. If surprised close up, and much terrified, it simply runs away as hard as it can, at a gait not materially different from that of any other game animal under like circumstances, while its head is thrust forward and held down, and the tail is raised perpendicularly. But normally its mode of progression, whether it trots or gallops, is entirely unique. In trotting, the head and tail are both held erect, and the animal throws out its legs with a singularly proud and free motion, bringing the feet well up, while at every step there is an indescribable spring. In the canter or gallop the head and tail are also held erect, the flashing white brush being very conspicuous. Three or four low, long, marvellously springy bounds are taken, and then a great leap is made high in the air, which is succeeded by three or four low bounds, and then by another high leap. A whitetail going through the brush in this manner is a singularly beautiful sight. It has been my experience that they are not usually very much frightened by an ordinary slow track-hound, and I have seen a buck play along in front of one, alternately trotting and cantering, head and flag up, and evidently feeling very little fear.

To my mind the chase of the whitetail, as it must usually be carried on, offers less attraction than the chase of any other kind of our large game. But this is a mere matter of taste, and such men as Judge Caton and Mr. George Bird Grinnell have placed it above all others as a game animal. Personally I feel that the chase of any animal has in it two chief elements of attraction. The first is the chance given to be in the wilderness; to see the sights and hear the sounds of wild nature. The second is the demand made by the particular kind of chase upon the qualities of manliness and hardihood. As regards the first, some kinds of game, of course, lead the hunter into particularly remote and wild localities; and the farther one gets into the wilderness, the greater is the attraction of its lonely freedom. Yet to camp out at all implies some measure of this delight. The keen, fresh air, the breath of the pine forests, the glassy stillness of the lake at sunset, the glory of sunrise among the mountains, the shimmer of the endless prairies, the ceaseless rustle of the cottonwood leaves where the wagon is drawn up on the low bluff of the shrunken river—all these appeal intensely to any man, no matter what may be the game he happens to be following. But there is a wide variation, and indeed contrast, in the qualities called for in the chase itself, according as one quarry or another is sought.

The qualities that make a good soldier are, in large part, the qualities that make a good hunter. Most important of all is the ability to shift for one's self, the mixture of hardihood and resourcefulness which enables a man to tramp all day in the right direction, and, when night comes, to make the best of whatever opportunities for shelter and warmth may be at hand. Skill in the use of the rifle is another trait; quickness in seeing game, another; ability to take advantage of cover, yet another; while patience, endurance, keenness of observation, resolution, good nerves, and instant readiness in an emergency, are all indispensable to a really good hunter.

If a man lives on a ranch, or is passing some weeks in a lodge in a game country, and starts out for two or three days, he will often do well to carry nothing whatever but a blanket, a frying-pan, some salt pork, and some hardtack. If the hunting-ground is such that he can use a wagon or a canoe, and the trip is not to be too long, he can carry about anything he chooses, including a tent, any amount of bedding, and if it is very cold, a small, portable stove, not to speak of elaborate cooking apparatus. If he goes with a pack-train, he will also be able to carry a good deal; but in such a case he must rely on the judgment of the trained packers, unless he is himself an expert in the diamond hitch. If it becomes necessary to go on foot for any length of time, he must be prepared to do genuine roughing, and must get along with the minimum of absolute necessities.

It is hardly necessary to point out that the hunter worthy of the name should be prepared to shift for himself in emergencies. A ranchman, or any other man whose business takes him much in the mountains and out on the great plains or among the forests, ought to be able to get along entirely on his own account. But this cannot usually be done by those whose existence is habitually more artificial. When a man who normally lives a rather over-civilized life, an over-luxurious life—especially in the great cities—gets off for a few weeks' hunting, he cannot expect to accomplish much in the way of getting game without calling upon the services of a trained guide, woodsman, plainsman, or mountain man, whose life-work it has been to make himself an adept in all the craft of the wilderness. Until a man unused to wilderness life, even though a good sportsman, has actually tried it, he has no idea of the difficulties and hardships of shifting absolutely for himself, even for only two or three days. Not only will the local guide have the necessary knowledge as to precisely which one of two seemingly similar places is most apt to contain game; not only will he possess the skill in packing horses, or handling a canoe in rough water, or finding his way through the wilderness, which the amateur must lack; but even the things which the amateur does, the professional will do so much more easily and rapidly, as in the one case to leave, and in the other case not to leave, ample time for the hunting proper. Therefore the ordinary amateur sportsman, especially if he lives in a city, must count upon the services of trained men, possibly to help him in hunting, certainly to help him in travelling, cooking, pitching camp, and the like; and this he must do, if he expects to get good sport, no matter how hardy he may be, and no matter how just may be the pride he ought to take in his own craft, skill, and capacity to undergo fatigue and exposure. But while normally he must take advantage of the powers of others, he should certainly make a point of being able to shift for himself whenever the need arises; and he can only be sure of possessing this capacity by occasionally exercising it. It ought to be unnecessary to point out that the wilderness is not a place for those who are dependent upon luxuries, and above all for those who make a camping trip an excuse for debauchery. Neither the man who wants to take a French cook and champagne on a hunting trip, nor his equally objectionable though less wealthy brother who is chiefly concerned with filling and emptying a large whiskey jug, has any place whatever in the real life of the wilderness.

The chase of an animal should rank according as it calls for the exercise in a high degree of a large number of these qualities. The grizzly is almost our only dangerous game, and under certain conditions shooting the grizzly calls for considerable courage on the part of the hunter. Disregarding these comparatively rare occasions, the chase of mountain game, especially the bighorn, demands more hardihood, power of endurance, and moral and physical soundness than any other kind of sport, and so must come first. The wapiti and mule-deer rank next, for they too must be killed by stalking as a result of long tramps over very rough ground. To kill a moose by still hunting is a feat requiring a high degree of skill, and entailing severe fatigue. When game is followed on horseback, it means that the successful hunter must ride well and boldly.

The whitetail is occasionally found where it yields a very high quality of sport. But normally it lives in regions where it is extremely difficult to kill it legitimately, as the wapiti and mule-deer are killed, and yet comparatively easy to kill it under circumstances which make no demand for any particular prowess on the part of the hunter. It is far more difficult to still hunt successfully in the dense brushy timber frequented by the whitetail than in the open glades, the mountains, and the rocky hills, through which the wapiti and mule-deer wander. The difficulty arises, however, because the chief requirement is stealth, noiselessness. The man who goes out into the hills for a mule-deer must walk hard and far, must be able to bear fatigue, and possibly thirst and hunger, must have keen eyes, and be a good shot. He does not need to display the extraordinary power of stealthy advance which is necessary to the man who would creep up to and kill a whitetail in thick timber. Now, the qualities of hardihood and endurance are better than the quality of stealth, and though all three are necessary in both kinds of chase, yet it is the chase of the mule-deer which most develops the former, and the chase of the whitetail which most develops the latter. When the woods are bare and there is some snow on the ground, however, still hunting the whitetail becomes not only possible, but a singularly manly and attractive kind of sport. Where the whitetail can be followed with horse and hound, the sport is also of a very high order. To be able to ride through woods and over rough country at full speed, rifle or shotgun in hand, and then to leap off and shoot at a running object, is to show that one has the qualities which made the cavalry of Forrest so formidable in the Civil War. There could be no better training for the mounted rifleman, the most efficient type of modern soldier.

By far the easiest way to kill the whitetail is in one or other of certain methods which entail very little work or skill on the part of the hunter. The most noxious of these, crusting in the deep snows, has already been spoken of. No sportsman worthy of the name would ever follow so butcherly a method. Fire hunting must also normally be ruled out. It is always mere murder if carried on by a man who sits up at a lick, and is not much better where the hunter walks through the fields—not to mention the fact that on such a walk he is quite as apt to kill stock as to kill a deer. But fire hunting from a boat, or jacking, as it is called, though it entails absolutely no skill in the hunter, and though it is, and ought to be, forbidden, as it can best be carried on at the season when nursing does are particularly apt to be the victims, nevertheless has a certain charm of its own. The first deer I ever killed, when a boy, was obtained in this way, and I have always been glad to have had the experience, though I have never been willing to repeat it. I was at the time camped out in the Adirondacks.

Two or three of us, all boys of fifteen or sixteen, had been enjoying what was practically our first experience in camping out, having gone out with two guides, Hank Martin and Mose Sawyer, from Paul Smith's on

Lake St. Regis. My brother and cousin were fond of fishing and I was
not, so I was deputed to try to bring in a deer. I had a double-barrelled
12-bore gun, French pinfire, with which I had industriously collected
"specimens" on a trip to Egypt and Palestine and on Long Island; except
for three or four enthralling but not over-successful days after woodcock
and quail, I had done no game shooting. As to every healthy boy with a
taste for outdoor life, the Northern forests were to me a veritable land of
enchantment. We were encamped by a stream among the tall pines, and I
had enjoyed everything; poling and paddling the boat, tramping through
the woods, the cries of chickaree and chipmunk, of jay, woodpecker,
chickadee, nuthatch, and cross-bill, which broke the forest stillness; and,
above all, the great reaches of sombre woodland themselves. The heart-
shaped footprints which showed where the deer had come down to drink
and feed on the marshy edges of the water made my veins thrill; and the
nights around the flickering camp-fire seemed filled with romance.

Around my ranch I very rarely tried to still-hunt whitetail, because it
was always easier to get mule-deer or prongbuck, if I had time to go off
for an all-day's hunt. There were whitetail on the very bottom on which
the ranch-house stood, as well as on the bottom opposite, and on those
to the right and left up and down stream. Occasionally I have taken the
hounds out alone, and then as they chevied the whitetail around the bottom, have endeavored by rapid running on foot or on horseback to get
to some place from which I could obtain a shot. The deer knew perfectly
well that the hounds could not overtake them, and they would usually do
a great deal of sneaking round and round through the underbrush and
cottonwoods before they finally made up their minds to leave the bottom.
On one occasion a buck came sneaking down a game trail through the
buck brush where I stood, going so low that I could just see the tips of
his antlers, and though I made desperate efforts I was not able to get into
a position from which I could obtain a shot. On another occasion, while
I was looking intently into a wood through which I was certain a deer
would pass, it deliberately took to the open ground behind me, and I did
not see it until it was just vanishing. Normally, the end of my efforts was
that the deer went off and the hounds disappeared after it, not to return
for six or eight hours. Once or twice things favored me; I happened to

take the right turn or go in the right direction, and the deer happened to blunder past me; and then I returned with venison for supper. Two or three times I shot deer about nightfall or at dawn, in the immediate neighborhood of the ranch, obtaining them by sneaking as noiselessly as possible along the cattle trails through the brush and timber, or by slipping along the edge of the river bank. Several times I saw deer while I was sitting on the piazza or on the doorstep of the ranch, and on one occasion I stepped back into the house, got the rifle, and dropped the animal from where I stood.

On yet other occasions I obtained whitetail which lived not on the river bottoms but among the big patches of brush and timber in the larger creeks. When they were found in such country I hunted them very much as I hunted the mule-deer, and usually shot one when I was expecting as much to see a mule-deer as a whitetail. When the game was plentiful I would often stay on my horse until the moment of obtaining the shot, especially if it was in the early morning or late evening. My method then was to ride slowly and quietly down the winding valleys and across the spurs, hugging the bank, so that, if deer were feeding in the open, I would get close up before either of us saw the other. Sometimes the deer would halt for a moment when it saw me, and sometimes it would bound instantly away. In either case my chance lay in the speed with which I could jump off the horse and take my shot. Even in favorable localities this method was of less avail with whitetail than mule-deer, because the former were so much more apt to skulk.

As soon as game became less plentiful my hunting had to be done on foot. My object was to be on the hunting-ground by dawn, or else to stay out there until it grew too dark to see the sights of my rifle. Often all I did was to keep moving as quietly as possible through likely ground, ever on the alert for the least trace of game; sometimes I would select a lookout and carefully scan a likely country to see if I could not detect something moving. On one occasion I obtained an old whitetail buck by the simple exercise of patience. I had twice found him in a broad basin, composed of several coulees, all running down to form the head of a big creek, and all of them well timbered. He dodged me on both occasions, and I made up my mind that I would spend a whole day in watching for him from a little natural ambush of sage-bush and cedar on a high point which overlooked the entire basin. I crept up to my ambush with the utmost caution early in the morning, and there I spent the entire day, with my lunch and a water-bottle, continually scanning the whole region most carefully with the glasses. The day passed less monotonously than it sounds, for every now and then I would catch a glimpse of wild life; once a fox, once a coyote, and once a badger; while the little chipmunks had a fine time playing all around me. At last, about mid-afternoon, I suddenly saw the buck come quietly out of the dense thicket in which he had made his midday bed, and deliberately walk up a hillside and lie down in a thin clump of ash where the sun could get at him—for it was in September, just before the rut began. There was no chance of stalking him in the place he had chosen, and all I could do was to wait. It was nearly sunset before he moved again, except that I occasionally saw him turn his head. Then he got up, and after carefully scrutinizing all the neighborhood, moved down into a patch of fairly thick brush, where I could see him standing and occasionally feeding, all the time moving slowly up the valley. I now slipped most cautiously back and trotted nearly a mile until I could come up behind one of the ridges bounding the valley in which he was. The wind had dropped and it was almost absolutely still when I crawled flat on my face to the crest, my hat in my left hand, my rifle in my right. There was a big sage-bush conveniently near, and under this I peered. There was a good deal of brush in the valley below, and if I had not known that the buck was there, I would never have discovered him. As it was, I watched for a quarter of an hour, and had about made up my mind that he must have gone somewhere else, when a slight movement nearly below me attracted my attention, and I caught a glimpse of him nearly three hun-dred yards off, moving quietly along by the side of a little dry watercourse which was right in the middle of the brush. I waited until he was well past, and then again slipped back with the utmost care, and ran on until I was nearly opposite the head of the coulee, when I again approached the ridge-line. Here there was no sage-bush, only tufts of tall grass, which were stirring in the little breeze which had just sprung up, fortunately in the right direction. Taking advantage of a slight inequality in the soil, I managed to get behind one of these tufts, and almost immediately saw the buck. Toward the head of the coulee the brush had become scanty and low, and he was now walking straight forward, evidently keeping a sharp lookout. The sun had just set. His course took him past me at a distance of eighty yards. When directly opposite I raised myself on my elbows, drawing up the rifle, which I had shoved ahead of me. The movement of course caught his eye at once; he halted for one second to look around and see what it was, and during that second I pulled the trigger. Away he went, his white flag switching desperately, and though he galloped over the hill, I felt he was mine. However, when I got to the top of the rise over which he had gone, I could not see him, and as there was a deep though narrow coulee filled with brush on the other side, I had a very ugly feeling that I might have lost him, in spite of the quantity of blood he had left along his trail. It was getting dark, and I plunged quickly into the coulee. Usually a wounded deer should not be followed until it has had time to grow stiff, but this was just one of the cases where the rule would have worked badly; in the first place, because darkness was coming on, and in the next place, because the animal was certain to die shortly, and all that I wanted was to see where he was. I followed his trail into the coulee, and expected to find that he had turned down it, but a hurried examination in the fading light showed me that he had taken the opposite course, and I scrambled hastily out on the other side, and trotted along, staring into the brush, and now and then shouting or throwing in a clod of earth. When nearly at the head there was a crackling in the brush, and out burst the wounded buck. He disappeared behind a clump of elms, but he had a hard hill to go up, and the effort was too much for him. When I next saw him he had halted, and before I could fire again down he came.

On another occasion I spied a whole herd of whitetail feeding in a natural meadow, right out in the open, in mid-afternoon, and was able to get up so close that when I finally shot a yearling buck (which was one of the deer farthest away from me, there being no big buck in the outfit), the remaining deer, all does and fawns, scattered in every direction, some galloping right past me in their panic. Once or twice I was able to perform a feat of which I had read, but in which I scarcely believed. This was, to creep up to a deer while feeding in the open, by watching when it shook its tail, and then remaining motionless. I cannot say whether the habit is a universal one, but on two occasions at least I was able thus to creep up to the feeding deer, because before lifting its head it invariably shook its tail, thereby warning me to stay without moving until it had lifted its head, scrutinized the landscape, and again lowered its head to graze. The eyesight of the whitetail, as compared with that of the prong-horn antelope, is poor. It notes whatever is in motion, but it seems unable to distinguish clearly anything that is not in motion. On the occasions in question no antelope that I have ever seen would have failed to notice me at once and to take alarm. But the whitetail, although it scrutinized me narrowly, while I lay motionless with my head toward it, seemed in each case to think that I must be harmless, and after a while it would go on feeding. In one instance the animal fed over a ridge and walked off before I could get a shot; in the other instance I killed it.

In 1894, on the last day I spent at the ranch, and with the last bul-let I fired from my rifle, I killed a fine whitetail buck. I left the ranch-house early in the afternoon on my favorite pony, Muley, my foreman, Sylvane Ferris, riding with me. We forded the shallow river and rode up a long winding coulee, with belts of timber running down its bottom. After going a couple of miles, by sheer good luck we stumbled on three whitetail—a buck, a doe and a fawn. When we saw them they were trying to sneak off, and immediately my foreman galloped toward one end of the belt of timber in which they were, and started to ride down through it, while I ran Muley to the other end to intercept them. They were, of course, quite likely to break off to one side; but this happened to be one of the occasions when everything went right. When I reached the spot from which I covered the exits from the timber, I leaped off, and immediately afterward heard a shout from my foreman that told me the deer were on foot. Muley was a pet horse, and enjoyed immensely the gallop after game; but his nerves invariably failed him at the shot. On this occasion he stood snorting beside me, and finally, as the deer came in sight, away he tore—only to go about 200 yards, however, and stand and watch us, snorting, with his ears pricked forward until, when I needed him, I went for him. At the moment, however, I paid no heed to Muley, for a cracking in the brush told me the game was close, and I caught the shadowy outlines of the doe and the fawn as they scudded through the timber. By good luck, the buck, evidently flurried, came right on the edge of the woods next to me, and as he passed, running like a quarter-horse, I held well ahead of him and pulled trigger. The bullet broke his neck and down he went—a fine fellow with a handsome ten-point head, and fat as a prize sheep; for it was just before the rut. Then we rode home, and I sat in a rocking-chair on the ranch-house veranda, looking across the wide, sandy river bed at the strangely shaped buttes and the groves of shimmering cottonwoods until the sun went down and the frosty air bade me go in.

10

Red Letter Days in British Columbia

by Lt. Townsend Whelen

Townsend Whelen (1877–1967) was an avid outdoorsman best remembered today for his detailed magazine articles on guns and hunting. He contributed to all the top outdoor magazines of his time, including Sports Afield *and* American Rifleman. *The best full biographical article on Whelen was written by Dave Petzal and published in* Field & Stream *in June 2006.*

In the month of July, 1901, my partner, Bill Andrews, and I were at a small Hudson Bay post in the northern part of British Columbia, outfitting for a long hunting and exploring trip in the wild country to the North. The official map showed this country as "unexplored," with one or two rivers shown by dotted lines. This map was the drawing card which had brought us thousands of miles by rail, stage and pack train to this out-of-the-way spot. By the big stove in the living room of the factor's house we listened to weird tales of this north country, of its enormous mountains and glaciers, its rivers and lakes and of the quantities of game and fish. The factor told us of three men who had tried to get through there in the Klondike rush several years before and had not been heard from yet. The trappers and Siwashes could tell us of trails which ran up either side of the Scumscum, the river on which the post stood, but no one knew what lay between that and the Yukon to the north.

We spent two days here outfitting and on the morning of the third said goodbye to the assembled population and started with our pack train up the east bank of the Scumscum. We were starting out to live and travel in an unknown wilderness for over six months, and our outfit may perhaps interest my readers: We had two saddle horses, four pack horses and a dog. A small tent formed one pack cover. We had ten heavy army blankets, which we used for saddle blankets while traveling, they being kept clean by using canvas sweat pads under them. We were able to pack 150 pounds of grub on each horse, divided up as nearly as I can remember as follows: One hundred and fifty pounds flour, 50 pounds sugar, 30 pounds beans, 10 pounds rice, 10 pounds dried apples, 20 pounds prunes, 30 pounds corn meal, 20 pounds oatmeal, 30 pounds potatoes, 10 pounds onions, 50 pounds bacon, 25 pounds salt, 1 pound pepper, 6 cans baking powder, 10 pounds soap, 10 pounds tobacco, 10 pounds tea, and a few little incidentals weighing probably 10 pounds. We took two extra sets of shoes for each horse, with tools for shoeing, 2 axes, 25 boxes of wax matches, a large can of gun oil, canton flannel for gun rags, 2 cleaning rods, a change of underclothes, 6 pairs of socks and 6 moccasins each, with buckskin for resoling, toilet articles, 100 yards of fishing line, 2 dozen fish hooks, an oil stove, awl, file, screw-driver, needles and thread, etc.

For cooking utensils we had 2 frying pans, 3 kettles to nest, 2 tin cups, 3 tin plates and a gold pan. We took 300 cartridges for each of our rifles. Bill carried a .38-55 Winchester, model '94, and I had my old .40-72 Winchester, model '95, which had proved too reliable to relinquish for a high-power small bore. Both rifles were equipped with Lyman sights and carefully sighted. As a precaution we each took along extra front sights, firing pins and main-springs, but did not have a chance to use them. I loaded the ammunition for both rifles myself, with black powder, smokeless priming, and lead bullets. Both rifles proved equal to every emergency.

Where the post stood the mountains were low and covered for the most part with sage brush, with here and there a grove of pines or quaking aspen. As our pack train wound its way up the narrow trail above the river bank we saw many Siwashes spearing salmon, a very familiar sight in that country. These gradually became fewer and fewer, then we passed a miner's cabin and a Siwash village with its little log huts and its hay fields, from which grass is cut for the winter consumption of the horses. Gradually all signs of civilization disappeared, the mountains rose higher and higher, the valley became a canon, and the roar of the river increased, until finally the narrowing trail wound around an outrageous corner with the river a thousand feet below, and looming up in front of us appeared a range of snow-capped mountains, and thus at last we were in the haven where we would be.

That night we camped on one of the little pine-covered benches above the canon. My, but it was good to get the smell of that everlasting sage out of our nostrils, and to take long whiffs of the balsam-ladened air! Sunset comes very late at this latitude in July, and it was an easy matter to wander up a little draw at nine in the evening and shoot the heads of three grouse. After supper it was mighty good to lie and smoke and listen to the tinkle of the horse bells as they fed on the luscious mountain grass. We were old campmates, Bill and I, and it took us back to many trips we had had before, which were, however, to be surpassed many times by this one. I can well remember how as a boy, when I first took to woods loafing, I used to brood over a little work which we all know so well, entitled, "Woodcraft," by that grand old man, "Nessmuk," and particularly that part where he relates about his eight-day tramp through the then virgin wilderness of Michigan. But here we were, starting out on a trip which was to take over half a year, during which time we were destined to cover over 1,500 miles of unexplored mountains, without the sight of a human face or an axe mark other than our own.

The next day after about an hour's travel, we passed the winter cabin of an old trapper, now deserted, but with the frames for stretching bear skins and boards for marten pelts lying around—betokening the owner's occupation. The dirt roof was entirely covered with the horns of deer and mountain sheep, and we longed to close our jaws on some good red venison. Here the man-made trails came to an end, and henceforth we used the game trails entirely. These intersect the country in every direction, being made by the deer, sheep and caribou in their migrations between the high and low altitudes. In some places they were hardly discernible, while in others we followed them for days, when they were as plainly marked as the bridle paths in a city park. A little further on we saw a whole family of goats sunning themselves on a high bluff across the river, and that night we dined on the ribs of a fat little spike buck which I shot in the park where we pitched our tent.

To chronicle all the events which occurred on that glorious trip would, I fear, tire my readers, so I will choose from the rich store certain ones which have made red-letter days in our lives. I can recollect but four days when we were unable to kill enough game or catch enough fish to keep the table well supplied, and as luck would have it, those four days came together, and we nearly starved. We had been camped for about a week in a broad wooded valley, having a glorious loaf after a hard struggle across a mountain pass, and were living on trout from a little stream alongside camp, and grouse which were in the pine woods by the thousands. Tiring of this diet we decided to take a little side trip and get a deer or two, taking only our three fattest horses and leaving the others behind to fatten up on the long grass in the valley, for they had become very poor owing to a week's work high up above timber line. The big game here was all high up in the mountains to escape the heat of the valley. So we started one morning, taking only a little tea, rice, three bannocks, our bedding and rifles, thinking that we would enjoy living on meat straight for a couple of days. We had along with us a black mongrel hound named Lion, belonging to Bill. He was a fine dog on grouse but prone to chase a deer once in a while.

About eight miles up the valley could be seen a high mountain of green serpentine rock and for many days we had been speculating on the many fine bucks which certainly lay in the little ravines around the base, so we chose this for our goal. We made the top of the mountain about three in the afternoon, and gazing down on the opposite side we saw a little lake with good horse feed around it and determined to camp there. About half way down we jumped a doe and as it stood on a little hummock Bill blazed away at it and undershot. This was too much for Lion, the hound, and he broke after the deer, making the mountainside ring with his baying for half an hour. Well, we hunted all the next day, and the next, and never saw a hair. That dog had chased the deer all out of the country with his barking.

By this time our little grub-stake of rice, bannocks and tea was exhausted, and, to make things worse, on the third night we had a terrific hail storm, the stones covering the ground three inches deep. Breakfast the next morning consisted of tea alone and we felt pretty glum as we started out, determining that if we did not find game that day we would pull up stakes for our big camp in the valley. About one o'clock I struck a fresh deer trail and had not followed it long before three or four others joined it, all traveling on a game trail which led up a valley. This valley headed up about six miles from our camp in three little ravines, each about four miles long. When I got to the junction of these ravines it was getting dark and I had to make for camp. Bill was there before me and had the fire going and some tea brewing, but nothing else. He had traveled about twenty miles that day and had not seen a thing. I can still see the disgusted look on his face when he found I had killed nothing. We drank our tea in silence, drew our belts tighter and went to bed.

The next morning we saddled up our horses and pulled out. We had not tasted food for about sixty hours and were feeling very faint and weak. I can remember what an effort it was to get into the saddle and how sick and weak I felt when old Baldy, my saddle horse, broke into a trot. Our way back led near the spot where I had left the deer trail the night before, and we determined to ride that way hoping that perhaps we might get a shot at them. Bill came first, then Loco, the pack horse, and I brought up the rear. As we were crossing one of the little ravines at the head of the main valley Loco bolted and Bill took after him to drive him back into the trail. I sat on my horse idly watching the race, when suddenly I saw a mouse-colored flash and then another and heard the thump, thump of cloven feet. Almost instantly the whole ravine seemed to be alive with deer. They were running in every direction. I leaped from my horse and cut loose at the nearest, which happened to be a doe. She fell over a log and I could see her tail waving in little circles and knew I had her. Then I turned on a big buck on the other side of the ravine and at the second shot he stumbled and rolled into the little stream. I heard Bill shooting off to the left and yelled to him that we had enough, and he soon joined me, saying he had a spike buck down. It was the work of but a few minutes to dress the deer and soon we had a little fire going and the three livers hanging in little strips around it. Right here we three, that is, Bill, the dog and myself, disposed of a liver apiece, and my! how easily and quickly it went—the first meat in over a week. Late that night we made our horse camp in the lower valley, having to walk all the way as our horses packed the meat. The next day was consumed entirely with jerking meat, cooking and eating. We consumed half the spike buck that day. When men do work such as we were doing their appetites are enormous, even without a fast of four days to sharpen them up.

One night I well remember after a particularly hard day with the pack train through a succession of wind-falls. We killed a porcupine just before camping and made it into a stew with rice, dough balls, onions and thick gravy, seasoned with curry. It filled the kettle to within an inch of the top and we ate the whole without stopping, whereat Bill remarked that it was enough for a whole boarding-house. According to the catalogue of Abercrombie and Fitch that kettle held eight quarts.

We made it the rule while our horses were in condition, to travel four days in the week, hunt two and rest one. Let me chronicle a day of traveling; it may interest some of you who have never traveled with a pack train. Arising at the first streak of dawn, one man cooked the breakfast while the other drove in the horses. These were allowed to graze free at every camping place, each horse having a cow bell around its neck, only Loco being hobbled, for he had a fashion of wandering off on an exploring expedition of his own and leading all the other horses with him. The horses were liable to be anywhere within two miles of camp, and it was necessary to get behind them to drive them in. Four miles over these mountains would be considered a pretty good day's work in the East. Out here it merely gave one an appetite for his breakfast. If you get behind a pack of well-trained horses they will usually walk right straight to camp, but on occasions I have walked, thrown stones and cussed from seven until twelve before I managed to get them in. Sometimes a bear will run off a pack of horses. This happened to us once and it took two days to track them to the head of a canon, fifteen miles off, and then we had to break Loco all over again.

Breakfast and packing together would take an hour, so we seldom got started before seven o'clock. One of us rode first to pick out the trail, then followed the four pack horses and the man in the rear, whose duty it was to keep them in the trail and going along. Some days the trail was fine, running along the grassy south hillsides with fine views of the snowcapped ranges, rivers, lakes and glaciers; and on others it was one continual struggle over fallen logs, boulders, through ice-cold rivers, swifter than the Niagara rapids, and around bluffs so high that we could scarcely distinguish the outlines of the trees below. Suppose for a minute that you have the job of keeping the horses in the trail. You ride behind the last horse, lazily watching the train. You do not hurry them as they stop for an instant to catch at a whiff of bunch grass beside the trail. Two miles an hour is all the speed you can hope to make. Suddenly one horse will leave the trail enticed by some particularly green grass a little to one side, and leaning over in your saddle you pick up a stone and hurl it at the delinquent, and he falls into line again. Then everything goes well until suddenly one of the pack horses breaks off on a faint side trail going for all he is worth. You dig in your spurs and follow him down the mountain side over rocks and down timber until he comes to a stop half a mile below in a thicket of quaking aspen. You extricate him and drive him back. The next thing you know one of the horses starts to buck and you notice that his pack is turning; then everything starts at once. The pack slides between the horse's legs, he bucks all the harder, the frying pan comes loose, a side pack comes off and the other horses fly in every direction. Perhaps in an hour you have corralled the horses, repacked the cause of your troubles and are hitting the trail again. In another day's travel the trail may lead over down timber and big boulders and for eight solid hours you are whipping the horses to make them jump the obstructions, while your companion is pulling at the halters.

Rustling with a pack train is a soul-trying occupation. Where possible we always aimed to go into camp about three in the afternoon. Then the horses got a good feed before dark—they will not feed well at night—and we had plenty of time to make a comfortable camp and get a good supper. We seldom pitched our tent on these one-night camps unless the weather looked doubtful, preferring to make a bed of pine boughs near the fire. The blankets were laid on top of a couple of pack sheets and the tent over all.

For several days we had been traveling thus, looking for a pass across a long snow-capped mountain range which barred our way to the north. Finally we found a pass between two large peaks where we thought we could get through, so we started up. When we got up to timber-line the wind was blowing so hard that we could not sit on our horses. It would take up large stones the size of one's fist and hurl them down the mountain side. It swept by us cracking and roaring like a battery of rapid-fire guns. To cross was impossible, so we back-tracked a mile to a spot where a little creek crossed the trail, made camp and waited. It was three days before the wind went down enough to allow us to cross.

The mountain sheep had made a broad trail through the pass and it was easy to follow, being mostly over shale rock. That afternoon, descending the other side of the range, we camped just below timber line by a little lake of the most perfect emerald hue I have ever seen. The lake was about a mile long. At its head a large glacier extended way up towards the peaks. On the east was a wall of bright red rock, a thousand feet high, while to the west the hillside was covered with dwarf pine trees, some of them being not over a foot high and full-grown at that. Below our camp the little stream, the outlet of the lake, bounded down the hillside in a succession of waterfalls. A more beautiful picture I have yet to see. We stayed up late that night watching it in the light of the full moon and thanked our lucky stars that we were alive. It was very cold; we put on all the clothes we owned and turned in under seven blankets. The heavens seemed mighty near, indeed, and the stars crackled and almost exploded with the still silver mountains sparkling all around. We could hear the roar of the waterfalls below us and the bells of the horses on the hillside above. Our noses were very cold. Far off a coyote howled and so we went to sleep—and instantly it was morning.

I arose and washed in the lake. It was my turn to cook, but first of all I got my telescope and looked around for signs of game. Turning the glass to the top of the wooded hillside, I saw something white moving, and getting a steady position, I made it out to be the rump of a mountain sheep. Looking carefully I picked out four others. Then I called Bill. The sheep were mine by right of discovery, so we traded the cook detail and I took my rifle and belt, stripped to trousers, moccasins and shirt, and started out, going swiftly at first to warm up in the keen mountain air. I kept straight up the hillside until I got to the top and then started along the ridge toward the sheep. As I crossed a little rise I caught sight of them five hundred yards ahead, the band numbering about fifty. Some were feeding, others were bedded down in some shale. From here on it was all stalking, mostly crawling through the small trees and bushes which were hardly knee-high. Finally, getting within one hundred and fifty yards, I got a good, steady prone position between the bushes, and picking out the largest ram, I got the white Lyman sight nicely centered behind his shoulder and very carefully and gradually I pressed the trigger. The instant the gun went off I knew he was mine, for I could call the shot exactly. Instantly the sheep were on the move. They seemed to double up, bunch and then vanish. It was done so quickly that I doubt if I could have gotten in another shot even if I had wished it. The ram I had fired at was knocked completely off its feet, but picked himself up instantly and started off with the others; but after he had run about a hundred yards I saw his head drop and turning half a dozen somersaults, he rolled down the hill and I knew I had made a heart shot. His horns measured 16½ inches at the base, and the nose contained an enormous bump, probably caused in one of his fights for the supremacy of the herd.

I dressed the ram and then went for the horses. Bill, by this time, had everything packed up, so after going up the hill and loading the sheep on my saddle horse, we started down the range for a region where it was warmer and less strenuous and where the horse feed was better. That night we had mountain sheep ribs—the best meat that ever passed a human's mouth—and I had a head worth bringing home. A 16½-inch head is very rare in these days. I believe the record head measured about 19 inches. I remember distinctly, however, on another hunt in the Lillooet district of British Columbia, finding in the long grass of a valley the half-decayed head of an enormous ram. I measured the pith of the skull where the horn had been and it recorded 18 inches. The horn itself must have been at least 21 inches. The ram probably died of old age or was unable to get out of the high altitude when the snow came.

We journeyed on and on, having a glorious time in the freedom of the mountains. We were traveling in a circle, the diameter of which was about three hundred miles. One day we struck an enormous glacier and had to bend way off to the right to avoid it. For days as we travelled that glacier kept us company. It had its origin way up in a mass of peaks and perpetual snow, being fed from a dozen valleys. At least six moraines could be distinctly seen on its surface, and the air in its vicinity was decidedly cool. Where we first struck it it was probably six miles wide and I believe it was not a bit less than fifty miles long. We named it Chilco glacier, because it undoubtedly drained into a large lake of that name near the coast. At this point we were not over two hundred miles from the Pacific Ocean.

As the leaves on the aspen trees started to turn we gradually edged around and headed toward our starting point, going by another route, however, trusting to luck and the careful map we had been making to bring us out somewhere on the Scumscum river above the post. The days were getting short now and the nights very cold. We had to travel during almost all the daylight and our horses started to get poor. The shoes we had taken for them were used up by this time and we had to avoid as much as possible the rocky country. We travelled fast for a month until we struck the headwaters of the Scumscum; then knowing that we were practically safe from being snowed up in the mountain we made a permanent camp on a hillside where the horsefeed was good and started to hunt and tramp to our hearts' delight, while our horses filled up on the grass. We never killed any more game than we could use, which was about one animal every ten days. In this climate meat will keep for a month if protected from flies in the daytime and exposed to the night air after dark.

We were very proud of our permanent camp. The tent was pitched under a large pine tree in a thicket of willows and quaking aspen. All around it was built a windbreak of logs and pine boughs, leaving in front a yard, in the center of which was our camp fire. The windbreak went up six feet high and when a fire was going in front of the tent we were as warm as though in a cabin, no matter how hard the wind blew. Close beside the tent was a little spring, and a half a mile away was a lake full of trout from fifteen pounds down. We spent three days laying in a supply of firewood. Altogether it was the best camp I ever slept in. The hunting within tramping distance was splendid. We rarely hunted together, each preferring to go his own way. When we did not need meat we hunted varmints, and I brought in quite a number of prime coyote pelts and one wolf. One evening Bill staggered into camp with a big mountain lion over his shoulders. He just happened to run across it in a little pine thicket. That was the only one we saw on the whole trip, although their tracks were everywhere and we frequently heard their mutterings in the still evenings. The porcupines at this camp were unusually numerous. They would frequently get inside our wind break and had a great propensity for eating our soap. Lion, the hound, would not bother them; he had learned his lesson well. When they came around he would get an expression on his face as much as to say, "You give me a pain."

The nights were now very cold. It froze every night and we bedded ourselves down with lots of skins and used enormous logs on the fire so that it would keep going all night. We shot some marmots and made ourselves fur caps and gloves and patched up our outer garments with buckskin. And still the snow did not come.

One day while out hunting I saw a big goat on a bluff off to my right and determined to try to get him for his head, which appeared through my telescope to be an unusually good one. He was about half a mile off when I first spied him and the bluff extended several miles to the south-west like a great wall shutting off the view in that direction. I worked up to the foot of the bluffs and then along; climbing up several hundred feet I struck a shelf which appeared to run along the face at about the height I had seen the goat. It was ticklish work, for the shelf was covered with slide rock which I had to avoid disturbing, and then, too, in places it dwindled to a ledge barely three feet wide with about five hundred feet of nothing underneath. After about four hundred yards of this work I heard a rock fall above me and looking up saw the billy leaning over an outrageous corner looking at me. Aiming as nearly as I could straight up I let drive at the middle of the white mass. There was a grunt, a scramble and a lot of rocks, and then down came the goat, striking in between the cliff and a big boulder and not two feet from me. I fairly shivered for fear he would jump up and butt me off the ledge, but he only gave one quiver and lay still. The 330-grain bullet entering the stomach, had broken the spine and killed instantly. He was an old grandfather and had a splendid head, which I now treasure very highly. I took the head, skin, fat and some of the meat back to camp that night, having to pack it off the bluff in sections. The fat rendered out into three gold-pans full of lard. Goat-fat is excellent for frying and all through the trip it was a great saving on our bacon.

Then one night the snow came. We heard it gently tapping on the tent, and by morning there was three inches in our yard. The time had come only too soon to pull out, which we did about ten o'clock, bidding good-bye to our permanent camp with its comfortable windbreak, its fireplace, table and chairs. Below us the river ran through a canon and we had to cross quite a high mountain range to get through. As we ascended the snow got deeper and deeper. It was almost two feet deep on a level on top of the range. We had to go down a very steep hog-back, and here had trouble in plenty. The horses' feet balled up with snow and they were continually sliding. A pack horse slid down on top of my saddle horse and started him. I was on foot in front and they knocked me down and the three of us slid until stopped by a fallen tree. Such a mess I never saw. One horse was on top of another. The pack was loose and frozen ropes tangled up with everything. It took us half an hour to straighten up the mess and the frozen lash ropes cut our hands frightfully. My ankle had become slightly strained in the mix-up and for several days I suffered agonies with it. There was no stopping—we had to hit the trail hard or get snowed in. One day we stopped to hunt. Bill went out while I nursed my leg. He brought in a fine seven-point buck.

Speaking of the hunt he said: "I jumped the buck in a flat of down timber. He was going like mad about a hundred yards off when I first spied him. I threw up the old rifle and blazed away five times before he tumbled. Each time I pulled I was conscious that the sights looked just like that trademark of the Lyman sight showing the running deer and the sight. When I went over to look at the buck I had a nice little bunch of five shots right behind the shoulder. Those Lyman sights are surely the sights for a hunting rifle." Bill was one of the best shots on game I ever saw. One day I saw him cut the heads off of three grouse in trees while he sat in the saddle with his horse walking up hill. Both our rifles did mighty good work. The more I use a rifle the more I become convinced of the truth of the saying, "Beware of the man with one gun." Get a good rifle to suit you exactly. Fix the trigger pull and sights exactly as you wish them and then stick to that gun as long as it will shoot accurately and you will make few misses in the field.

Only too soon we drove our pack-train into the post. As we rode up two men were building a shack. One of them dropped a board and we nearly jumped out of our skins at the terrific noise. My! how loud everything sounded to our ears, accustomed only to the stillness of those grand mountains. We stayed at the post three days, disposing of our horses and boxing up our heads and skins, and then pulled out for civilization. Never again will such experiences come to us. The day of the wilderness hunter has gone for good. And so the hunt of our lives came to an end.

11

The Road to Tinkhamtown

by Corey Ford

If you own a copy of the June 1970 issue of Field & Stream *magazine, consider yourself lucky. That was the 75th anniversary issue, a fine thing. But that's not the reason that issue was so precious. Illustrated with a painting by Howard Terpning, Corey Ford's story "The Road to Tinkhamtown" makes that issue a classic. A blurb written by the editors and displayed on the pages tells the story: "This story by the late Corey Ford, here published for the first time anywhere, is a moving tale which will not soon be forgotten. It is for all those who mourned his death that we present this farewell from the creator of 'The Lower Forty.'" A few months after he wrote this story in 1969, Ford passed away. He never saw "Tinkhamtown" in print. Ford's stories and his "Lower Forty" column were* Field & Stream *favorites. His setters provided the background of many of his tales. "Tinkhamtown" was his masterpiece, written in the evening of his life, written with skill and love, a dog story unlike any other. More than any story I know, this one brings to mind the great William Faulkner quote: "The past is never dead. It's not even past."*

IT WAS A LONG WAY, BUT HE KNEW WHERE HE WAS GOING. HE WOULD follow the road through the woods and over the crest of a bill and down the hill to the stream, and cross the sagging timbers of the bridge, and on the other side would be the place called Tinkhamtown. He was going back to Tinkhamtown.

He walked slowly at first, his legs dragging with each step. He had not walked for almost a year, and his flanks had shriveled and wasted away from lying in bed so long; he could fit his fingers around his thigh, Doc Towle had said he would never walk again, but that was Doc for you, always on the pessimistic side. Why, now he was walking quite easily, once he had started. The strength was coming back into his legs, and he did not have to stop for breath so often. He tried jogging a few steps, just to show he could, but he slowed again because he had a long way to go.

It was hard to make out the old road, choked with alders and covered by matted leaves, and he shut his eyes so he could see it better. He could always see it when he shut his eyes. Yes, here was the beaver dam on the right, just as he remembered it, and the flooded stretch where he had picked his way from hummock to hummock while the dog splashed unconcernedly in front of him. The water had been over his boot tops in one place, and sure enough, as he waded it now his left boot filled with water again, the same warm squdgy feeling. Everything was the way it had been that afternoon, nothing had changed in ten years. Here was the blowdown across the road that he had clambered over, and here on a knoll was the clump of thorn apples where a grouse had flushed as they passed. Shad had wanted to look for it, but he had whistled him back. They were looking for Tinkhamtown.

He had come across the name on a map in the town library. He used to study the old maps and survey charts of the state; sometimes they showed where a farming community had flourished, a century ago, and around the abandoned pastures and in the orchards grown up to pine the birds would be feeding undisturbed. Some of his best grouse covers had been located that way. The map had been rolled up in a cardboard cylinder; it crackled with age as he spread it out. The date was 1857. It was the sector between Cardigan and Kearsarge Mountains, a wasteland of slash and second-growth timber without habitation today, but evidently it had supported a number of families before the Civil War. A road was marked on the map, dotted with X's for homesteads, and the names of the owners were lettered beside them: Nason J. Tinkharn, Allard, R. Tinkham. Half the names were Tinkham. In the center of the map—the paper was so yellow that he could barely make it out—was the word "Tinkhamtown."

He had drawn a rough sketch on the back of an envelope, nothing where the road left the highway and ran north to a fork and then turned east and crossed a stream that was not even named; and the next morning he and Shad had set out together to find the place. They could not drive very far in the jeep, because washouts had gutted the roadbed and laid bare the ledges and boulders. He had stuffed the sketch in his hunting-coat pocket, and hung his shotgun over his forearm and started walking, the setter trotting ahead with the bell on his collar tinkling. It was an old-fashioned sleigh bell, and it had a thin silvery note that echoed through the woods like peepers in the spring. He could follow the sound in the thickest cover, and when it stopped he would go to where he heard it last and Shad would be on point. After Shad's death, he had put the bell away. He'd never had another dog.

It was silent in the woods without the bell, and the way was longer than he remembered. He should have come to the big hill by now. Maybe he'd taken the wrong turn back at the fork. He thrust a hand into his hunting coat; the envelope with the sketch was still in the pocket. He sat down on a flat rock to get his bearings, and then he realized, with a surge of excitement, that he had stopped on this very rock for lunch ten years ago. Here was the waxed paper from his sandwich, tucked in a crevice, and here was the hollow in the leaves where Shad had stretched out beside him, the dog's soft muzzle flattened on his thigh. He looked up, and through the trees he could see the hill.

He rose and started walking again, carrying his shotgun. He had left the gun standing in its rack in the kitchen when he had been taken to the state hospital, but now it was hooked over his arm by the trigger guard; he could feel the solid heft of it. The woods grew more dense as he climbed, but here and there a shaft of sunlight slanted through the trees. "And there were forests ancient as the hills," he thought "enfolding sunny spots of greenery." Funny that should come back to him now; he hadn't read it since he was a boy. Other things were coming back to him, the smell of dank leaves and sweet fern and frosted apples, the sharp contrast of sub and cool shade, the November stillness before snow. He walked faster feeling the excitement swell within him.

He paused on the crest of the hill, straining his ears for the faint mutter of the stream below him, but he could not hear it because of the voices. He wished they would stop talking, so he could hear the stream. Someone was saying his name over and over, "Frank, Frank," and he opened his eyes reluctantly and worried, and there was nothing to worry about. He tried to tell her where he was going, but when he moved his lips the words would not form. "What did you say, Frank?" she asked, bending her head lower. "I don't understand." He couldn't make the words any clearer, and she straightened and said to Doc Towle: "It sounded like Tinkhamtown."

"Tinkhamtown?" Doc shook his head, "Never heard him mention any place by that name."

He smiled to himself. Of course he'd never mentioned it to Doc. Things like a secret grouse cover you didn't mention to anyone, not even to as close a friend as Doc was. No, he and Shad were the only ones who knew. They found it together, that long ago afternoon, and it was their secret.

They had come to the stream—he shut his eyes so he could see it again—and Shad had trotted across the bridge. He had followed more cautiously, avoiding the loose planks and walking along a beam with his shotgun held out to balance himself. On the other side of the stream the road mounted steeply to a clearing in the woods, and he halted before the split-stone foundations of a house, the first of the series of farms shown on the map. It must have been a long time since the building had fallen in; the cottonwoods growing in the cellar hole were twenty, maybe thirty years old. His boot overturned a rusted axe blade, and the handle of a china cup in the grass; that was all. Beside the doorstep was a lilac bush, almost as tall as the cottonwoods. He thought of the wife who had set it out, a little shrub then, and the husband who had chided her for wasting time on such frivolous things with all the farmwork to be done. But the work had come to nothing, and still the lilac bloomed each spring, the one thing that had survived.

Shad's bell was moving along the stone wall at the edge of the clearing, and he strolled after him, not hunting, wondering about the people who had gone away and left their walls to crumble and their buildings to collapse under the winter snows. Had they ever come back to Tinkhamtown? Were they here now, watching him unseen? His toe stubbed against a block of hewn granite hidden by briers, part of the sill of the old barn. Once it had been a tight barn, warm with cattle steaming in their stalls, rich with the blend of hay and manure and harness leather. He liked to think of it the way it was; it was more real than this bare rectangle of blocks and the emptiness inside. He'd always felt that way about the past. Doc used to argue that what's over is over, but he would insist Doc was wrong. Everything is the way it was, he'd tell Doc. The past never changes. You leave it and go on to the present, but it is still there, waiting for you to come back to it.

He had been so wrapped in his thoughts that he had not realized Shad's bell had stopped. He hurried across the clearing holding his gun ready. In a corner of the stone wall an ancient apple tree had littered the ground with fallen fruit, and beneath it Shad was standing motionless. The white fan of his tail was lifted a little and his backline was level, the neck craned forward, one foreleg cocked. His flanks were trembling with the nearness of grouse, and a thin skein of drool hung from his jowls. The dog did not move as he approached, but the brown eyes rolled back until their whites showed, looking for him. "Steady, boy," he called. His throat was tight, the way it always got when Shad was on point, and he had to swallow hard, "Steady, I'm coming."

"I think his lips moved just now," his sister's voice said. He did not open his eyes, because he was waiting for the grouse to get up in front of Shad, but he knew Doc Towle was looking at him. "He's sleeping," Doc said after a moment. "Maybe you better get some sleep yourself, Mrs. Duncombe." He heard Doc's heavy footsteps cross the room. "Call me if there's any change," Doc said, and closed the door, and in the silence he could hear his sister's chair creaking beside him, her silk dress rustling regularly as she breathed.

What was she doing here, he wondered. Why had she come all the way from California to see him? It was the first time they had seen each other since she had married and moved out West. She was his only relative, but they had never been very close; they had nothing in common, really. He heard from her now and then, but it was always the same letter:

Why didn't he sell the old place, it was too big for him now that the folks had passed on, why didn't he take a small apartment in town where he wouldn't be alone? But he liked the big house, and he wasn't alone, not with Shad. He had closed off all the other rooms and moved into the kitchen so everything would be handy. His sister didn't approve of his bachelor ways, but it was very comfortable with his cot by the stove and Shad curled on the floor near him at night, whinnying and scratching, the linoleum with his claws as he chased a bird in a dream. He wasn't alone when he heard that.

He had never married. He had looked after the folks as long as they lived; maybe that was why. Shad was his family. They were always together—Shad was short for Shadow—and there was a closeness between them that he did not feel for anyone else, not his sister or Doc even. He and Shad used to talk without words, each knowing what the other was thinking, and they could always find one another in the woods. He still remembered the little things about him: the possessive thrust of his jaw, the way he false-yawned when he was vexed, the setter stubbornness sometimes, the clownish grin when they were going hunting, the kind eyes. That was it: Shad was the kindest person he had ever known.

They had not hunted again after Tinkhamtown. The old dog had stumbled several times, walking back to the jeep, and he had to carry him in his arms the last hundred yards. It was hard to realize he was gone. He liked to think of him the way he was; it was like the barn, it was more real than the emptiness. Sometimes at night, lying awake with the pain in his legs, he would hear the scratch of claws on the linoleum, and he would turn on the light and the hospital room would be empty. But when he turned the light off he would hear the scratching again, and he would be content and drop off to sleep, or what passed for sleep in these days and nights that ran together without dusk or dawn.

Once he asked Doc point-blank if he would ever get well. Doc was giving him something for the pain, and he hesitated a moment and finished what he was doing and cleaned the needle and then looked at him and said: "I'm afraid not, Frank." They had grown up in the town together, and Doc knew him too well to lie. "I'm afraid there's nothing to do." Nothing to do but lie there and wait till it was over. "Tell me, Doc," he whispered, for his voice wasn't very strong, "what happens when it's over?" And Doc fumbled with the catch of his black bag and closed it and said well he supposed you went on to someplace else called the Hereafter. But he shook his head: He always argued with Doc. "No, it isn't someplace else," he told him, "it's someplace you've been where you want to be again." Doc didn't understand, and he couldn't explain it any better. He knew what he meant, but the shot was taking effect and he was tired.

He was tired now, and his legs ached a little as he started down the hill, trying to find the stream. It was too dark under the trees to see the sketch he had drawn, and he could not tell direction by the moss on the north side of the trunks. The moss grew all around them, swelling them out of size, and huge blowdowns blocked his way. Their upended roots were black and misshapen, and now instead of excitement he felt a surge of panic. He floundered through a pile of slash, his legs throbbing with pain as the sharp points stabbed him, but he did not have the strength to get to the other side and he had to back out again and circle. He did not know where he was going. It was getting late, and he had lost the way.

There was no sound in the woods, nothing to guide him, nothing but his sister's chair creaking and her breath catching now and then in a dry sob. She wanted him to turn back, and Doc wanted him to, they all wanted him to turn back. He thought of the big house; if he left it alone it would fall in with the winter snows and cottonwoods would grow in the cellar hole. And there were all the other doubts, but most of all there was the fear. He was afraid of the darkness, and being alone, and not knowing where he was going. It would be better to turn around and go back. He knew the way back.

And then he heard it, echoing through the woods like peepers in the spring, the thin silvery tinkle of a sleigh bell. He started running toward it, following the sound down the hill. His legs were strong again, and he hurdled the blowdowns, he leapt over fallen logs, he put one fingertip on a pile of slash and sailed over it like a grouse skimming. He was getting nearer and the sound filled his ears, louder than a thousand church bells ringing, louder than all the choirs in the sky, as loud as the pounding of his heart. The fear was gone; he was not lost. He had the bell to guide him now.

He came to the stream, and paused for a moment at the bridge. He wanted to tell them he was happy, if they only knew how happy he was, but when he opened his eyes he could not see them anymore. Everything else was bright, but the room was dark.

The bell had stopped and he looked across the stream. The other side was bathed in sunshine, and he could see the road mounting steeply, and the clearing in the woods, and the apple tree in a corner of the stone wall. Shad was standing motionless beneath it, the white fan of his tails lifted, his neck craned forward and one foreleg cocked. The whites of his eyes showed as he looked back. waiting for him.

"Steady," he called, "steady, boy." He started across the bridge. "I'm coming."

12

The Mountain Goat at Home

by William T. Hornaday, ScD

Author William T. Hornaday, ScD (1854–1937) was a pioneering conservationist and zoologist. His field trips inspired the detailed observations on backcountry terrain and wildlife that he captured in his published prose.

JOHN PHILLIPS AND I WERE SCRAMBLING ALONG THE STEEP AND ROUGH eastern face of Bald Mountain, a few yards below timberline, half-way up 'twixt creek and summit. He was light of weight, well-seasoned and nimble-footed; I was heavy, ill-conditioned, and hungry for more air. Between the sliderock, down timber and brush, the going had been undeniably bad, and in spite of numerous rests I was almost fagged.

Far below us, at the bottom of the V-shaped valley, the horse-bell faintly tinkled, and as Mack and Charlie whacked out the trail, the pack-train crept forward. We were thankful that the camping-place, on Goat Pass, was only a mile beyond.

Presently we heard a voice faintly shouting to us from below.

"Look above you—at the goats!"

Hastily we moved out of a brush-patch, and looked aloft. At the top of the precipice that rose above our slope, a long, irregular line of living forms perched absurdly on the skyline, and looked over the edge, at us. Quickly we brought our glasses to bear, and counted fourteen living and wild Rocky Mountain goats.

"All nannies, young billies, and kids," said Mr. Phillips. "They are trying to guess what kind of wild animals we are." I noticed that he was quite calm; but I felt various things which seemed to sum themselves up in the formula—"the Rocky Mountain goat—at last!"

For fully ten minutes, the entire fourteen white ones steadfastly gazed down upon us, with but few changes of position, and few remarks. Finally, one by one they drew back from the edge of the precipice, and quietly drifted away over the bald crest of the mountain.

For twenty years I had been reading the scanty scraps of mountain-goat literature that at long intervals have appeared in print. I had seen seven specimens alive in captivity, and helped to care for four of them. With a firm belief that the game was worth it, I had traveled twenty-five hundred miles or more in order to meet this strange animal in its own home, and cultivate a close acquaintance with half a dozen wild flocks.

At three o'clock we camped at timberline, on a high and difficult pass between the Elk River and the Bull. That night we christened the ridge Goat Pass. While the guides and the cook unpacked the outfit and pitched the tents, Mr. Phillips hurried down the western side of the divide. Fifteen minutes later he and Kaiser—in my opinion the wisest hunting-dog in British Columbia—had twenty-eight nanny goats and kids at bay on the top of a precipice, and were photographing them at the risk of their lives.

Rifle and glass in hand, I sat down on a little knoll a few yards above the tents, to watch a lame billy goat who was quietly grazing and limping along the side of a lofty ridge that came down east of us from Phillips Peak. A lame wild animal in a country wherein a shot had not been fired for five years, was, to all of us, a real novelty; and with my glasses I watched the goat long and well. It was his left foreleg that was lame, and it was the opinion of the party that the old fellow was suffering from an accident received on the rocks. Possibly a stone had been rolled down upon him, by another goat.

Suddenly sharp cries of surprise came up from the camp, and I sprang up to look about. Three goats were running past the tents at top speed—a big billy, and two smaller goats.

"Hi, there! Goats! Goats!" cried Smith and Norboe.

The cook was stooping over the fire, and looking under his right arm he saw the bunch charging straight toward him, at a gallop. A second later, the big billy was almost upon him.

"Hey! You son-of-a-gun!" yelled Huddleston, and as the big snow-white animal dashed past him he struck it across the neck with a stick of firewood. The goat's tracks were within six feet of the campfire.

The billy ran straight through the camp, then swung sharply to the left, and the last I saw of him was his humpy hindquarters wildly bobbing up and down among the dead jack pines, as he ran for Bald Mountain.

The two smaller goats held their course, and one promptly disappeared. The other leaped across our water-hole, and as it scrambled out of the gully near my position, and paused for a few seconds to look backward, instinctively I covered it with my rifle. But only for an instant. "Come as they may," thought I, "my first goat shall not be a small one!" And as the goat turned and raced on up, my .303 Savage came down.

We laughed long at the utter absurdity of three wild goats actually breaking into the privacy of our camp, on our first afternoon in Goatland. In the Elk Valley, Charlie Smith had promised me that we would camp "right among the goats," and he had royally kept his word.

At evening, when we gathered round the campfire, and counted up, we found that on our first day in Goatland, we had seen a total of fifty-three goats; and no one had fired a shot. As for myself, I felt quite set up over my presence of mind in not firing at the goat which I had "dead to rights" after it had invaded our camp, and which might have been killed as a measure of self-defence.

Our camp was pitched in a most commanding and awe-inspiring spot. We were precisely at timberline, in a grassy hollow on the lowest summit between Bald and Bird Mountains, on the north, and Phillips Peak, on the south. From our tents the ground rose for several hundred feet, like the cables of the Brooklyn Bridge, until it stopped against a rock wall which went on up several hundred feet more. In a notch quite near us was a big bank of eternal ice. In that country, such things are called glaciers; and its melting foot was the starting-point of Goat Creek. Fifty paces taken eastward from our tents brought us to a projecting point from which we looked down a hundred feet to a rope of white water, and on down Goat Creek as it drops five hundred feet to the mile, to the point where it turns a sharp corner to the right, and disappears.

Westward of camp, after climbing up a hundred feet or so, through dead standing timber, the ridge slopes steeply down for a mile and a half to the bottom of a great basin half filled with green timber, that opens toward Bull River. It was on this slope, at a point where a wall of rock cropped out, that Mr. Phillips cornered his flock of goats and photographed them.

At our camp, water and wood were abundant; there was plenty of fine grass for our horses, spruce boughs for our beds, scenery for millions, and what more could we ask?

The day following our arrival on Goat Pass was dull and rainy, with a little snow, and we all remained in camp. At intervals, someone would stroll out to our lookout point above Goat Creek, and eye-search the valley below "to see if an old silver-tip could come a-moochin' up, by accident," as Guide Smith quaintly phrased it.

That gray day taught me something of color values in those mountains. As seen from our lookout point, the long, even stretch of house-roof mountain-slope on the farther side of Goat Creek was a revelation. In the full sunlight of a clear day, its tints were nothing to command particular attention. Strong light seemed to take the colors out of everything. But a cloudy day, with a little rain on the face of nature, was like new varnish on an old oil-painting.

During the forenoon, fleecy white clouds chased each other over the pass and through our camp, and for much of the time the Goat Creek gorge was cloud-filled. At last, however, about noon, they rose and drifted away, and then the mountain opposite revealed a color pattern that was exquisitely beautiful.

For a distance of a thousand yards the ridge-side stretched away down the valley, straight and even; and in that distance it was furrowed from top to bottom by ten or twelve gullies, and ribbed by an equal number of ridges. At the bottom of the gorge was a dense green fringe of tall, obelisk spruces, very much alive. In many places, ghostly processions of dead spruces, limbless and gray, forlornly climbed the ridges, until half-way up the highest stragglers stopped. Intermixed with these tall poles were patches of trailing juniper of a dark olive-green color, growing tightly to the steep slope.

The apex of each timbered ridge was covered with a solid mass of great willow-herb or "fireweed" (*Chamaenerion anguistifolium*), then in its brightest autumn tints of purple and red. The brilliant patches of color which they painted on the mountainside would have rejoiced the heart of an artist. This glorious plant colored nearly every mountainside in that region during our September there.

Below the fireweed, the ridges were dotted with small, cone-shaped spruces, and trailing junipers (*Juniperus prostrata*), of the densest and richest green. The grassy sides of the gullies were all pale yellow—green, softly blended at the edges with the darker colors that framed them in. At the bottom of each washout was a mass of light-gray sliderock, and above all this rare pattern of soft colors loomed a lofty wall of naked carboniferous limestone rock, gray, grim and forbidding.

It seemed to me that I never elsewhere had seen mountains so rich in colors as the ranges between the Elk and the Bull in that particular September.

The rain and the drifting clouds were with us for one day only. Very early on the second morning, while Mr. Phillips and I lay in our sleeping-bags considering the grave question of getting or not getting up, Mack Norboe's voice was heard outside, speaking low but to the point:

"Director, there's an old billy goat, lying right above our camp!"

It was like twelve hundred volts. We tumbled out of our bags, slipped on our shoes, and ran out. Sure enough, a full-grown male goat was lying on the crest of the divide that led up to the summit of Bald Mountain, seventy-five feet above us, and not more than two hundred and fifty yards away. The shooting of him was left to me.

I think I could have bagged that animal as he lay; but what would there have been in that of any interest to a sportsman? I had not asked any goats to come down to our camp, and lie down to be shot!

Not caring greatly whether I got that goat or not, I attempted a stalk along the western side of the ridge, through the dead timber, and well below him. But the old fellow was not half so sleepy as he looked. When finally I came up to a point that was supposed to command his works, I found that he had winded me. He had vanished from his resting-place, and was already far up the side of Bald Mountain, conducting a masterly retreat.

After a hurried breakfast, we made ready for a day with the goats on the northern mountains. Although there are many things in favor of small parties—the best consisting of one guide and one hunter—we all went together—Mr. Phillips, Mack, Charlie and I. Our leader declared a determination to "see the Director shoot his first goat," and I assured the others that the services of all would be needed in carrying home my spoils.

As we turned back toward camp, and took time to look "at the sceneries," the view westward, toward Bull River, disclosed a cloud effect so beautiful that Mr. Phillips insisted upon photographing it, then and there. To give the "touch of life" which he always demanded, I sat in, as usual.

By Mr. Phillips' advice, I put on suspenders and loosened my cartridge-belt, in order to breathe with perfect freedom. We wore no leggings. Our shoes were heavily hobnailed, and while I had thought mine as light as one dared use in that region of ragged rocks, I found that for cliff-climbing they were too heavy, and too stiff in the soles. Of course knee-breeches are the thing, but they should be so well cut that in steep climbing they will not drag on the knees, and waste the climber's horse-power; and there should be a generous opening at the knee.

In those mountains, four things, and only four, are positively indispensable to every party: rifles, axes, fieldglasses and blankets. Each member of our hunting party carried a good glass, and never stirred from camp without it. For myself, I tried an experiment. Two months previously Mrs. Hornaday selected for me, in Paris, a very good opera-glass, made by Lemaire, with a field that was delightfully large and clear. While not quite so powerful a magnifier as the strongest binoculars now on the market, its field was so much clearer that I thought I would prefer it. It was much smaller than any regulation fieldglass, and I carried it either in a pocket of my trousers, or loose inside my hunting-shirt, quite forgetful of its weight.

It proved a great success. We found much interest in testing it with binoculars five times as costly, and the universal verdict was that it would reveal an animal as far as a hunter could go to it, and find it. I mention this because in climbing I found it well worthwhile to be free from a dangling leather case that is always in the way, and often is too large for comfort.

From our camp we went north, along the top of the eastern wall of Bald Mountain. Two miles from home we topped a sharp rise, and there directly ahead, and only a quarter of a mile away on an eastern slope lay a band of eleven goats, basking in the welcome sunshine. The flock was composed of nannies, yearling billies and kids, with not even one old billy among those present. Two old chaperons lay with their heads well up, on the lookout, but all the others lay full length upon the grass, with their backs uphill. Three of the small kids lay close against their mothers.

They were on the northerly point of a fine mountain meadow, with safety rocks on three sides. Just beyond them lay a ragged hogback of rock, both sides of which were so precipitous that no man save an experienced mountaineer would venture far upon it. It was to this rugged fortress that the goats promptly retreated for safety when we left off watching them, and rose from our concealment. Their sunning-ground looked like a sheep-yard, and we saw that goats had many times lain upon that spot.

Nearby, behind a living windbreak, was a goat-bed, that looked as if goats had lain in it five hundred times. By some curious circumstance, a dozen stunted spruces had woven themselves together, as if for mutual support, until they formed a tight evergreen wall ten feet long and eight feet high. It ranged north and south, forming an excellent hedge-like shield from easterly winds, while the steep mountain partially cut off the winds from the west. On the upper side of that natural windbreak, the turf had been worn into dust, and the droppings were several inches deep. Apparently it was liked because it was a good shelter, in the center of a fine sky-pasture, and within a few jumps of ideal safety rocks.

From the spot where the goats had lain, looking ahead and to our left, we beheld a new mountain. Later on we christened it Bird Mountain, because of the flocks of ptarmigan we found upon its summit. Near its summit we saw five more goats, all females and kids. At our feet lay a deep, rich-looking basin, then a low ridge, another basin with a lakelet in it, and beyond that another ridge, much higher than the first. Ridge No. 2 had dead timber upon it, but it was very scattering, for it was timberline; and its upper end snugged up against the eastern wall of Bird Mountain. Later on we found that the northern side of that ridge ended in a wall of rock that was scalable by man in one place only.

"Yonder are two big old billies!" said someone with a glass in action.

"Yes sir; there they are; all alone, and heading this way, too. Those are your goats this time, Director, sure enough."

"Now boys," said I, "if we can stalk those two goats successfully, and bag them both, neatly and in quick time, we can call it genuine goat-hunting!"

They were distant about a mile and a half, jogging along down a rocky hill, through a perfect maze of gullies, ridges, grassplots and rocks, one of them keeping from forty to fifty feet behind the other.

Even at that distance they looked big, and very, very white. Clearly, they were heading for Bird Mountain. We planned to meet them wherever they struck the precipitous side of the mountain ahead of us, and at once began our stalk.

From the basin which contained the little two-acre tarn, the rocky wall of Bird Mountain rose almost perpendicularly for about eight hundred feet. As we were passing between the lake and the cliff, we heard bits of loose rock clattering down.

"Just look yonder!" said Mr. Phillips, with much fervor.

Close at hand, and well within fair rifle-shot, were four goats climbing the wall; and two more were at the top, looking down as if deeply interested. The climbers had been caught napping, and being afraid to retreat either to right or left, they had elected to seek safety by climbing straight up! It was a glorious opportunity to see goats climb in a difficult place, and forthwith we halted and watched as long as the event lasted, utterly oblivious of our two big billies. Our binoculars brought them down to us wonderfully well, and we saw them as much in detail as if we had been looking a hundred feet with the unaided eye.

The wall was a little rough, but the angle of it seemed not more than 10 degrees from perpendicular. The footholds were merely narrow edges

of rock, and knobs the size of a man's fist. Each goat went up in a generally straight course, climbing slowly and carefully all the while. Each one
chose its own course, and paid no attention to those that had gone before.
The eyes looked ahead to select the route, and the front hoofs skillfully
sought for footholds. It seemed as if the powerful front legs performed
three-fourths of the work, reaching up until a good foothold was secured,
then lifting the heavy body by main strength, while the hindlegs "also
ran." It seemed that the chief function of the hind limbs was to keep what
the forelegs won. As an exhibition of strength of limb, combined with
surefootedness and nerve, it was marvelous, no less.

Often a goat would reach toward one side for a new foothold, find
none, then rear up and pivot on its hindfeet, with its neck and stomach
pressed against the wall, over to the other side. Occasionally a goat would
be obliged to edge off five or ten feet to one side in order to scramble on
up. From first to last, no goat slipped and no rocks gave way under their
feet, although numerous bits of loose sliderock were disturbed and sent
rattling down.

It was a most inspiring sight, and we watched it with breathless
interest. In about ten minutes the four goats had by sheer strength and
skill climbed about two hundred feet of the most precipitous portion of
the cliff, and reached easy going. After that they went on up twice as
rapidly as before, and soon passed over the summit, out of our sight. Then
we compared notes.

Mr. Phillips and I are of the opinion that nothing could have induced
mountain sheep to have made that appalling climb, either in the presence
of danger or otherwise. Since that day we have found that there are many
mountain hunters who believe that as a straightaway cliff-climber, the
goat does things that are impossible for sheep.

As soon as the goat-climbing exhibition had ended, we hurried on
across the basin, and up the side of Ridge No. 2. This ridge bore a thin
sprinkling of low spruces, a little fallen timber, much purple fireweed and
some good grass. As seen at a little distance, it was a purple ridge. The
western end of it snugged up against the mountain, and it was there that
we met our two big billy goats. They had climbed nearly to the top of
our ridge, close up to the mountain, and when we first sighted them they

were beginning to feed upon a lace-leaved anemone (*Pulsatilla occidenta-lis*), at the edge of their newly found pasture. We worked toward them, behind a small clump of half-dead spruces, and finally halted to wait for them to come within range.

After years of waiting, Rocky Mountain goats, at last! How amazingly white and soft they look; and how big they are! The high shoulder hump, the big, round barrel of the body, and the knee-breeches on the legs make the bulk of the animal seem enormous. The whiteness of "the driven snow," of cotton and of paper seem by no means to surpass the incomparable white of those soft, fluffy-coated animals as they appear in a setting of hard, gray limestone, rugged sliderock and dark-green vegetation. They impressed me as being the whitest living objects I ever beheld, and far larger than I had expected to find them. In reality, their color had the effect of magnifying their size; for they looked as big as two-year-old buffaloes.

Of course only Mr. Phillips and I carried rifles; and we agreed that the left man should take the left animal.

"It's a hundred and fifty yards!" said Mack Norboe, in a hoarse whisper.

My goat was grazing behind the trunk of a fallen tree, which shielded his entire body. I waited, and waited; and there he stood, with his head down, and calmly cropped until I became wildly impatient. I think he stood in one spot for five minutes, feeding upon Pulsatilla.

"Why don't you shoot?" queried Phillips, in wonder.

"I can't! My goat's hiding behind a tree."

"Well, fire when you're ready, Gridley, and I'll shoot when you do!"

It must have been five minutes, but it seemed like twenty-five, before that goat began to feel a thrill of life along his keel, and move forward. The annoying suspense had actually made me unsteady; besides which, my Savage was a new one, and unchristened. Later on I found that the sights were not right for me, and that my first shooting was very poor.

At last my goat stood forth, in full view—white, immaculate, high of hump, low of head, big and bulky. I fired for the vitals behind the shoulder.

"You've overshot!" exclaimed Norboe, and

"Bang!" said Mr. Phillips' Winchester.

Neither of us brought down our goat at the first fire!

I fired again, holding much lower, and the goat reared up a foot. Mr. Phillips fired again, whereupon his goat fell over like a sack of oats, and went rolling down the hill. My goat turned to run, and as he did so I sent two more shots after him. Then he disappeared behind some rocks. Mack, John and I ran forward, to keep him in sight, and fire more shots if necessary. But no goat was to be seen.

"He can't get away!" said Norboe, reassuringly.

"He's dead!" said I, by way of an outrageous bluff. "You'll find him down on the sliderock!" But inwardly I was torn by doubts.

We hurried down the steep incline, and presently came to the top of a naked wall of rock. Below that was a wide expanse of sliderock.

"Thar he is!" cried Norboe. "Away down yonder, out on the sliderock, dead as a wedge."

From where he stood when I fired, the goat had run back about two hundred feet, where he fell dead, and then began to roll. We traced him by a copious stream of blood on the rocks. He fell down the rock wall, for a hundred feet, in a slanting direction, and then—to my great astonishment—he rolled two hundred feet farther (by measurement) on that ragged, jagged slide-rock before he fetched up against a particularly large chunk of stone, and stopped. We expected to find his horns broken, but they were quite uninjured. The most damage had been inflicted upon his nose, which was badly cut and bruised. The bullet that ended his life (my second shot) went squarely through the valves of his heart; but I regret to add that one thigh-bone had been broken by another shot, as he ran from me.

Mr. Phillips' goat behaved better than mine. It rolled down the grassy slope, and lodged on a treacherous little shelf of earth that overhung the very brink of the precipice. One step into that innocent-looking fringe of green juniper bushes meant death on the sliderock below; and it made me nervous to see Mack and Charlie stand there while they skinned the animal.

As soon as possible we found the only practicable route down the rock wall, and scrambled down. The others say that I slid down the last twenty feet; but that is quite immaterial. I reached the goat a few paces in advance of the others, and thought to divert my followers by reciting a celebrated quotation beginning, "To a hunter, the moment of triumph," etc. As I laid my hand upon the goat's hairy side and said my little piece, I heard a deadly "click."

"Got him!" cried Mr. Phillips; and then three men and a dog laughed loud and derisively. Since seeing the picture I have altered that quotation, to this: "To a hunter, the moment of humiliation is when the first sees his idiotic smile on a surreptitious plate." It is inserted solely to oblige Mr. Phillips, as evidence of the occasion when he got ahead of me.

The others declared that the goat was "a big one, though not the very biggest they ever grow." Forthwith we measured him; and in taking his height we shoved his foreleg up until the elbow came to the position it occupies under the standing, living animal. The measurements were as follows:

Rocky Mountain Goat
Oreamnos montanus
Male, six years old. Killed September 8, 1905, near the Bull River, British Columbia.

	Inches
Standing height at shoulder	38
Length, nose to root of tail	59.25
Length of tail vertebrae	3.50
Girth behind foreleg	55
Girth around abdomen	58
Girth of neck behind ears (unskinned)	18
Circumference of forearm, skinned	11.25
Width of chest	14
Length of horn on curve	9.75
Spread of horns at tips	5
Circumference of horn at base	5.60
Circumference of front hoof	10.50
Circumference of rear hoof	7.75
Base of ear to end of nostrils	10.50
Front corner of eye to rear corner	9
Nostril opening	7

Widest spread of ears, tip to tip — 15
Total weight of animal by scales, allowing 8 lbs.
  for blood lost — 258 lbs.

The black and naked glands in the skin behind the horn were on that date small, and inconspicuous; but they stood on edge, with the naked face of each closely pressed against the base of the horn in front of it.

On another occasion I shot a thin old goat that stood forty-two inches high at the shoulders, and Mr. Phillips shot another that weighed two hundred and seventy-six pounds. After we had thoroughly dissected my goat, weighed it, examined the contents of its stomach, and saved a good sample of its food for close examination at camp, we tied up the hindquarters, head and pelt, and set out for camp.

And thus ended our first day in the actual hunting of mountain goats, in the course of which we saw a total of forty-two animals. The stalking, killing and dissecting of our two goats was very interesting, but the greatest event of the day was our opportunity to watch those five goats climb an almost perpendicular cliff.

This day, also, was the eleventh of September ...

Mr. Phillips, Charlie Smith and I descended the steep side of Goat Pass, crossed the basin and slowly climbed the grassy divide that separates it from the source of Avalanche Creek. When half way down the southern side of that divide, we looked far up the side of Phillips Peak and saw two big old billy goats of shootable size. They were well above timberline, lying where a cloud-land meadow was suddenly chopped off at a ragged precipice. The way up to them was long, and very steep.

"That's a long climb, Director," said Mr. Phillips; "but there are no bad rocks."

I said that I could make it, in time—as compared with eternity—if the goats would wait for me.

"Oh, they'll wait! We'll find 'em there, all right," said Charlie, confidently. So we started.

As nearly as I can estimate, we climbed more than a mile, at an angle that for the upper half of the distance was about 30 degrees—a very steep ascent. At first our way up led through green timber, over smooth ground that was carpeted with needles of spruce and pine. That was comparatively easy, no more difficult, in fact, than climbing the stairs of four Washington monuments set one upon another.

At climbing steep mountains, Mr. Phillips, Charlie Smith and the two Norboes are perfect friends. They are thin, tough and long-winded, and being each of them fully forty pounds under my weight, I made no pretence at trying to keep up with them. As it is in an English workshop, the slowest workman set the pace.

In hard climbing, almost every Atlantic-coast man perspires freely, and is very extravagant in the use of air. It frequently happened that when half way up a high mountain, my lungs consumed the air so rapidly that a vacuum was created around me, and I would have to stop and wait for a new supply of oxygen to blow along. My legs behaved much better than my lungs, and to their credit be it said that they never stopped work until my lungs ran out of steam.

As I toiled up that long slope, I thought of a funny little engine that I saw in Borneo, pulling cars over an absurd wooden railway that ran from the bank of the Sadong River to the coalmines. It would run about a mile at a very good clip, then suddenly cease pulling, and stop. Old Walters, the superintendent, said:

"There's only one thing ails that engine. The bloomin' little thing can't make steam fast enough!"

I was like that engine. I couldn't "keep steam"; and whenever my lungs became a perfect vacuum, I had to stop and rest, and collect air. Considering the fact that there was game above us, I thought my comrades were very considerate in permitting me to set the pace. Now had someone glared at me with the look of a hungry cannibal, and hissed between his teeth, *"Step lively!"* it would have made me feel quite at home.

In due time we left the green timber behind us, and started up the last quarter of the climb. There we found stunted spruces growing like scraggy brush, three feet high, gnarled and twisted by the elements, and enfeebled by the stony soil on which they bravely tried to grow. Only the bravest of trees could even rear their heads on that appalling steep, scorched by the sun, rasped by the wind, drenched by the rains and frozen by the snow. But after a hundred yards or so, even the dwarf spruces gave up the struggle. Beyond them, up to our chosen point, the mountain-roof was smooth and bare, except for a sprinkle of fine, flat sliderock that was very treacherous stuff to climb over.

"Let me take your rifle, Director!" said Charlie, kindly.

"No, thank you. I'll carry it up, or stay down. But you may keep behind me if you will, and catch me if I start to roll!"

On steep slopes, such as that was, my companions had solemnly warned me not to fall backward and start rolling; for a rolling man gathers no moss. A man bowling helplessly down a mountainside at an angle of 30 degrees quickly acquires a momentum which spells death. Often have I looked down a horribly steep stretch, and tried to imagine what I would feel, and think, were I to overbalance backward, and go bounding down. A few hours later we saw a goat carcass take a frightful roll down a slope not nearly so steep as where we climbed up, and several times it leaped six feet into the air.

To keep out of the sight of the goats it was necessary for us to bear well toward our left; and this brought us close to the edge of the precipice, where the mountainside was chopped off. In view of the loose stones underfoot, I felt liked edging more to the right; for the twin chances of a roll down and a fall over began to abrade my nerves. Mr. Phillips and Charlie climbed along so close to the drop that I found myself wondering which of them would be the first to slip and go over.

"Keep well over this way, Director, or the goats may wind you!" said Charlie, anxiously.

"That's all right, Charlie; he's winded now!" said John.

I said we would rest on that; and before I knew the danger, Mr. Phillips had taken a picture of me, resting, and smiling a most idiotic smile.

At last we reached the pinnacle which we had selected when we first sighted our game. As nearly as we could estimate, afterward, by figuring up known elevations, we were at a height of about nine thousand feet, and though not the highest, it was the dizziest point I ever trod. Except when we looked ahead, we seemed to be fairly suspended in mid-air! To look down under one's elbow was to look into miles of dizzy, bottomless space.

The steep slope had led us up to the sharp point of a crag that stuck up like the end of a man's thumb and terminated in a crest as sharp as the comb of a houseroof. Directly in front, and also on the left, was a sheer drop. From the right, the ragged edge of the wall ran on up, to the base of Phillips Peak. Beyond our perch, twelve feet away, there yawned a great basin-abyss, and on beyond that rocky gulf rose a five-hundred-foot wall at the base of the Peak. A little to the right of our position another ragged pinnacle thrust its sharp apex a few feet higher than ours, and eventually caused me much trouble in securing my first shot.

We reached the top of our crag, and peered over its highest rocks just in time to see our two goats quietly walk behind a ragged point of rock farther up the wall, and disappear. They were only a hundred and fifty yards distant; but they had not learned of our existence, and were not in the least alarmed. Naturally, we expected them to saunter back into view, for we felt quite sure they did not mean to climb down that wall to the bottom of the basin. So we lay flat upon the slope, rifles in hand, and waited, momentarily expecting the finish. They were due to cross a grassy slope between two crags, not more than forty feet wide, and if not fired at within about ten seconds of their reappearance, they would be lost behind the rocks! The chance was not nearly so good as it looked.

But minutes passed, and no goats returned. It became evident that the dawdling pair had lain down behind the sheltering crag, for a siesta in the sun. We composed ourselves to await their pleasure, and in our first breath of opportunity, looked off southeasterly, over the meadow whereon the two goats had been feeding. And then we saw a sight of sights.

Rising into view out of a little depression on the farther side of the meadow, lazily sauntering along, there came ten big, snow-white billy goats! They were heading straight toward us, and there was not a nanny, nor a kid, nor even a young billy in the bunch. The air was clear; the sun was shining brightly, the meadow was like dark olive-brown plush, and how grandly those big, pure-white creatures did loom up! When first seen they were about four hundred yards away, but our glasses made the distance seem only one-third of that.

For more than an hour we lay flat on our pinnacle, and watched those goats. No one thought of time. It was a chance of a lifetime. My companions were profoundly surprised by the size of the collection; for previous to that moment, no member of our party ever had seen more than four big male goats in one bunch.

The band before us was at the very top of a sky-meadow of unusual luxuriance, which climbed up out of the valley on our right, and ran on up to the comb of rock that came down from Phillips Peak. In area the meadow was five hundred yards wide, and half a mile long. Afterward, when we walked over it, we found it was free from stones, but full of broad steps, and covered with a dense, greenish-purple matting of ground verdure that was as soft to the foot as the thickest pile carpet. The main body of this verdure is a moss-like plant called mountain avens, closely related to cinquefoil, and known botanically as *Dryas octopetala*. It has a very pretty leaf measuring about 7⁄16 by 3⁄16 inches, with finely serrated edges. In September a mass of it contains a mixture of harmonious colors: olive-green, brown, gray and purple. On this the goats were feeding. This plant is very common in those mountains above timberline, especially on southern slopes; but it demands a bit of ground almost exclusively for itself, and thrives best when alone.

Along with this there grew a moss-like saxifrage (*Saxifraga austro-montana*), which to any one not a botanist seems to be straight moss. It grows in cheerful little clumps of bright green, and whenever it is found on a mountain-pasture, one is pleased to meet it.

I record these notes here, because our ten goats had been in no hurry. They were more than deliberate; they were almost stagnant. In an hour, the farthest that any one of them moved was about one hundred yards, and most of them accomplished even less than that. They were already so well fed that they merely minced at the green things around them. Evidently they had fed to satiety in the morning hours, before we reached them.

As they straggled forward, they covered about two acres of ground. Each one seemed steeped and sodden in laziness. When out grazing, our giant tortoises move faster than they did on that lazy afternoon. When the leader of this band of weary Willies reached the geographical center of the sky-meadow, about two hundred yards from us, he decided to take a sunbath on the most luxurious basin possible to him. Slowly he focussed his mind upon a level bench of earth, about four feet wide. It contained an old goat-bed of loose earth, and upon this he lay down, with his back uphill.

At this point, however, he took a sudden resolution. After about a minute of reflection, he decided that the head of his bed was too high and too humpy; so, bracing himself back with his right foreleg, like an ancient Roman senator at a feast, he set his left leg in motion and flung out from under his breast a quantity of earth. The loose soil rose in a black shower, two feet high, and the big hoof flung it several feet down the hill. After about a dozen rakes, he settled down to bask in the warm sunshine, and blink at the scenery of Avalanche Valley.

Five minutes later, a little higher up the slope, another goat did the same thing; and eventually two or three others laid down. One, however, deliberately sat down on his haunches, dog-fashion, with his back uphill. For fully a quarter of an hour he sat there in profile, slowly turning his head from side to side, and gazing at the scenery while the wind blew through his whiskers.

So far as I could determine, no sentinel was posted. There was no leader, and no individual seemed particularly on the alert for enemies. One and all, they felt perfectly secure.

In observing those goats one fact became very noticeable. At a little distance, their legs looked very straight and stick-like, devoid of all semblance of gracefulness and of leaping power. The animals were very white and immaculate—as were all the goats that we saw—and they stood out with the sharpness of clean snow-patches on dark rock. Nature may have known about the much overworked principle of "protective coloration" when she fashioned the mountain goat, but if so, she was guilty of cruelty to goats in clothing this creature with pelage which, in the most comfortable season for hunting, renders it visible for three miles or more. Even the helpless kidling is as white as cotton, and a grand mark for eagles.

That those goats should look so stiff and genuinely ungraceful on their legs, gave me a distinct feeling of disappointment. From that moment I gave up all hope of ever seeing a goat perform any feats requiring either speed or leaping powers; for we saw that of those short, thick legs—nearly as straight as four Indian clubs—nothing is to be expected save power in lifting and sliding, and rocklike steadfastness. In all the two hundred and thirty-nine goats that we saw, we observed nothing to disprove the conclusive evidence of that day regarding the physical powers of the mountain goat.

While we watched the band of mountain loafers, still another old billy goat, making No. 13, appeared across the rock basin far to our left. From the top of the northern ridge, he set out to walk across the wide rock wall that formed the western face of Phillips Peak. From where we were the wall seemed almost smooth, but to the goat it must have looked otherwise. Choosing a narrow, light-gray line of stratification that extended across the entire width of the wall, the solitary animal set out on its promenade. The distance to be traversed to reach the uppermost point of our sky-pasture was about fifteen hundred feet, and the contour line chosen was about four hundred feet above our position. The incident was like a curtain-raiser to a tragic play.

That goat's walk was a very tame performance. The animal plodded steadily along, never faster, never slower, but still with a purposeful air, like a postman delivering mail. For a mountain goat, not pursued or frightened, it was a rapid walk, probably three miles an hour. Its legs swung to and fro with the regularity and steadiness of four pendulums, and I think they never once paused. The animal held to that one line of stratification, until near the end of its promenade. There a great mass of rock had broken away from the face of the cliff, and the goat was forced to climb down about fifty feet, then up again, to regain its chosen route. A few minutes later its ledge ran out upon the apex of the sky-meadow. There Billy paused for a moment, to look about him; then he picked out a soft spot, precisely where the steep slope of the meadow ended against the rocky peak, and lay down to rest.

Up to that time, Mr. Phillips and I had killed only one goat each, and as we lay there we had time to decide upon the future. He resolved to kill one fine goat as a gift to the Carnegie Museum, and I wished two more for my own purposes. We decided that at a total of three goats each—two less than our lawful right—we would draw the line, and kill no more.

The first shot at the pair of invisible goats was to be mine; and as already suggested, the circumstances were like those surrounding a brief moving target in a shooting-gallery. Before us were two rocky crag-points, and behind the one on the left, the animals lay hidden for full an hour. Between the two crags the V-shaped spot of the meadow, across which I knew my goat would walk or run, looked very small. If he moved a yard too far, the right-hand crag would hide him from me until he would be three hundred yards away. I was compelled to keep my rifle constantly ready, and one eye to the front, in order to see my goat in time to get a shot at him while he crossed that forty feet of ground.

And after all, I came ever so near to making a failure of my vigil. I was so absorbed in watching that unprecedented band of billies that before I knew it, the two goats were in the center of the V-shaped stage, and moving at a good gait across it. Horrors!

Hurriedly I exclaimed to Mr. Phillips, "There they are!" took a hurried aim at the tallest goat, and just as his head was going out of sight, let go. He flinched upward at the shoulders, started forward at a trot, and instantly disappeared from my view.

The instant my rifle cracked, Mr. Phillips said, imperatively,

"Don't move! Don't make a sound, and those goats will stay right where they are."

Instantly we "froze." All the goats sprang up, and stood at attention. All looked fixedly in our direction, but the distant eleven were like ourselves, frozen into statues. In that band not a muscle moved for fully three minutes.

Finally the goats decided that the noise they had heard was nothing at which to be alarmed. One by one their heads began to move, and in five minutes their fright was over. Some went on feeding, but three or four of the band decided that they would saunter down our way and investigate that noise.

But what of my goat?

John slid over to my left, to look as far as possible behind the intercepting crag. Finally he said,

"He's done for! He's lying out there, dead."

As soon as possible I looked at him; and sure enough, he lay stretched upon the grass, back uphill, and apparently very dead. The other goat had gone on and joined the ten.

The investigating committee came walking down toward us with a briskness which soon brought them within rifle-shot; and then Mr. Phillips picked out his Carnegie Museum goat and opened fire, at a range of about three hundred yards. The first shot went high, but at the next the goat came down, hit behind the shoulder. This greatly alarmed all the other goats, but they were so confused that three of them came down toward us at a fast trot. At two hundred yards I picked out one, and fired. At my third shot, it fell, but presently scrambled up, ran for the edge of the precipice and dropped over out of sight. It landed, mortally wounded, on some ragged rocks about fifty feet down, and to end its troubles a shot from the edge quickly finished it.

Mr. Phillips killed his first goat, and before the bunch got away, broke the leg of another. This also got over the edge of the precipice, and had to be finished up from the edge.

But a strange thing remains to be told.

By the time Mr. Phillips and I had each fired about two shots of the last round, in the course of which we ran well over to the right in order to command the field, to our blank amazement my first goat—the dead one!—staggered to his feet, and started off toward the edge of the precipice. It was most uncanny to see a dead animal thus come to life!

"Look, Director," cried Charlie Smith, "your first goat's come to life! Kill him again! Kill him again, quick!"

I did so; and after the second killing he remained dead. I regret to say that in my haste to get those goats measured, skinned and weighed before night, I was so absorbed that I forgot to observe closely where my first shot struck the goat that had to be killed twice. I think however, that it went through his liver and other organs without touching the vital portions of the lungs.

My first goat was the tallest one of the six we killed on that trip, but not the heaviest. He was a real patriarch, and decidedly on the downhill side of life. He was so old that he had but two incisor teeth remaining, and they were so loose they were almost useless. He was thin in flesh, and his pelage was not up to the mark in length. But in height he was tall, for he stood forty-two inches at the shoulders, with the foreleg pushed up where it belongs in a standing animal.

Mr. Phillips' Carnegie Museum goat was the heaviest one shot on that trip, its gross weight being two hundred and seventy-six pounds.

Charlie decided to roll the skinned carcass of my goat down the mountain, if possible within rifle-shot of the highest point of green timber, in the hope that a grizzly might find it, and thereby furnish a shot. He cut off the legs at the knees, and started the body rolling on the sky-pasture, end over end. It went like a wheel, whirling down at a terrific rate, sometimes jumping fifty feet. It went fully a quarter of a mile before it reached a small basin, and stopped. The other carcass, also, was rolled down. It went sidewise, like a bag of grain, and did not roll quite as far as the other.

By the time we had finished our work on the goats—no trifling task—night was fast approaching, and leaving all the heads, skins and meat for the morrow, we started for our new camp, five miles away.

We went down the meadow (thank goodness!), and soon struck the green timber; and then we went on down, down, and still farther down, always at thirty degrees, until it seemed to me we never would stop going down, never reach the bottom and the trail. But everything earthly has an end. At the end of a very long stretch of plunging and sliding, we reached Avalanche Creek, and drank deeply of the icy-cold water for which we had so long been athirst.

After three miles of travel down the creek, over sliderock, through green timber, yellow willows, more green timber and some down timber, we heard the cheerful whack of Huddleston's axe, and saw on tree-trunk and bough the ruddy glow of the new campfire.

The new camp was pitched in one of the most fascinating spots I ever camped within. The three tents stood at the southern edge of a fine, open grove of giant spruces that gave us good shelter on rainy days. Underneath the trees there was no underbrush, and the ground was deeply carpeted with dry needles. Grand mountains rose on either hand, practically from our campfire, and for our front view a fine valley opened southward for six miles, until its lower end was closed by the splendid mass of Roth Mountain and Glacier. Close at hand was a glorious pool of icewater, and firewood "to burn." Yes, there was one other feature, of great moment, abundant grass for our horses, in the open meadow in front of the tents.

To crown all these luxuries, Mr. Phillips announced that, according to mountain customs already established, and precedents fully set, that camp would then and there be named in my honor—"Camp Hornaday." What more could any sportsman possibly desire?

13

The Oregon Trail

by Francis Parkman Jr.

The Oregon Trail: Sketches of Prairie and Rocky Mountain Life
by Francis Parkman Jr. (1823–1893) is one of America's oldest and
most treasured books on the opening of the West. First published in
1849, the book details Parkman's incredible journey into the great unknown of the American West when he was only twenty-three years
old. Much of the best prose centers on his adventures with a band of
Oglala Sioux.

THE COUNTRY BEFORE US WAS NOW THRONGED WITH BUFFALO, AND A
sketch of the manner of hunting them will not be out of place. There
are two methods commonly practised, "running" and "approaching." The
chase on horseback, which goes by the name of "running," is the more
violent and dashing mode of the two, that is to say, when the buffalo are
in one of their wild moods; for otherwise it is tame enough. A practised
and skilful hunter, well mounted, will sometimes kill five or six cows in a
single chase, loading his gun again and again as his horse rushes through
the tumult. In attacking a small band of buffalo, or in separating a single
animal from the herd and assailing it apart from the rest, there is less
excitement and less danger. In fact, the animals are at times so stupid
and lethargic that there is little sport in killing them. With a bold and
well-trained horse the hunter may ride so close to the buffalo that as
they gallop side by side he may touch him with his hand; nor is there
much danger in this as long as the buffalo's strength and breath continue

unabated; but when he becomes tired and can no longer run with ease, with his tongue lolls out and the foam flies from his jaws, then the hunter had better keep a more respectful distance; the distressed brute may turn upon him at any instant; and especially at the moment when he fires his gun. The horse then leaps aside, and the hunter has need of a tenacious seat in the saddle, for if he is thrown to the ground there is no hope for him. When he sees his attack defeated, the buffalo resumes his flight, but if the shot is well directed he soon stops; for a few moments he stands still, then totters and falls heavily upon the prairie.

The chief difficulty in running buffalo, as it seems to me, is that of loading the gun or pistol at full gallop. Many hunters for convenience's sake carry three or four bullets in the mouth; the powder is poured down the muzzle of the piece, the bullet dropped in after it, the stock struck hard upon the pommel of the saddle, and the work is done. The danger of this is obvious. Should the blow on the pommel fail to send the bullet home, or should the bullet, in the act of aiming, start from its place and roll towards the muzzle, the gun would probably burst in discharging. Many a shattered hand and worse casualties besides have been the result of such an accident. To obviate it, some hunters make use of a ramrod, usually hung by a string from the neck, but this materially increases the difficulty of loading. The bows and arrows which the Indians use in running buffalo have many advantages over firearms, and even white men occasionally employ them.

The danger of the chase arises not so much from the onset of the wounded animal as from the nature of the ground which the hunter must ride over. The prairie does not always present a smooth, level, and uniform surface; very often it is broken with hills and hollows, intersected by ravines, and in the remoter parts studded by the stiff wild-sage bushes. The most formidable obstructions, however, are the burrows of wild animals, wolves, badgers, and particularly prairie-dogs, with whose holes the ground for a very great extent is frequently honeycombed. In the blindness of the chase the hunter rushes over it unconscious of danger; his horse, at full career, thrusts his leg deep into one of the burrows; the bone snaps, the rider is hurled forward to the ground and probably killed. Yet accidents in buffalo running happen less frequently than one would suppose; in the recklessness of the chase, the hunter enjoys all the impunity of a drunken man, and may ride in safety over gullies and declivities, where, should he attempt to pass in his sober senses, he would infallibly break his neck.

The method of "approaching," being practised on foot, has many advantages over that of "running"; in the former, one neither breaks down his horse nor endangers his own life; he must be cool, collected, and watchful; must understand the buffalo, observe the features of the country and the course of the wind, and be well skilled in using the rifle. The buffalo are strange animals; sometimes they are so stupid and infatuated that a man may walk up to them in full sight on the open prairie, and even shoot several of their number before the rest will think it necessary to retreat. At another moment they will be so shy and wary that in order to approach them the utmost skill, experience, and judgment are necessary. Kit Carson, I believe, stands preeminent in running buffalo; in approaching, no man living can bear away the palm from Henry Chatillon.

After Tête Rouge had alarmed the camp, no further disturbance occurred during the night. The Arapahoes did not attempt mischief, or if they did the wakefulness of the party deterred them from effecting their purpose. The next day was one of activity and excitement, for about ten o'clock the man in advance shouted the gladdening cry of "Buffalo, buffalo!" and in the hollow of the prairie just below us, a band of bulls was grazing. The temptation was irresistible, and Shaw and I rode down upon them. We were badly mounted on our travelling horses, but by hard lashing we overtook them, and Shaw, running alongside a bull, shot into him both balls of his double-barrelled gun. Looking round as I galloped by, I saw the bull in his mortal fury rushing again and again upon his antagonist, whose horse constantly leaped aside, and avoided the onset. My chase was more protracted, but at length I ran close to the bull and killed him with my pistols. Cutting off the tails of our victims by way of trophy, we rejoined the party in about a quarter of an hour after we had left it. Again and again that morning rang out the same welcome cry of "Buffalo, buffalo!" Every few moments, in the broad meadows along the river, we saw bands of bulls, who, raising their shaggy heads, would gaze in stupid amazement at the approaching horsemen, and then breaking into a clumsy gallop, file off in a long line across the trail in front, towards the rising prairie on the left. At noon, the plain before us was alive with thousands of buffalo—bulls, cows, and calves—all moving rapidly as we drew near; and far off beyond the river the swelling prairie was darkened with them to the very horizon. The party was in gayer spirits than ever. We stopped for a nooning near a grove of trees by the river.

"Tongues and hump-ribs tomorrow," said Shaw, looking with contempt at the venison steaks which Deslauriers placed before us. Our meal finished, we lay down to sleep. A shout from Henry Chatillon aroused us, and we saw him standing on the cart-wheel, stretching his tall figure to its full height, while he looked towards the prairie beyond the river. Following the direction of his eyes, we could clearly distinguish a large, dark object, like the black shadow of a cloud, passing rapidly over swell after swell of the distant plain; behind it followed another of similar appearance, though smaller, moving more rapidly, and drawing closer and closer to the first. It was the hunters of the Arapahoe camp chasing a band of buffalo. Shaw and I caught and saddled our best horses, and went plunging through sand and water to the farther bank. We were too late. The hunters had already mingled with the herd, and the work of slaughter was nearly over. When we reached the ground we found it strewn far and near with numberless carcasses, while the remnants of the herd, scattered in all directions, were flying away in terror, and the Indians still rushing in pursuit. Many of the hunters, however, remained upon the spot, and among the rest was our yesterday's acquaintance, the chief of the village. He had alighted by the side of a cow, into which he had shot five or six arrows, and his woman, who had followed him on horseback to the hunt, was giving him a draught of water from a canteen, purchased or plundered from some volunteer soldier. Recrossing the river, we overtook the party, who were already on their way.

We had gone scarcely a mile when we saw an imposing spectacle. From the river-bank on the right, away over the swelling prairie on the left, and in front as far as the eye could reach, was one vast host of buffalo. The outskirts of the herd were within a quarter of a mile. In many parts they were crowded so densely together that in the distance their rounded backs presented a surface of uniform blackness; but elsewhere they were more scattered, and from amid the multitude rose little columns of dust where some of them were rolling on the ground. Here and there a battle was going forward among the bulls. We could distinctly see them rushing against each other, and hear the clattering of their horns and their hoarse bellowing. Shaw was riding at some distance in advance, with Henry Chatillon; I saw him stop and draw the leather covering from his gun. With such a sight before us, but one thing could be thought of. That morning I had used pistols in the chase. I had now a mind to try the virtue of a gun. Deslauriers had one, and I rode up to the side of the cart; there he sat under the white covering, biting his pipe between his teeth and grinning with excitement.

"Lend me your gun, Deslauriers."

"Oui, Monsieur, oui," said Deslauriers, tugging with might and main to stop the mule, which seemed obstinately bent on going forward. Then everything but his moccasons disappeared as he crawled into the cart and pulled at the gun to extricate it.

"Is it loaded?" I asked.

"Oui, bien chargé; you'll kill, mon bourgeois; yes, you'll kill—c'est un bon fusil."

I handed him my rifle and rode forward to Shaw.

"Are you ready?" he asked.

"Come on," said I.

"Keep down that hollow," said Henry, "and then they won't see you till you get close to them."

The hollow was a kind of wide ravine; it ran obliquely towards the buffalo, and we rode at a canter along the bottom until it became too shallow; then we bent close to our horses' necks, and, at last, finding that it could no longer conceal us, came out of it and rode directly towards the herd. It was within gunshot; before its outskirts, numerous grizzly old bulls were scattered, holding guard over their females. They glared at us in anger and astonishment, walked towards us a few yards, and then turning slowly round, retreated at a trot which afterwards broke into a clumsy gallop. In an instant the main body caught the alarm. The buffalo began to crowd away from the point towards which we were approaching, and a gap was opened in the side of the herd. We entered it, still restraining our excited horses. Every instant the tumult was thickening. The buffalo, pressing together in large bodies, crowded away from us on every hand. In front and on either side we could see dark columns and masses, half hidden by clouds of dust, rushing along in terror and confusion, and hear the tramp and clattering of ten thousand hoofs. That countless multitude of powerful brutes, ignorant of their own strength, were flying in a panic from the approach of two feeble horsemen. To remain quiet longer was impossible.

"Take that band on the left," said Shaw; "I'll take these in front."

He sprang off, and I saw no more of him. A heavy Indian whip was fastened by a band to my wrist; I swung it into the air and lashed my horse's flank with all the strength of my arm. Away she darted, stretching close to the ground. I could see nothing but a cloud of dust before me, but I knew that it concealed a band of many hundreds of buffalo. In a moment I was in the midst of the cloud, half suffocated by the dust and stunned by the trampling of the flying herd; but I was drunk with the chase and cared for nothing but the buffalo. Very soon a long dark mass became visible, looming through the dust; then I could distinguish each bulky carcass, the hoofs flying out beneath, the short tails held rigidly erect. In a moment I was so close that I could have touched them with my gun. Suddenly, to my amazement, the hoofs were jerked upwards, the tails flourished in the air, and amid a cloud of dust the buffalo seemed to sink into the earth before me. One vivid impression of that instant remains upon my mind. I remember looking down upon the backs of several buffalo dimly visible through the dust. We had run unawares upon a ravine. At that moment I was not the most accurate judge of depth and width, but when I passed it on my return, I found it about twelve feet deep and not quite twice as wide at the bottom. It was impossible to stop; I would have done so gladly if I could; so, half sliding, half plunging, down went the little mare. She came down on her knees in the loose sand at the bottom; I was pitched forward against her neck and nearly thrown over her head among the buffalo, who amid dust and confusion came tumbling in all around. The mare was on her feet in an instant and scrambling like a cat up the opposite side. I thought for a moment that she would have fallen back and crushed me, but with a violent effort she clambered out and gained the hard prairie above. Glancing back, I saw the huge head of a bull clinging as it were by the forefeet at the edge of the dusty gulf. At length I was fairly among the buffalo. They were less densely crowded than before, and I could see nothing but bulls, who always run at the rear of a herd to protect their females. As I passed among them they would lower their heads, and turning as they ran, try to gore my horse; but as they were already at full speed there was no force in their onset, and as Pauline ran faster than they, they were always thrown behind her in the effort. I soon began to distinguish cows amid the throng. One just in front of me seemed to my liking, and I pushed close to her side. Dropping the reins, I fired, holding the muzzle of the gun within a foot of her shoulder. Quick as lightning she sprang at Pauline; the little mare dodged the attack, and I lost sight of the wounded animal amid the tumult. Immediately after, I selected another, and urging forward Pauline, shot into her both pistols in succession. For a while I kept her in view, but in attempting to load my gun, lost sight of her also in the confusion. Believing her to be mortally wounded and unable to keep up with the herd, I checked my horse. The crowd rushed onwards. The dust and tumult passed away, and on the prairie, far behind the rest, I saw a solitary buffalo galloping heavily. In a moment I and my victim were running side by side. My firearms were all empty, and I had in my pouch nothing but rifle bullets, too large for the pistols and too small for the gun. I loaded the gun, however, but as often as I levelled it to fire, the bullets would roll out of the muzzle and the gun returned only a report like a squib, as the powder harmlessly exploded. I rode in front of the buffalo and tried to turn her back; but her eyes glared, her mane bristled, and lowering her head, she rushed at me with the utmost fierceness and activity. Again and again I rode before her, and again and again she repeated her furious charge. But little Pauline was in her element. She dodged her enemy at every rush, until at length the buffalo stood still, exhausted with her own efforts, her tongue lolling from her jaws.

Riding to a little distance, I dismounted, thinking to gather a handful of dry grass to serve the purpose of wadding, and load the gun at my leisure. No sooner were my feet on the ground than the buffalo came bounding in such a rage towards me that I jumped back again into the saddle and with all possible despatch. After waiting a few minutes more, I made an attempt to ride up and stab her with my knife; but Pauline was near being gored in the attempt. At length, bethinking me of the fringes at the seams of my buckskin trousers, I jerked off a few of them, and, reloading the gun, forced them down the barrel to keep the bullet in its place; then approaching, I shot the wounded buffalo through the heart. Sinking to her knees, she rolled over lifeless on the prairie. To my astonishment, I found that, instead of a cow, I had been slaughtering a stout yearling bull. No longer wondering at his fierceness, I opened his throat, and cutting out his tongue, tied it at the back of my saddle. My mistake was one which a more experienced eye than mine might easily make in the dust and confusion of such a chase.

Then for the first time I had leisure to look at the scene around me. The prairie in front was darkened with the retreating multitude, and on either hand the buffalo came filing up in endless columns from the low plains upon the river. The Arkansas was three or four miles distant. I turned and moved slowly towards it. A long time passed before, far in the distance, I distinguished the white covering of the cart and the little black specks of horsemen before and behind it. Drawing near, I recognized Shaw's elegant tunic, the red flannel shirt, conspicuous far off. I overtook the party, and asked him what success he had had. He had assailed a fat cow, shot her with two bullets, and mortally wounded her. But neither of us was prepared for the chase that afternoon, and Shaw, like myself, had no spare bullets in his pouch; so he abandoned the disabled animal to Henry Chatillon, who followed, despatched her with his rifle, and loaded his horse with the meat.

We encamped close to the river. The night was dark, and as we lay down we could hear, mingled with the howling of wolves, the hoarse bellowing of the buffalo, like the ocean beating upon a distant coast.

No one in the camp was more active than Jim Gurney, and no one half so lazy as Ellis. Between these two there was a great antipathy. Ellis never stirred in the morning until he was compelled, but Jim was always on his feet before daybreak; and this morning as usual the sound of his voice awakened the party.

"Get up, you booby! up with you now, you're fit for nothing but eating and sleeping. Stop your grumbling and come out of that buffalo-robe, or I'll pull it off for you."

Jim's words were interspersed with numerous expletives, which gave them great additional effect. Ellis drawled out something in a nasal tone from among the folds of his buffalo-robe; then slowly disengaged himself, rose into a sitting posture, stretched his long arms, yawned hideously, and, finally raising his tall person erect, stood staring about him to all the four quarters of the horizon. Deslauriers's fire was soon blazing, and the horses and mules, loosened from their pickets, were feeding on the neighboring meadow. When we sat down to breakfast the prairie was still in the dusky light of morning; and as the sun rose we were mounted and on our way again.

"A white buffalo!" exclaimed Munroe.

"I'll have that fellow," said Shaw, "if I run my horse to death after him."

He threw the cover of his gun to Deslauriers and galloped out upon the prairie.

"Stop, Mr. Shaw, stop!" called out Henry Chatillon, "you'll run down your horse for nothing; it's only a white ox."

But Shaw was already out of hearing. The ox, which had no doubt strayed away from some of the government wagon trains, was standing beneath some low hills which bounded the plain in the distance. Not far from him a band of veritable buffalo bulls were grazing; and startled at Shaw's approach, they all broke into a run, and went scrambling up the hillsides to gain the high prairie above. One of them in his haste and terror involved himself in a fatal catastrophe. Along the foot of the hills was a narrow strip of deep marshy soil, into which the bull plunged and hopelessly entangled himself. We all rode to the spot. The huge carcass was half sunk in the mud, which flowed to his very chin, and his shaggy mane was outspread upon the surface. As we came near, the bull began to struggle with convulsive strength; he writhed to and fro, and in the energy of his fright and desperation would lift himself for a moment half out of the slough, while the reluctant mire returned a sucking sound as he strained to drag his limbs from its tenacious depths. We stimulated his exertions by getting behind him and twisting his tail; nothing would do. There was clearly no hope for him. After every effort his heaving sides were more deeply embedded, and the mire almost overflowed his nostrils; he lay still at length, and looking round at us with a furious eye, seemed to resign himself to fate. Ellis slowly dismounted, and, levelling his boasted yager, shot the old bull through the heart; then lazily climbed back again to his seat, pluming himself no doubt on having actually killed a buffalo. That day the invincible yager drew blood for the first and last time during the whole journey.

The morning was a bright and gay one, and the air so clear that on the farthest horizon the outline of the pale blue prairie was sharply drawn against the sky. Shaw was in the mood for hunting; he rode in advance of the party, and before long we saw a file of bulls galloping at full speed upon a green swell of the prairie at some distance in front. Shaw came scouring along behind them, arrayed in his red shirt, which looked very well in the distance; he gained fast on the fugitives, and as the foremost bull was disappearing behind the summit of the swell, we saw him in the act of assailing the hindmost; a smoke sprang from the muzzle of his gun and floated away before the wind like a little white cloud; the bull turned upon him, and just then the rising ground concealed them both from view.

We were moving forward until about noon, when we stopped by the side of the Arkansas. At that moment Shaw appeared riding slowly down the side of a distant hill; his horse was tired and jaded, and when he threw his saddle upon the ground, I observed that the tails of two bulls were dangling behind it. No sooner were the horses turned loose to feed than Henry, asking Munroe to go with him, took his rifle and walked quietly away. Shaw, Tête Rouge, and I sat down by the side of the cart to discuss the dinner which Deslauriers placed before us, and we had scarcely finished when we saw Munroe walking towards us along the river-bank. Henry, he said, had killed four fat cows, and had sent him back for horses to bring in the meat. Shaw took a horse for himself and another for Henry, and he and Munroe left the camp together. After a short absence all three of them came back, their horses loaded with the choicest parts of the meat. We kept two of the cows for ourselves, and gave the others to Munroe and his companions. Deslauriers seated himself on the grass before the pile of meat, and worked industriously for some time to cut it into thin broad sheets for drying, an art in which he had all the skill of an Indian woman. Long before night, cords of raw hide were stretched around the camp, and the meat was hung upon them to dry in the sunshine and pure air of the prairie. Our California companions were less successful at the work; but they accomplished it after their own fashion, and their side of the camp was soon garnished in the same manner as our own.

We meant to remain at this place long enough to prepare provisions for our journey to the frontier, which, as we supposed, might occupy about a month. Had the distance been twice as great and the party ten times as large, the rifle of Henry Chatillon would have supplied meat enough for the whole within two days; we were obliged to remain, however, until it should be dry enough for transportation; so we pitched our tent and made other arrangements for a permanent camp. The California men, who had no such shelter, contented themselves with arranging their packs on the grass around their fire. In the mean time we had nothing to do but amuse ourselves. Our tent was within a rod of the river, if the broad sand-beds, with a scanty stream of water coursing here and there along their surface, deserve to be dignified with the name of river. The vast flat plains on either side were almost on a level with the sand-beds, and they were bounded in the distance by low, monotonous hills, parallel to the course of the stream. All was one expanse of grass; there was no wood in view, except some trees and stunted bushes upon two islands which rose from the wet sands of the river. Yet far from being dull and tame, the scene was often a wild and animated one; for twice a day, at sunrise and at noon, the buffalo came issuing from the hills, slowly advancing in their grave processions to drink at the river. All our amusements were to be at their expense. An old buffalo bull is a brute of unparalleled ugliness. At first sight of him every feeling of pity vanishes. The cows are much smaller and of a gentler appearance, as becomes their sex. While in this camp we forbore to attack them, leaving to Henry Chatillon, who could better judge their quality, the task of killing such as we wanted for use; but against the bulls we waged an unrelenting war. Thousands of them might be slaughtered without causing any detriment to the species, for their numbers greatly exceed those of the cows; it is the hides of the latter alone which are used for the purposes of commerce and for making the lodges of the Indians; and the destruction among them is therefore greatly disproportionate.

Our horses were tired, and we now usually hunted on foot. While we were lying on the grass after dinner, smoking, talking, or laughing at Tête Rouge, one of us would look up and observe, far out on the plains beyond the river, certain black objects slowly approaching. He would inhale a parting whiff from the pipe, then rising lazily, take his rifle, which leaned against the cart, throw over his shoulder the strap of his pouch and powder-horn, and with his moccasons in his hand, walk across the sand towards the opposite side of the river. This was very easy; for though the sands were about a quarter of a mile wide, the water was nowhere more than two feet deep. The farther bank was about four or five feet high, and quite perpendicular, being cut away by the water in spring. Tall grass grew along its edge. Putting it aside with his hand, and cautiously looking through it, the hunter can discern the huge shaggy back of the bull slowly swaying to and fro, as, with his clumsy, swinging gait, he advances towards the river. The buffalo have regular paths by which they come down to drink. Seeing at a glance along which of these his intended victim is moving, the hunter crouches under the bank within fifteen or twenty yards, it may be, of the point where the path enters the river. Here he sits down quietly on the sand. Listening intently, he hears the heavy, monotonous tread of the approaching bull. The moment after, he sees a motion among the long weeds and grass just at the spot where the path is channelled through the bank. An enormous black head is thrust out, the horns just visible amid the mass of tangled mane. Half sliding, half plunging, down comes the buffalo upon the river-bed below. He steps out in full sight upon the sands. Just before him a runnel of water is gliding, and he bends his head to drink. You may hear the water as it gurgles down his capacious throat. He raises his head, and the drops trickle from his wet beard. He stands with an air of stupid abstraction, unconscious of the lurking danger. Noiselessly the hunter cocks his rifle. As he sits upon the sand, his knee is raised, and his elbow rests upon it, that he may level his heavy weapon with a steadier aim. The stock is at his shoulder; his eye ranges along the barrel. Still he is in no haste to fire. The bull, with slow deliberation, begins his march over the sands to the other side. He advances his foreleg, and exposes to view a small spot, denuded of hair, just behind the point of his shoulder; upon this the hunter brings the sight of his rifle to bear; lightly and delicately his finger presses the hair-trigger. The spiteful crack of the rifle responds to his touch, and instantly in the middle of the bare spot appears a small red dot. The buffalo shivers; death has overtaken him, he cannot tell from whence; still he does not fall, but walks heavily forward, as if nothing had happened. Yet before he has gone far out upon the sand, you see him stop; he totters; his knees bend under him, and his head sinks forward to the ground. Then his whole vast bulk sways to one side; he rolls over on the sand, and dies with a scarcely perceptible struggle.

Waylaying the buffalo in this manner, and shooting them as they come to water, is the easiest method of hunting them. They may also be approached by crawling up ravines or behind hills, or even over the open prairie. This is often surprisingly easy; but at other times it requires the utmost skill of the most experienced hunter. Henry Chatillon was a man of extraordinary strength and hardihood; but I have seen him return to camp quite exhausted with his efforts, his limbs scratched and wounded, and his buckskin dress stuck full of the thorns of the prickly-pear, among which he had been crawling. Sometimes he would lie flat upon his face, and drag himself along in this position for many rods together.

On the second day of our stay at this place, Henry went out for an afternoon hunt. Shaw and I remained in camp, until, observing some bulls approaching the water upon the other side of the river, we crossed over to attack them. They were so near, however, that before we could get under cover of the bank our appearance as we walked over the sands alarmed them. Turning round before coming within gun-shot, they began to move off to the right in a direction parallel to the river. I climbed up the bank and ran after them. They were walking swiftly, and before I could come within gun-shot distance they slowly wheeled about and faced me. Before they had turned far enough to see me I had fallen flat on my face. For a moment they stood and stared at the strange object upon the grass;

then turning away, again they walked on as before; and I, rising immediately, ran once more in pursuit. Again they wheeled about, and again I fell prostrate. Repeating this three or four times, I came at length within a hundred yards of the fugitives, and as I saw them turning again, I sat down and levelled my rifle. The one in the centre was the largest I had ever seen. I shot him behind the shoulder. His two companions ran off. He attempted to follow, but soon came to a stand, and at length lay down as quietly as an ox chewing the cud. Cautiously approaching him, I saw by his dull and jelly-like eye that he was dead.

When I began the chase, the prairie was almost tenantless; but a great multitude of buffalo had suddenly thronged upon it, and looking up I saw within fifty rods a heavy, dark column stretching to the right and left as far as I could see. I walked towards them. My approach did not alarm them in the least. The column itself consisted almost entirely of cows and calves, but a great many old bulls were ranging about the prairie on its flank, and as I drew near they faced towards me with such a grim and ferocious look that I thought it best to proceed no farther. Indeed, I was already within close rifle-shot of the column, and I sat down on the ground to watch their movements. Sometimes the whole would stand still, their heads all one way; then they would trot forward, as if by a common impulse, their hoofs and horns clattering together as they moved. I soon began to hear at a distance on the left the sharp reports of a rifle, again and again repeated; and not long after, dull and heavy sounds succeeded, which I recognized as the familiar voice of Shaw's double-barreled gun. When Henry's rifle was at work there was always meat to be brought in. I went back across the river for a horse, and, returning, reached the spot where the hunters were standing. The buffalo were visible on the distant prairie. The living had retreated from the ground, but ten or twelve carcasses were scattered in various directions. Henry, knife in hand, was stooping over a dead cow, cutting away the best and fattest of the meat.

When Shaw left me he had walked down for some distance under the river-bank to find another bull. At length he saw the plains covered with the host of buffalo, and soon after heard the crack of Henry's rifle. Ascending the bank, he crawled through the grass, which for a rod or two from the river was very high and rank. He had not crawled far before to his astonishment he saw Henry standing erect upon the prairie, almost surrounded by the buffalo. Henry was in his element. Quite unconscious that any one was looking at him, he stood at the full height of his tall figure, one hand resting upon his side, and the other arm leaning carelessly on the muzzle of his rifle. His eye was ranging over the singular assemblage around him. Now and then he would select such a cow as suited him, level his rifle, and shoot her dead; then quietly reloading, he would resume his former position. The buffalo seemed no more to regard his presence than if he were one of themselves; the bulls were bellowing and butting at each other, or rolling about in the dust. A group of buffalo would gather about the carcass of a dead cow, snuffing at her wounds; and sometimes they would come behind those that had not yet fallen, and endeavor to push them from the spot. Now and then some old bull would face towards Henry with an air of stupid amazement, but none seemed inclined to attack or fly from him. For some time Shaw lay among the grass, looking in surprise at this extraordinary sight; at length he crawled cautiously forward, and spoke in a low voice to Henry, who told him to rise and come on. Still the buffalo showed no sign of fear; they remained gathered about their dead companions. Henry had already killed as many cows as he wanted for use, and Shaw, kneeling behind one of the carcasses, shot five bulls before the rest thought it necessary to disperse.

The frequent stupidity and infatuation of the buffalo seems the more remarkable from the contrast it offers to their wildness and wariness at other times. Henry knew all their peculiarities; he had studied them as a scholar studies his books, and derived quite as much pleasure from the occupation. The buffalo were in a sense companions to him, and, as he said, he never felt alone when they were about him. He took great pride in his skill in hunting. He was one of the most modest of men; yet in the simplicity and frankness of his character, it was clear that he looked upon his pre-eminence in this respect as a thing too palpable and well established to be disputed. But whatever may have been his estimate of his own skill, it was rather below than above that which others placed upon it. The only time that I ever saw a shade of scorn darken his face was when two volunteer soldiers, who had just killed a buffalo for the first time, undertook to instruct him as to the best method of "approaching." Henry always seemed to think that he had a sort of prescriptive right to the buffalo, and to look upon them as something belonging to himself. Nothing excited his indignation so much as any wanton destruction committed among the cows, and in his view shooting a calf was a cardinal sin.

Henry Chatillon and Tête Rouge were of the same age; that is, about thirty. Henry was twice as large, and about six times as strong as Tête Rouge. Henry's face was roughened by winds and storms; Tête Rouge's was bloated by sherry-cobblers and brandy-toddy. Henry talked of Indians and buffalo; Tête Rouge of theatres and oyster-cellars. Henry had led a life of hardship and privation; Tête Rouge never had a whim which he would not gratify at the first moment he was able. Henry moreover was the most disinterested man I ever saw; while Tête Rouge, though equally good natured in his way, cared for nobody but himself. Yet we would not have lost him on any account; he served the purpose of a jester in a feudal castle; our camp would have been lifeless without him. For the past week he had fattened in a most amazing manner; and, indeed, this was not at all surprising, since his appetite was inordinate. He was eating from morning till night; half the time he would be at work cooking some private repast for himself, and he paid a visit to the coffee-pot eight or ten times a day. His rueful and disconsolate face became jovial and rubicund, his eyes stood out like a lobster's, and his spirits, which before were sunk to the depths of despondency, were now elated in proportion; all day he was singing, whistling, laughing, and telling stories. Being mortally afraid of Jim Gurney, he kept close in the neighborhood of our tent. As he had seen an abundance of low fast life, and had a considerable fund of humor, his anecdotes were extremely amusing, especially since he never hesitated to place himself in a ludicrous point of view, provided he could raise a laugh by doing so. Tête Rouge, however, was sometimes rather troublesome; he had an inveterate habit of pilfering provisions at all times of the day. He set ridicule at defiance, and would never have given over his tricks, even if they had drawn upon him the scorn of the whole party. Now and then, indeed, something worse than laughter fell to his share; on these occasions he would exhibit much contrition, but half an hour after we would generally observe him stealing round to the box at the back of the cart, and slyly making off with the provisions which Deslauriers had laid by for supper. He was fond of smoking; but having no tobacco of his own, we used to provide him with as much as he wanted, a small piece at a time. At first we gave him half a pound together; but this experiment proved an entire failure, for he invariably lost not only the tobacco, but the knife intrusted to him for cutting it, and a few minutes after he would come to us with many apologies and beg for more.

We had been two days at this camp, and some of the meat was nearly fit for transportation, when a storm came suddenly upon us. About sunset the whole sky grew as black as ink, and the long grass at the edge of the river bent and rose mournfully with the first gusts of the approaching hurricane. Munroe and his two companions brought their guns and placed them under cover of our tent. Having no shelter for themselves, they built a fire of driftwood that might have defied a cataract, and, wrapped in their buffalo-robes, sat on the ground around it to bide the fury of the storm. Deslauriers esconced himself under the cover of the cart. Shaw and I, together with Henry and Tête Rouge, crowded into the little tent; but first of all the dried meat was piled together, and well protected by buffalo-robes pinned firmly to the ground. About nine o'clock the storm broke amid absolute darkness; it blew a gale, and torrents of rain roared over the boundless expanse of open prairie. Our tent was filled with mist and spray beating through the canvas, and saturating everything within. We could only distinguish each other at short intervals by the dazzling flashes of lightning, which displayed the whole waste around us with its momentary glare. We had our fears for the tent; but for an hour or two it stood fast, until at length the cap gave way before a furious blast; the pole tore through the top, and in an instant we were half suffocated by the cold and dripping folds of the canvas, which fell down upon us. Seizing upon our guns, we placed them erect, in order to lift the saturated cloth above our heads. In this agreeable situation, involved among wet blankets and buffalo-robes, we spent several hours of the night, during which the storm would not abate for a moment, but pelted down with merciless fury. Before long the water gathered beneath us in a pool two or three inches deep; so that for a considerable part of the night we were partially immersed in a cold bath. In spite of all this, Tête Rouge's flow of spirits did not fail him; he laughed, whistled, and sang in defiance of the storm, and that night paid off the long arrears of ridicule which he owed us. While we lay in silence, enduring the infliction with what philosophy we could muster, Tête Rouge, who was intoxicated with animal spirits, cracked jokes at our expense by the hour together. At about three o'clock in the morning, preferring "the tyranny of the open night" to such a wretched shelter, we crawled out from beneath the fallen canvas. The wind had abated, but the rain fell steadily. The fire of the California men still blazed amid the darkness, and we joined them as they sat around it. We made ready some hot coffee by way of refreshment; but when some of the party sought to replenish their cups, it was found that Tête Rouge, having disposed of his own share, had privately abstracted the coffee-pot and drunk the rest of the contents out of the spout.

In the morning, to our great joy, an unclouded sun rose upon the prairie. We presented a rather laughable appearance, for the cold and clammy buck-skin, saturated with water, clung fast to our limbs. The light wind and warm sunshine soon dried it again, and then we were all encased in armor of intolerable stiffness. Roaming all day over the prairie and shooting two or three bulls, were scarcely enough to restore the stiffened leather to its usual pliancy.

Besides Henry Chatillon, Shaw and I were the only hunters in the party. Munroe this morning made an attempt to run a buffalo, but his horse could not come up to the game. Shaw went out with him, and being better mounted, soon found himself in the midst of the herd. Seeing nothing but cows and calves around him, he checked his horse. An old bull came galloping on the open prairie at some distance behind, and turning, Shaw rode across his path, levelling his gun as he passed, and shooting him through the shoulder into the heart.

A great flock of buzzards was usually soaring about a few trees that stood on the island just below our camp. Throughout the whole of yesterday we had noticed an eagle among them; today he was still there; and Tête Rouge, declaring that he would kill the bird of America, borrowed Deslauriers's gun and set out on his unpatriotic mission. As might have been expected, the eagle suffered no harm at his hands. He soon returned, saying that he could not find him, but had shot a buzzard instead. Being required to produce the bird in proof of his assertion, he said he believed that he was not quite dead, but he must be hurt, from the swiftness with which he flew off.

"If you want," said Tête Rouge, "I'll go and get one of his feathers; I knocked off plenty of them when I shot him."

Just opposite our camp, was another island covered with bushes, and behind it was a deep pool of water, while two or three considerable streams coursed over the sand not far off. I was bathing at this place in the afternoon when a white wolf, larger than the largest Newfoundland dog, ran out from behind the point of the island, and galloped leisurely over the sand not half a stone's-throw distant. I could plainly see his red eyes and the bristles about his snout; he was an ugly scoundrel, with a bushy tail, a large head, and a most repulsive countenance. Having neither rifle to shoot nor stone to pelt him with, I was looking after some missile for his benefit, when the report of a gun came from the camp, and the ball threw up the sand just beyond him; at this he gave a slight jump, and stretched away so swiftly that he soon dwindled into a mere speck on the distant sand-beds. The number of carcasses that by this time were lying about the neighboring prairie summoned the wolves from every quarter; the spot where Shaw and Henry had hunted together soon became their favorite resort, for here about a dozen dead buffalo were fermenting under the hot sun. I used often to go over the river and watch them at their meal. By lying under the bank it was easy to get a full view of them. There were three different kinds: the white wolves and the gray wolves, both very large, and besides these the small prairie wolves, not much bigger than spaniels. They would howl and fight in a crowd around a single carcass, yet they were so watchful, and their senses so acute, that I never was able to crawl within a fair shooting distance; whenever I attempted it, they would all scatter at once and glide silently away through the tall grass. The air above this spot was always full of turkey-buzzards or black vultures; whenever the wolves left a carcass they would descend upon it, and cover it so densely that a rifle bullet shot at random among the gormandizing crowd would generally strike down two or three of them. These birds would often sail by scores just above our camp, their broad black wings seeming half transparent as they expanded them against the bright sky. The wolves and the buzzards thickened about us every hour, and two or three eagles also came to the feast. I killed a bull within rifle-shot of the camp; that night the wolves made a fearful howling close at hand, and in the morning the carcass was completely hollowed out by these voracious feeders.

After remaining four days at this camp we prepared to leave it. We had for our own part about five hundred pounds of dried meat, and the California men had prepared some three hundred more; this consisted of the fattest and choicest parts of eight or nine cows, a small quantity only being taken from each, and the rest abandoned to the wolves. The pack animals were laden, the horses saddled, and the mules harnessed to the cart. Even Tête Rouge was ready at last, and slowly moving from the ground, we resumed our journey eastward. When we had advanced about a mile, Shaw missed a valuable hunting-knife, and turned back in search of it, thinking that he had left it at the camp. The day was dark and gloomy. The ashes of the fires were still smoking by the river-side; the grass around them was trampled down by men and horses, and strewn with all the litter of a camp. Our departure had been a gathering signal to the birds and beasts of prey; Shaw assured me that literally dozens of wolves were prowling about the smouldering fires, while multitudes were roaming over the neighboring prairie; they all fled as he approached, some running over the sand-beds and some over the grassy plains. The vultures in great clouds were soaring overhead, and the dead bull near the camp was completely blackened by the flock that had alighted upon it; they flapped their broad wings, and stretched upwards their crested heads and long skinny necks, fearing to remain, yet reluctant to leave their disgusting feast. As he searched about the fires he saw the wolves seated on the hills waiting for his departure. Having looked in vain for his knife, he mounted again, and left the wolves and the vultures to banquet freely upon the carrion of the camp.

14

My Most Memorable Hunting Dog

by Archibald Rutledge

We introduced Mr. Rutledge earlier in this book with his turkey-hunting story. Poet laureate of South Carolina and author of numerous stories and books, Rutledge was a man who led two lives. In one life he grew up on Hampton Plantation and returned there for lengthy Christmas vacations every year. His other life was as an English pro-fessor at Mercersburg Academy in Pennsylvania. His years of hunting experience were as diverse as bobwhite quail and ruffed grouse. This Rutledge classic was presented in my friend Jim Casada's book Bird Dog Days, Wingshooting Ways *(2016), a bountiful collection of Rutledge upland hunting stories. It includes the best short biography of Archibald Rutledge I've ever seen.*

DURING THE YEARS OF MY YOUNG MANHOOD, WHEN I WAS A TEACHER IN the beautiful Cumberland Valley of Pennsylvania, I hunted quail and grouse a great deal, and I raised and trained a good many bird dogs.

Animals can occasionally be as memorable as human beings; among dogs I give the first place to Mike. Although he was no beauty, he was a joy forever. There was a pathos about him as if he were aware of his unpromising looks.

In those early years I inevitably hunted quail but finally gave it up, for I love the birds too much. One year I went quite overboard in buying a registered pointer with the proud name of Savannah Count. He arrived in a crate that looked like a palace. He was huge, handsome, and supercilious. For some reason, he seemed especially oblivious to me.

On the first day of the season I took His Majesty into the fields. At the first shot he vanished over the rolling countryside. The lordly Count was gun-shy. I did not retrieve him for days.

I was reminded of a dog I took to old Galboa to correct the same fault. Galboa had a way with animals. Telling the old man my troubles, I left the dog with him for two weeks. When

I returned, he gestured with contempt toward the dog lying in the grass. "You must learn," he said, "that nothing can be done about a fool."

There are few plights worse for a quail hunter than to have no bird dog when the season opens. When Count defected, I at once called up a Pennsylvania Game protector, a good friend of mine, to ask him if he could relieve my emergency. He raised bird dogs "on the side," and I had bought several good ones from him. But his report was disappointing. "I did have two dandies," he said, "but I sold both last week. I haven't got a thing now but Mike, and I don't like to sell him to you. You and I have been good friends."

Although this seemed like a sinister introduction, I said, "Ship him to me." As if to sink Mike even lower in my estimation, my friend said, "I could not change you more than $15.00 for this mutt." (I had paid $100.00 for my airborne Savannah Count.)

When Mike arrived, I found him, in appearance, no "hound of heaven." Undersized, angular, with bristly red and yellow hair, for a bird dog he appeared to be put together wrong. His ears were small and peaked; someone had cut off more than half his tail. No one had lately taken him to a beauty parlor. But, as a judge once said to me, about the possible verdict of a jury, "Brother, you never know."

As if he had everything else against him, Mike's feet were too large, so that he walked as if he had snowshoes on. Despite all these adverse factors, Mike had qualities to admire, and, for me, a human and lovable nature. He had a good head, which should presage wisdom and a keen nose. Mike had, too, like some people, a certain air about him; an ugly air, but unique and unforgettable.

Of course, Mike had not any social background. To gracious living, he was alien. Yet already I could feel his loyalty to me. He was also courageous. As I led him up to my home, which was near the express office, we met a big dog that I knew to be a mean one. The big dog, bristling, made some invidious remarks about Mike's mother. Mike bristled also, took a step forward, growling. He was ready for a fight.

I never learned anything of Mike's ancestry; but somewhere in it a blooded pointer probably could be found. He looked to be all cur; but there was something about him that made me know that he wasn't. He had ways and wiles about him.

I have owned many good dogs, but Mike was a character. He was always surprising me with the things he did, which he had thought out all by himself, things that endeared him to me. For example, one afternoon we were crossing a field when we came to a rather cold dark stream with steep banks. Mike did not like the looks of it; but his heart must have kept saying, "Whither thou goest, I will go." I managed to slip down the bank, cross the water with the aid of some limbs, and literally crawled up the farther bank. I then looked for Mike and called him.

Having estimated the problem, and disliking cold water, he had calmly walked away from the creek in a straight line, just as a high jumper or a pole vaulter would, in order to afford himself a speedy run for his takeoff. He went about thirty yards, turned, and came running full speed for the creek. There was a break in the trees so that I could watch him land safely. I was surprised how high he went.

A wild white-tailed deer has been known to jump forty-two feet; a horse, thirty-six feet; a man, twenty-eight feet. I am sure that Mike jumped between twenty and twenty-five feet, and he did so with certainty and grace.

The same week I took a friend hunting quail. Every time he shot, he missed. Meanwhile Mike disappeared. I was not surprised, as his russet coloring blended perfectly with those of the autumn. When I found him he was lying flat in a ditch, his head on his outstretched paws. He looked at me with eyes that seemed to express disappointment, chagrin, and even disgust. He was not able to take any more strong doses of missing! It made him sick; besides, all his work was going for nothing. Of course,

I may have misinterpreted his expression; but it looked like humiliating regret to me. Indeed, Mike's expression was so forlorn it would not have surprised me if big dash tears had rolled down his cheeks.

As we approached an old rail fence one day, Mike sprang up to the top rail. It must have been at that moment that one of the top rails began to swing at right angles to the line of the fence. Just at that moment the hot and heavy scent of a covey of quail, almost beneath him, assailed Mike's nostrils. He crept forward a step to make certain, and found himself with all four feet on the swaying fence rail. Mike's game was to keep his balance and also not to frighten the covey. I can still see him, the picture of shrewd loyalty and devotion, holding his balance until I could come up. He was rocking perfectly.

On another occasion I missed him. After a few minutes he came creeping and crawling back to me. On reaching me, he whined, turned around and started back the way he had come. He paused, looking back to make sure I understood his message and was following. His gait was very peculiar. He was walking as if he were stepping on eggs. He led me to a big covey of quail. He must have known that I could not see him; so he came and got me!

One day Mike and I were out on a sandy road when a big crowd of frolicking young people came by. Purely in jest, one of them threw a pine cone at Mike. It did not hit him; but even if it had, it could not have hurt him. But it wounded his dignity; and he never forgot it.

Except for the one who threw the cone, all the others could enter my yard in perfect safety. But the one who threw the cone would stop outside the gate and call for someone please to "tie Mike up." Really gentle by disposition, Mike would not let anyone take liberties with him.

When I hunted in Pennsylvania, there were some ringneck pheasants there. We were allowed to kill only the cock birds, which are easily distinguished by their gaudy colors and their long tails. It is characteristic of these birds that they will often run long distances on the ground before taking flight. One afternoon, in a wild valley, Mike struck a trail. I knew at once it must be a pheasant because of the distance he was going. At last he came to a stand. I walked carefully to flush the bird. After all our long walk, it was a hen! Of course, I did not shoot. As I stood idly there, Mike, apparently in anger, whirled on me and barked in the most disgusted fashion! There was no mistaking what he meant: "After all my careful work, what in the world is the matter with you?" Some dogs are certainly capable of rebuking their masters—if the provocation is great.

Once when Mike and I were hunting in a field of wheat stubble near a thicket of blackberry canes, he came back to me whining, and he seemed to be cringing. Something had scared him, and he was not a dog easily scared. I was wearing my corduroy trousers; and he took hold of the cuff of one leg, to pull me back, or at least to delay me. But feeling I should investigate, I literally dragged Mike through the stubble. As we drew near the briar patch, I heard what had frightened Mike; then I saw the snake, that ashen heap of death. I have lost dogs that have been struck by rattlers, and have located these lethal serpents by dogs which barked at them—being wary enough to keep their distance. I looked at Mike. In his eyes was a distinct warning. I had dealt with dogs all my life, but what kind of a dog was this? I have had a good dog "take on" a wild boar that had personal designs on me. Yet I doubt if that brave dog was really defending me. With Mike it was different. He cautiously warned me against what he knew was deadly danger. Is it any wonder that I love and honor his memory?

Early in our acquaintance he gave me a good idea of his unusualness. Early one damp morning, I drove out in a buggy (I had no car) to hunt quail. Mike lay in the bottom of the buggy and a robe covered him and my knees. About a mile from town a heavy Osage orange hedge stood on the left of the road. As we were passing this, something happened— something for which I could not at first account. The robe had risen off my knees. Mike was standing up. As soon as I saw the trance-like look in his eyes, I knew that he had winded quail, and had pointed them from the buggy! For precaution's sake, I drove forward a few paces, where I got out of the buggy. But as he was still pointing, I had to lift him down to the roadway. He was still pointing, and as stiff as a board.

When his feet touched the ground he began a curious stiff-legged walk back down the road. Then he came to a perfect point. As the grass was rather thin, I saw the quail on the ground, a beautiful covey of about sixteen birds. When they rose and whirled over the hedge, I did not shoot—partly, I think, because of the strange magic of Mike's behavior.

On another occasion I took a friend duck hunting. Flight shooting was then permitted after sundown. I put my friend on a good stand and he blazed away for an hour. I shot only twice. But when dark came, and I started down the old bank on which we had been standing, I almost fell over a big pile of wild ducks. That was Mike's work. He had brought all my friend's ducks to me! He had original ideas about loyalty.

When the Great Depression came, I had three sons in college. I had already sold some heirloom furniture. Was there anything else that might bring in some money? There was Mike. Unfortunately a man of means had seen him work. He had several times approached me to buy him. Meanwhile the university treasurer kept bearing down on me. On a disastrous day I decided to let my dear Mike go. I felt worse than a sinner. While I was making the crate, Mike watched me curiously. When I put him in and nailed it shut, he must have had an inkling of what was coming. He lay flat on the bottom of the box, and looked at me with big misty eyes. I set the crate in the wheelbarrow, and rolled it down to the express office. I heard some subdued whimpering, but I really believe that Mike was weeping. Nor was he the only one. I left him at the office to be shipped out.

But I had hardly reached home when the enormity of my crime overcame me. I rushed back to the express office (although no train was due for several hours). "It's a mistake!" I exclaimed to the express agent. "I'm not going to sell him."

Not long after that I decided to stop quail shooting. By then Mike was getting old. The aspect of the approach of age is always sad with a dog as active and intelligent as Mike. While he was still strong, I could expect him always to meet me halfway down the avenue that led to my home. He apparently timed my arrival; but was usually an hour or so early, just lying there waiting. At other times, he would pull at my corduroy trousers, trying to get me started on a hunt, or would run down the avenue, barking, and looking expectantly toward the house for me to join him. But then came days when he did not meet me. And sometimes when I would seem to be getting ready to go for a hunt, he would lie in the sun by the steps, thump the ground with his tail, and look at me with a nameless wistfulness. He seemed to be acknowledging his own weakness, and doing so with tragic regret. His eyes spoke for him. Like King Lear, he was saying, "I am old now."

Then, too, Mike began to make mistakes in the field. One day he was holding a point on the briared bank of a ditch. I was sure he had a quail or a pheasant. But as I got near him he gave up the point, and turned back to me, his expression registering shame and apology. He crawled up to me whining, and rubbed against my boots, as if imploring forgiveness. He was abashed that he had been pointing an old land turtle! Yet the finest part of his life was yet to come. He had always loved children, and had been a great favorite with them. One of my grandsons was crazy about Mike; when, therefore, the boy's mother told me that another child was expected, I let them take him. "He might make a nurse for the baby," I said, never dreaming of the real import of my words.

In a pretty room on the second floor of my son's house all was made ready for the new baby. In the center of the room was the immaculate crib, all lacy and frilly. There was a mahogany footboard around the base. One day when the mother came into the room she was greeted by a low growl. Mike had taken possession of the little square box beneath the bassinet. Please don't ask me how he knew a baby was coming there. Perhaps he had dealt with a baby before, in another family. True, there was an unwonted air of suppressed excitement and expectancy, and he may have interpreted these. Do some animals, at certain times, have the eerie clairvoyance of premonition? At any rate, Mike planted himself under the bassinet, and would not leave. He had to be fed and watered there.

The mother was at the hospital two weeks. When she brought the tiny daughter home, Mike barked delightedly. And he took charge. Except for the mother, he would let no one else enter the room. When the baby cried, or even fretted, Mike barked. After some months had passed, and the baby began to crawl about the room, Mike would come close and lie down so that tiny Bonnie could sleep with him for a pillow. My daughter-in-law said, "I feel much safer with Mike than with a nurse."

When Bonnie was a year and a half old, she was allowed to run up and down the pavement in front of her house—but only if Mike went with her. He was not by then keeping up with the baby very well. He always stayed between her and the street. One day she threw a little rubber ball out into the road, and at once, like a fairy, ran after it. Mike was old then and not nearly so fast as he had once been. Two cars were coming from opposite directions. Mike, making the effort of his life, dashed between Bonnie and one car. She was saved, but he was struck and killed.

Mike was a dog that looked all wrong, but was all right. Ugly, he was loyal and smart. Many redeeming faults were his—those same human qualities that make people lovable. It is not hard for me to forget Savannah Count; but I shall always remember Mike.

15

Hunting the Grisly

by Theodore Roosevelt

As I mentioned in my Editor's Note, the misspelling of "grizzly" will be overlooked. President Theodore Roosevelt's adventures with the great bears stand as he wrote them, with passion and experience.

IF OUT IN THE LATE FALL OR EARLY SPRING, IT IS OFTEN POSSIBLE TO follow a bear's trail in the snow; having come upon it either by chance or hard hunting, or else having found where it leads from some carcass on which the beast has been feeding. In the pursuit one must exercise great caution, as at such times the hunter is easily seen a long way off, and game is always especially watchful for any foe that may follow its trail.

Once I killed a grisly in this manner. It was early in the fall, but snow lay on the ground, while the gray weather boded a storm. My camp was in a bleak, wind-swept valley, high among the mountains which form the divide between the head-waters of the Salmon and Clarke's Fork of the Columbia. All night I had lain in my buffalo-bag, under the lea of a windbreak of branches, in the clump of fir-trees, where I had halted the preceding evening. At my feet ran a rapid mountain torrent, its bed choked with ice-covered rocks; I had been lulled to sleep by the stream's splashing murmur, and the loud moaning of the wind along the naked cliffs. At dawn I rose and shook myself free of the buffalo robe, coated with hoar-frost. The ashes of the fire were lifeless; in the dim morning the air was bitter cold. I did not linger a moment, but snatched up my rifle, pulled on my fur cap and gloves, and strode off up a side ravine; as I walked I ate some mouthfuls of venison, left over from supper.

Two hours of toil up the steep mountain brought me to the top of a spur. The sun had risen, but was hidden behind a bank of sullen clouds. On the divide I halted, and gazed out over a vast landscape, inconceivably wild and dismal. Around me towered the stupendous mountain masses which make up the backbone of the Rockies. From my feet, as far as I could see, stretched a rugged and barren chaos of ridges and detached rock masses. Behind me, far below, the stream wound like a silver ribbon, fringed with dark conifers and the changing, dying foliage of poplar and quaking aspen. In front the bottoms of the valleys were filled with the somber evergreen forest, dotted here and there with black, ice-skimmed tarns; and the dark spruces clustered also in the higher gorges, and were scattered thinly along the mountain sides. The snow which had fallen lay in drifts and streaks, while, where the wind had scope it was blown off, and the ground left bare.

For two hours I walked onwards across the ridges and valleys. Then among some scattered spruces, where the snow lay to the depth of half a foot, I suddenly came on the fresh, broad trail of a grisly. The brute was evidently roaming restlessly about in search of a winter den, but willing, in passing, to pick up any food that lay handy. At once I took the trail, travelling above and to one side, and keeping a sharp look-out ahead. The bear was going across wind, and this made my task easy. I walked rapidly, though cautiously; and it was only in crossing the large patches of bare ground that I had to fear making a noise. Elsewhere the snow muffled my footsteps, and made the trail so plain that I scarcely had to waste a glance upon it, bending my eyes always to the front.

At last, peering cautiously over a ridge crowned with broken rocks, I saw my quarry, a big, burly bear, with silvered fur. He had halted on an open hillside, and was busily digging up the caches of some rock gophers or squirrels. He seemed absorbed in his work, and the stalk was easy.

Slipping quietly back, I ran towards the end of the spur, and in ten minutes struck a ravine, of which one branch ran past within seventy yards of where the bear was working. In this ravine was a rather close growth of stunted evergreens, affording good cover, although in one or two places I had to lie down and crawl through the snow. When I reached the point for which I was aiming, the bear had just finished rooting, and was starting off. A slight whistle brought him to a standstill, and I drew a bead behind his shoulder, and low down, resting the rifle across the crooked branch of a dwarf spruce. At the crack he ran off at speed, making no sound, but the thick spatter of blood splashes, showing clear on the white snow, betrayed the mortal nature of the wound. For some minutes I followed the trail; and then, topping a ridge, I saw the dark bulk lying motionless in a snow drift at the foot of a low rock-wall, from which he had tumbled.

The usual practice of the still-hunter who is after grisly is to toll it to baits. The hunter either lies in ambush near the carcass, or approaches it stealthily when he thinks the bear is at its meal.

One day while camped near the Bitter Root Mountains in Montana I found that a bear had been feeding on the carcass of a moose which lay some five miles from the little open glade in which my tent was pitched, and I made up my mind to try to get a shot at it that afternoon. I stayed in camp till about three o'clock, lying lazily back on the bed of sweet-smelling evergreen boughs, watching the pack ponies as they stood under the pines on the edge of the open, stamping now and then, and switching their tails. The air was still, the sky a glorious blue; at that hour in the afternoon even the September sun was hot. The smoke from the smouldering logs of the camp fire curled thinly upwards. Little chipmunks scuttled out from their holes to the packs, which lay in a heap on the ground, and then scuttled madly back again. A couple of drab-colored whisky-jacks, with bold mien and fearless bright eyes, hopped and fluttered round, picking up the scraps, and uttering an extraordinary variety of notes, mostly discordant; so tame were they that one of them lit on my outstretched arm as I half dozed, basking in the sunshine.

When the shadows began to lengthen, I shouldered my rifle and plunged into the woods. At first my route lay along a mountain side; then for half a mile over a windfall, the dead timber piled about in crazy confusion. After that I went up the bottom of a valley by a little brook, the ground being carpeted with a sponge of soaked moss. At the head of this brook was a pond covered with water-lilies; and a scramble through a rocky pass took me into a high, wet valley, where the thick growth of spruce was broken by occasional strips of meadow. In this valley the moose carcass lay, well at the upper end.

In moccasined feet I trod softly through the soundless woods. Under the dark branches it was already dusk, and the air had the cool chill of evening. As I neared the clump where the body lay, I walked with redoubled caution, watching and listening with strained alertness. Then I heard a twig snap; and my blood leaped, for I knew the bear was at his supper. In another moment I saw his shaggy, brown form. He was working with all his awkward giant strength, trying to bury the carcass, twisting it to one side and the other with wonderful ease. Once he got angry and suddenly gave it a tremendous cuff with his paw; in his bearing he had something half humorous, half devilish. I crept up within forty yards; but for several minutes he would not keep his head still. Then something attracted his attention in the forest, and he stood motionless looking towards it, broadside to me, with his fore-paws planted on the carcass. This gave me my chance. I drew a very fine bead between his eye and ear; and pulled trigger. He dropped like a steer when struck with a pole-axe.

If there is a good hiding-place handy it is better to lie in wait at the carcass. One day on the head-waters of the Madison, I found that a bear was coming to an elk I had shot some days before; and I at once determined to ambush the beast when he came back that evening. The carcass lay in the middle of a valley a quarter of a mile broad. The bottom of this valley was covered by an open forest of tall pines; a thick jungle of smaller evergreens marked where the mountains rose on either hand. There were a number of large rocks scattered here and there, one, of very convenient shape, being only some seventy or eighty yards from the carcass. Up this I clambered. It hid me perfectly, and on its top was a carpet of soft pine needles, on which I could lie at my ease.

Hour after hour passed by. A little black woodpecker with a yellow crest ran nimbly up and down the tree-trunks for some time and then flitted away with a party of chickadees and nut-hatches. Occasionally a Clarke's crow soared about overhead or clung in any position to the swaying end of a pine branch, chattering and screaming. Flocks of cross-bills, with wavy flight and plaintive calls, flew to a small mineral lick near by, where they scraped the clay with their queer little beaks.

As the westering sun sank out of sight beyond the mountains these sounds of bird-life gradually died away. Under the great pines the evening was still with the silence of primeval desolation. The sense of sadness and loneliness, the melancholy of the wilderness, came over me like a spell. Every slight noise made my pulses throb as I lay motionless on the rock gazing intently into the gathering gloom. I began to fear that it would grow too dark to shoot before the grisly came.

Suddenly and without warning, the great bear stepped out of the bushes and trod across the pine needles with such swift and silent footsteps that its bulk seemed unreal. It was very cautious, continually halting to peer around; and once it stood up on its hind legs and looked long down the valley towards the red west. As it reached the carcass I put a bullet between its shoulders. It rolled over, while the woods resounded with its savage roaring. Immediately it struggled to its feet and staggered off; and fell again to the next shot, squalling and yelling. Twice this was repeated; the brute being one of those bears which greet every wound with a great outcry, and sometimes seem to lose their feet when hit—although they will occasionally fight as savagely as their more silent brethren. In this case the wounds were mortal, and the bear died before reaching the edge of the thicket.

I spent much of the fall of 1889 hunting on the head-waters of the Salmon and Snake in Idaho, and along the Montana boundary line from the Big Hole Basin and the head of the Wisdom River to the neighborhood of Red Rock Pass and to the north and west of Henry's Lake. During the last fortnight my companion was the old mountain man, already mentioned, named Griffeth or Griffin—I cannot tell which, as he was always called either "Hank" or "Griff." He was a crabbedly honest old fellow, and a very skilful hunter; but he was worn out with age and rheumatism, and his temper had failed even faster than his bodily strength. He showed me a greater variety of game than I had ever seen before in so short a time; nor did I ever before or after make so successful a hunt. But he was an exceedingly disagreeable companion on account of his surly, moody ways. I generally had to get up first, to kindle the fire and make ready breakfast, and he was very quarrelsome. Finally, during my absence from camp one day, while not very far from Red Rock pass, he found my whisky-flask, which I kept purely for emergencies, and drank all the contents. When I came back he was quite drunk. This was unbearable, and after some high words I left him, and struck off homeward through the woods on my own account. We had with us four pack and saddle horses; and of these I took a very intelligent and gentle little bronco mare, which possessed the invaluable trait of always staying near camp, even when not hobbled. I was not hampered with much of an outfit, having only my buffalo sleeping-bag, a fur coat, and my washing kit, with a couple of spare pairs of socks and some handkerchiefs. A frying-pan, some salt pork, and a hatchet, made up a light pack, which, with the bedding, I fastened across the stock saddle by means of a rope and a spare packing cinch. My cartridges and knife were in my belt; my compass and matches, as always, in my pocket. I walked, while the little mare followed almost like a dog, often without my having to hold the lariat which served as halter.

The country was for the most part fairly open, as I kept near the foothills where glades and little prairies broke the pine forest. The trees were of small size. There was no regular trail, but the course was easy to keep, and I had no trouble of any kind save on the second day. That afternoon I was following a stream which at last "canyoned up," that is sank to the bottom of a canyon-like ravine impossible for a horse. I started up a side valley, intending to cross from its head coulies to those of another valley which would lead in below the canyon.

However, I got enmeshed in the tangle of winding valleys at the foot of the steep mountains, and as dusk was coming on I halted and camped in a little open spot by the side of a small, noisy brook, with crystal water. The place was carpeted with soft, wet, green moss, dotted red with the kinnikinnic berries, and at its edge, under the trees where the ground was dry, I threw down the buffalo bed on a mat of sweet-smelling pine needles. Making camp took but a moment. I opened the pack, tossed the bedding on a smooth spot, knee-haltered the little mare, dragged up a few dry logs, and then strolled off, rifle on shoulder, through the frosty gloaming, to see if I could pick up a grouse for supper.

For half a mile I walked quickly and silently over the pine needles, across a succession of slight ridges separated by narrow, shallow valleys. The forest here was composed of lodge-pole pines, which on the ridges grew close together, with tall slender trunks, while in the valleys the growth was more open. Though the sun was behind the mountains there was yet plenty of light by which to shoot, but it was fading rapidly.

At last, as I was thinking of turning towards camp, I stole up to the crest of one of the ridges, and looked over into the valley some sixty yards off. Immediately I caught the loom of some large, dark object; and another glance showed me a big grisly walking slowly off with his head down. He was quartering to me, and I fired into his flank, the bullet, as I afterwards found, ranging forward and piercing one lung. At the shot he uttered a loud, moaning grunt and plunged forward at a heavy gallop, while I raced obliquely down the hill to cut him off. After going a few hundred feet he reached a laurel thicket, some thirty yards broad, and two or three times as long which he did not leave. I ran up to the edge and there halted, not liking to venture into the mass of twisted, close-growing stems and glossy foliage. Moreover, as I halted, I head him utter a peculiar, savage kind of whine from the heart of the brush. Accordingly, I began to skirt the edge, standing on tiptoe and gazing earnestly to see if I could not catch a glimpse of his hide. When I was at the narrowest part of the thicket, he suddenly left it directly opposite, and then wheeled and stood broadside to me on the hill-side, a little above. He turned his head stiffly towards me; scarlet strings of froth hung from his lips; his eyes burned like embers in the gloom.

I held true, aiming behind the shoulder, and my bullet shattered the point or lower end of his heart, taking out a big nick. Instantly the great bear turned with a harsh roar of fury and challenge, blowing the blood foam from his mouth, so that I saw the gleam of his white fangs; and then he charged straight at me, crashing and bounding through the laurel bushes, so that it was hard to aim. I waited until he came to a fallen tree, raking him as he topped it with a ball, which entered his chest and went through the cavity of his body, but he neither swerved nor flinched, and at the moment I did not know that I had struck him. He came steadily on, and in another second was almost upon me. I fired for his forehead, but my bullet went low, entering his open mouth, smashing his lower jaw and going into the neck. I leaped to one side almost as I pulled trigger; and through the hanging smoke the first thing I saw was his paw as he made a vicious side blow at me. The rush of his charge carried him past. As he struck he lurched forward, leaving a pool of bright blood where his muzzle hit the ground; but he recovered himself and made two or three jumps onwards, while I hurriedly jammed a couple of cartridges into the magazine, my rifle holding only four, all of which I had fired. Then he tried to pull up, but as he did so his muscles seemed suddenly to give way, his head drooped, and he rolled over and over like a shot rabbit. Each of my first three bullets had inflicted a mortal wound.

It was already twilight, and I merely opened the carcass, and then trotted back to camp. Next morning I returned and with much labor took off the skin. The fur was very fine, the animal being in excellent trim, and unusually bright-colored. Unfortunately, in packing it out I lost the skull, and had to supply its place with one of plaster. The beauty of the trophy, and the memory of the circumstances under which I procured it, make me value it perhaps more highly than any other in my house.

This is the only instance in which I have been regularly charged by a grisly. On the whole, the danger of hunting these great bears has been much exaggerated. At the beginning of the present century, when white hunters first encountered the grisly, he was doubtless an exceedingly savage beast, prone to attack without provocation, and a redoubtable foe to persons armed with the clumsy, small-bore muzzle-loading rifles of the day. But at present bitter experience has taught him caution. He has been hunted for the bounty, and hunted as a dangerous enemy to stock, until, save in the very wildest districts, he has learned to be more wary than a deer and to avoid man's presence almost as carefully as the most timid kind of game. Except in rare cases he will not attack of his own accord, and, as a rule, even when wounded his object is escape rather than battle.

Still, when fairly brought to bay, or when moved by a sudden fit of ungovernable anger, the grisly is beyond peradventure a very dangerous antagonist. The first shot, if taken at a bear a good distance off and previously unwounded and unharried, is not usually fraught with much danger, the startled animal being at the outset bent merely on flight. It is always hazardous, however, to track a wounded and worried grisly into thick cover, and the man who habitually follows and kills this chief of American game in dense timber, never abandoning the bloody trail whithersoever it leads, must show no small degree of skill and hardihood, and must not too closely count the risk to life or limb. Bears differ widely in temper, and occasionally one may be found who will not show fight, no matter how much he is bullied; but, as a rule, a hunter must be cautious in meddling with a wounded animal which has retreated into a dense thicket, and had been once or twice roused; and such a beast, when it does turn, will usually charge again and again, and fight to the last with unconquerable ferocity. The short distance at which the bear can be seen through the underbrush, the fury of his charge, and his tenacity of life make it necessary for the hunter on such occasions to have steady nerves and a fairly quick and accurate aim. It is always well to have two men in following a wounded bear under such conditions. This is not necessary, however, and a good hunter, rather than lose his quarry, will, under ordinary circumstances, follow and attack it, no matter how tangled the fastness in which it has sought refuge; but he must act warily and with the utmost caution and resolution, if he wishes to escape a terrible and probably fatal mauling. An experienced hunter is rarely rash, and never heedless; he will not, when alone, follow a wounded bear into a thicket, if by that exercise of patience, skill, and knowledge of the game's habits he can avoid the necessity; but it is idle to talk of the feat as something which ought in no case to be attempted. While danger ought never to be needlessly incurred, it is yet true that the keenest zest in sport comes from its presence, and from the consequent exercise of the qualities necessary to overcome it. The most thrilling moments of an American hunter's life are those in which, with every sense on the alert, and with nerves strung to the highest point, he is following alone into the heart of its forest fastness the fresh and bloody footprints of an angered grisly; and no other triumph of American hunting can compare with the victory to be thus gained.

These big bears will not ordinarily charge from a distance of over a hundred yards; but there are exceptions to this rule. In the fall of 1890 my friend Archibald Rogers was hunting in Wyoming, south of the

Yellowstone Park, and killed seven bears. One, an old he, was out on a bare table-land, grubbing for roots, when he was spied. It was early in the afternoon, and the hunters, who were on a high mountain slope, examined him for some time through their powerful glasses before making him out to be a bear. They then stalked up to the edge of the wood which fringed on the table-land on one side, but could get no nearer than about three hundred yards, the plains being barren of all cover. After waiting for a couple of hours Rogers risked the shot, in despair of getting nearer, and wounded the bear, though not very seriously. The animal made off, almost broadside to, and Rogers ran forward to intercept it. As soon as it saw him it turned and rushed straight for him, not heeding his second shot, and evidently bent on charging home. Rogers then waited until it was within twenty yards, and brained it with his third bullet.

In fact bears differ individually in courage and ferocity precisely as men do, or as the Spanish bulls, of which it is said that not more than one in twenty is fit to stand the combat of the arena. One grisly can scarcely be bullied into resistance; the next may fight to the end, against any odds, without flinching, or even attack unprovoked. Hence men of limited experience in this sport, generalizing from the actions of the two or three bears each has happened to see or kill, often reach diametrically opposite conclusions as to the fighting temper and capacity of the quarry. Even old hunters—who indeed, as a class, are very narrow-minded and opinionated—often generalize just as rashly as beginners. One will portray all bears as very dangerous; another will speak and act as if he deemed them of no more consequence than so many rabbits. I knew one old hunter who had killed a score without ever seeing one show fight. On the other hand, Dr. James C. Merrill, U. S. A., who has had about as much experience with bears as I have had, informs me that he has been charged with the utmost determination three times. In each case the attack was delivered before the bear was wounded or even shot at, the animal being roused by the approach of the hunter from his day bed, and charging headlong at them from a distance of twenty or thirty paces. All three bears were killed before they could do any damage. There was a very remarkable incident connected with the killing of one of them. It occurred in the northern spurs of the Bighorn range. Dr. Merrill, in company with an old hunter, had climbed down into a deep, narrow canyon. The bottom was threaded with well-beaten elk trails. While following one of these the two men turned a corner of the canyon and were instantly charged by an old she-grisly, so close that it was only by good luck that one of the hurried shots disabled her and caused her to tumble over a cut bank where she was easily finished. They found that she had been lying directly across the game trail, on a smooth well beaten patch of bare earth, which looked as if it had been dug up, refilled, and trampled down. Looking curiously at this patch they saw a bit of hide only partially covered at one end; digging down they found the body of a well grown grisly cub. Its skull had been crushed, and the brains licked out, and there were signs of other injuries. The hunters pondered long over this strange discovery, and hazarded many guesses as to its meaning. At last they decided that probably the cub had been killed, and its brains eaten out, either by some old male-grisly or by a cougar, that the mother had returned and driven away the murderer, and that she had then buried the body and lain above it, waiting to wreak her vengeance on the first passer-by.

Old Tazewell Woody, during his thirty years' life as a hunter in the Rockies and on the great plains, killed very many grislies. He always exercised much caution in dealing with them; and, as it happened, he was by some suitable tree in almost every case when he was charged. He would accordingly climb the tree (a practice of which I do not approve however); and the bear would look up at him and pass on without stopping. Once, when he was hunting in the mountains with a companion, the latter, who was down in a valley, while Woody was on the hill-side, shot at a bear. The first thing Woody knew the wounded grisly, running up-hill, was almost on him from behind. As he turned it seized his rifle in its jaws. He wrenched the rifle round, while the bear still gripped it, and pulled trigger, sending a bullet into its shoulder; whereupon it struck him with its paw, and knocked him over the rocks. By good luck he fell in a snow bank and was not hurt in the least. Meanwhile the bear went on and they never got it.

Once he had an experience with a bear which showed a very curious mixture of rashness and cowardice. He and a companion were camped in a little tepee or wigwam, with a bright fire in front of it, lighting up the night. There was an inch of snow on the ground. Just after they went to bed a grisly came close to camp. Their dog rushed out and they could hear it bark round in the darkness for nearly an hour; then the bear drove it off and came right into camp. It went close to the fire, picking up the scraps of meat and bread, pulled a haunch of venison down from a tree, and passed and repassed in front of the tepee, paying no heed whatever to the two men, who crouched in the doorway talking to one another. Once it passed so close that Woody could almost have touched it. Finally his companion fired into it, and off it ran, badly wounded, without an attempt at retaliation. Next morning they followed its tracks in the snow, and found it a quarter or a mile away. It was near a pine and had buried itself under the loose earth, pine needles, and snow; Woody's companion almost walked over it, and putting his rifle to its ear blew out its brains. In all his experience Woody had personally seen but four men who were badly mauled by bears. Three of these were merely wounded. One was bitten terribly in the back. Another had an arm partially chewed off. The third was a man named George Dow, and the accident happened to him on the Yellowstone about the year 1878. He was with a pack animal at the time, leading it on a trail through a wood. Seeing a big she-bear with cubs he yelled at her; whereat she ran away, but only to cache her cubs, and in a minute, having hidden them, came racing back at him. His pack animal being slow he started to climb a tree; but before he could get far enough up she caught him, almost biting a piece out of the calf of his leg, pulled him down, bit and cuffed him two or three times, and then went on her way.

The only time Woody ever saw a man killed by a bear was once when he had given a touch of variety to his life by shipping on a New Bedford whaler which had touched at one of the Puget Sound ports. The whaler went up to a part of Alaska where bears were very plentiful and bold. One day a couple of boats' crews landed; and the men, who were armed only with an occasional harpoon or lance, scattered over the beach, one of them, a Frenchman, wading into the water after shell-fish. Suddenly a bear emerged from some bushes and charged among the astonished sailors, who scattered in every direction; but the bear, said Woody, "just had it in for that Frenchman," and went straight at him. Shrieking with terror he retreated up to his neck in the water; but the bear plunged in after him, caught him, and disembowelled him. One of the Yankee mates then fired a bomb lance into the bear's hips, and the savage beast hobbled off into the dense cover of the low scrub, where the enraged sailor folk were unable to get at it.

The truth is that while the grisly generally avoids a battle if possible, and often acts with great cowardice, it is never safe to take liberties with him; he usually fights desperately and dies hard when wounded and cornered, and exceptional individuals take the aggressive on small provocation.

During the years I lived on the frontier I came in contact with many persons who had been severely mauled or even crippled for life by grislies; and a number of cases where they killed men outright were also brought under my ken. Generally these accidents, as was natural, occurred to hunters who had roused or wounded the game.

A fighting bear sometimes uses his claws and sometimes his teeth. I have never known one to attempt to kill an antagonist by hugging, in spite of the popular belief to this effect; though he will sometimes draw an enemy towards him with his paws the better to reach him with his teeth, and to hold him so that he cannot escape from the biting. Nor does the bear often advance on his hind legs to the attack; though, if the man has come close to him in thick underbrush, or has stumbled on him in his lair unawares, he will often rise up in this fashion and strike a single blow. He will also rise in clinching with a man on horseback. In 1882 a mounted Indian was killed in this manner on one of the river bottoms some miles below where my ranch house now stands, not far from the junction of the Beaver and Little Missouri. The bear had been hunted into a thicket by a band of Indians, in whose company my informant, a white man, with whom I afterward did some trading, was travelling. One of them in the excitement of the pursuit rode across the end of the thicket; as he did so the great beast sprang at him with wonderful quickness, rising on its hind legs, and knocking over the horse and rider with a single sweep of its terrible fore-paws. It then turned on the fallen man and tore him open, and though the other Indians came promptly to his rescue and slew his assailant, they were not in time to save their comrade's life.

A bear is apt to rely mainly on his teeth or claws according to whether his efforts are directed primarily to killing his foe or to making good his own escape. In the latter event he trusts chiefly to his claws. If cornered, he of course makes a rush for freedom, and in that case he downs any man who is in his way with a sweep of his great paw, but passes on without stopping to bite him. If while sleeping or resting in thick brush some one suddenly stumbles on him close up he pursues the same course, less from anger than from fear, being surprised and startled. Moreover, if attacked at close quarters by men and dogs he strikes right and left in defence.

Sometimes what is called a charge is rather an effort to get away. In localities where he has been hunted, a bear, like every other kind of game, is always on the look-out for an attack, and is prepared at any moment for immediate flight. He seems ever to have in his mind, whether feeding, sunning himself, or merely roaming around, the direction—usually towards the thickest cover or most broken ground—in which he intends to run if molested. When shot at he instantly starts towards this place; or he may be so confused that he simply runs he knows not whither; and in either event he may take a line that leads almost directly to or by the hunter, although he had at first no thought of charging. In such a case he usually strikes a single knock-down blow and gallops on without halting, though that one blow may have taken life. If the claws are long and fairly sharp (as in early spring, or even in the fall, if the animal has been working over soft ground) they add immensely to the effect of the blow, for they cut like blunt axes. Often, however, late in the season, and if the ground has been dry and hard, or rocky, the claws are worn down nearly to the quick, and the blow is then given mainly with the under side of the paw; although even under this disadvantage a thump from a big bear will down a horse or smash in a man's breast. The hunter Hofer once lost a horse in this manner. He shot at and wounded a bear which rushed off, as ill luck would have it, past the place where his horse was picketed; probably more in fright than in anger it struck the poor beast a blow which, in the end, proved mortal.

If a bear means mischief and charges not to escape but to do damage, its aim is to grapple with or throw down its foe and bite him to death. The charge is made at a gallop, the animal sometimes coming on silently, with the mouth shut, and sometimes with the jaws open, the lips drawn back and teeth showing, uttering at the same time a succession of roars or of savage rasping snarls. Certain bears charge without any bluster and perfectly straight; while others first threaten and bully, and even when charging stop to growl, shake the head and bite at a bush or knock holes in the ground with their fore-paws. Again, some of them charge home with a ferocious resolution which their extreme tenacity of life renders especially dangerous; while others can be turned or driven back even by a shot which is not mortal. They show the same variability in their behavior when wounded. Often a big bear, especially if charging, will receive a bullet in perfect silence, without flinching or seeming to pay any heed to it; while another will cry out and tumble about, and if charging, even though it may not abandon the attack, will pause for a moment to whine or bite at the wound.

Sometimes a single bite causes death. One of the most successful bear hunters I ever knew, an old fellow whose real name I never heard as he was always called Old Ike, was killed in this way in the spring or early summer of 1886 on one of the head-waters of the Salmon. He was a very good shot, had killed nearly a hundred bears with the rifle, and, although often charged, had never met with any accident, so that he had grown somewhat careless. On the day in question he had met a couple of mining prospectors and was travelling with them, when a grisly crossed his path. The old hunter immediately ran after it, rapidly gaining, as the bear did not hurry when it saw itself pursued, but slouched slowly forwards, occasionally turning its head to grin and growl. It soon went into a dense grove of young spruce, and as the hunter reached the edge it charged fiercely out. He fired one hasty shot, evidently wounding the animal, but not seriously enough to stop or cripple it; and as his two companions ran forward they saw the bear seize him with its wide-spread jaws, forcing him to the ground. They shouted and fired, and the beast abandoned the fallen man on the instant and sullenly retreated into the spruce thicket, whither they dared not follow it. Their friend was at his last gasp; for the whole side of the chest had been crushed in by the one bite, the lungs showing between the rent ribs.

Very often, however, a bear does not kill a man by one bite, but after throwing him lies on him, biting him to death. Usually, if no assistance is at hand, such a man is doomed; although if he pretends to be dead, and has the nerve to lie quiet under very rough treatment, it is just possible that the bear may leave him alive, perhaps after half burying what it believes to be the body. In a very few exceptional instances men of extraordinary prowess with the knife have succeeded in beating off a bear, and even in mortally wounding it, but in most cases a single-handed struggle, at close quarters, with a grisly bent on mischief, means death.

Occasionally the bear, although vicious, is also frightened, and passes on after giving one or two bites; and frequently a man who is knocked down is rescued by his friends before he is killed, the big beast mayhap using his weapons with clumsiness. So a bear may kill a foe with a single blow of its mighty fore-arm, either crushing in the head or chest by sheer force of sinew, or else tearing open the body with its formidable claws; and so on the other hand he may, and often does, merely disfigure or maim the foe by a hurried stroke. Hence it is common to see men who have escaped the clutches of a grisly, but only at the cost of features marred beyond recognition, or a body rendered almost helpless for life. Almost every old resident of western Montana or northern Idaho has known two or three unfortunates who have suffered in this manner. I have myself met one such man in Helena, and another in Missoula; both were living at least as late as 1889, the date at which I last saw them. One had been partially scalped by a bear's teeth; the animal was very old and so the fangs did not enter the skull. The other had been bitten across the face, and the wounds never entirely healed, so that his disfigured visage was hideous to behold.

Most of these accidents occur in following a wounded or worried bear into thick cover; and under such circumstances an animal apparently hopelessly disabled, or in the death throes, may with a last effort kill one or more of its assailants. In 1874 my wife's uncle, Captain Alexander Moore, U. S. A., and my friend Captain Bates, with some men of the 2nd and 3rd Cavalry, were scouting in Wyoming, near the Freezeout Mountains. One morning they roused a bear in the open prairie and followed it at full speed as it ran towards a small creek. At one spot in the creek beavers had built a dam, and as usual in such places there was a thick growth of bushes and willow saplings. Just as the bear reached the edge of this little jungle it was struck by several balls, both of its forelegs being broken. Nevertheless, it managed to shove itself forward on its hind-legs, and partly rolled, partly pushed itself into the thicket, the bushes though low being so dense that its body was at once completely hidden. The thicket was a mere patch of brush, not twenty yards across in any direction. The leading troopers reached the edge almost as the bear tumbled in. One of them, a tall and powerful man named Miller, instantly dismounted and prepared to force his way in among the dwarfed willows, which were but breast-high. Among the men who had ridden up were Moore and Bates, and also the two famous scouts, Buffalo Bill—long a companion of Captain Moore,—and California Joe, Custer's faithful follower. California Joe had spent almost all his life on the plains and in the mountains, as a hunter and Indian fighter; and when he saw the trooper about to rush into the thicket he called out to him not to do so, warning him of the danger. But the man was a very reckless fellow and he answered by jeering at the old hunter for his over-caution in being afraid of a crippled bear. California Joe made no further effort to dissuade him, remarking quietly: "Very well, sonny, go in; it's your own affair." Miller then leaped off the bank on which they stood and strode into the thicket, holding his rifle at the port. Hardly had he taken three steps when the bear rose in front of him, roaring with rage and pain. It was so close that the man had no chance to fire. Its fore-arms hung useless and as it reared unsteadily on its hind-legs, lunging forward at him, he seized it by the ears and strove to hold it back. His strength was very great, and he actually kept the huge head from his face and braced himself so that he was not overthrown; but the bear twisted its muzzle from side to side, biting and tearing the man's arms and shoulders. Another soldier jumping down slew the beast with a single bullet, and rescued his comrade; but though alive he was too badly hurt to recover and died after reaching the hospital. Buffalo Bill was given the bear-skin, and I believe has it now.

The instances in which hunters who have rashly followed grislies into thick cover have been killed or severely mauled might be multiplied indefinitely. I have myself known of eight cases in which men have met their deaths in this manner.

It occasionally happens that a cunning old grisly will lie so close that the hunter almost steps on him; and he then rises suddenly with a loud, coughing growl and strikes down or seizes the man before the latter can fire off his rifle. More rarely a bear which is both vicious and crafty deliberately permits the hunter to approach fairly near to, or perhaps pass by, its hiding-place, and then suddenly charges him with such rapidity that he has barely time for the most hurried shot. The danger in such a case is of course great.

Ordinarily, however, even in the brush, the bear's object is to slink away, not to fight, and very many are killed even under the most unfavorable circumstances without accident. If an unwounded bear thinks itself unobserved it is not apt to attack; and in thick cover it is really astonishing to see how one of these large animals can hide, and how closely it will lie when there is danger. About twelve miles below my ranch there are some large river bottoms and creek bottoms covered with a matted mass of cottonwood, box-alders, bull-berry bushes, rosebushes, ash, wild plums, and other bushes. These bottoms have harbored bears ever since I first saw them; but, though often in company with a large party, I have repeatedly beaten through them, and though we must at times have been very near indeed to the game, we never so much as heard it run.

When bears are shot, as they usually must be, in open timber or on the bare mountain, the risk is very much less. Hundreds may thus be killed with comparatively little danger; yet even under these circumstances they will often charge, and sometimes make their charge good. The spice of danger, especially to a man armed with a good repeating rifle, is only enough to add zest to the chase, and the chief triumph is in outwitting the wary quarry and getting within range. Ordinarily the only excitement is in the stalk, the bear doing nothing more than keep a keen look-out and manifest the utmost anxiety to get away. As is but natural, accidents occasionally occur; yet they are usually due more to some failure in man or weapon than to the prowess of the bear. A good hunter whom

I once knew, at a time when he was living in Butte, received fatal injuries from a bear he attacked in open woodland. The beast charged after the first shot, but slackened its pace on coming almost up to the man. The latter's gun jambed, and as he was endeavoring to work it he kept stepping slowly back, facing the bear which followed a few yards distant, snarling and threatening. Unfortunately, while thus walking backwards the man struck a dead log and fell over it, whereupon the beast instantly sprang on him and mortally wounded him before help arrived.

On rare occasions men who are not at the time hunting it fall victims to the grisly. This is usually because they stumble on it unawares and the animal attacks them more in fear than in anger. One such case, resulting fatally, occurred near my own ranch. The man walked almost over a bear while crossing a little point of brush, in a bend of the river, and was brained with a single blow of the paw. In another instance which came to my knowledge the man escaped with a shaking up, and without even a fight. His name was Perkins, and he was out gathering huckleberries in the woods on a mountain side near Pend'Oreille Lake. Suddenly he was sent flying head over heels, by a blow which completely knocked the breath out of his body; and so instantaneous was the whole affair that all he could ever recollect about it was getting a vague glimpse of the bear just as he was bowled over. When he came to he found himself lying some distance down the hill-side, much shaken, and without his berry pail, which had rolled a hundred yards below him, but not otherwise the worse for his misadventure; while the footprints showed that the bear, after delivering the single hurried stoke at the unwitting disturber of its day-dreams, had run off up-hill as fast as it was able.

A she-bear with cubs is a proverbially dangerous beast; yet even under such conditions different grislies act in directly opposite ways. Some she-grislies, when their cubs are young, but are able to follow them about, seem always worked up to the highest pitch of anxious and jealous rage, so that they are likely to attack unprovoked any intruder or even passer-by. Others when threatened by the hunter leave their cubs to their fate without a visible qualm of any kind, and seem to think only of their own safety.

In 1882 Mr. Casper W. Whitney, now of New York, met with a very singular adventure with a she-bear and cub. He was in Harvard when I was, but left it and, like a good many other Harvard men of that time, took to cow-punching in the West. He went on a ranch in Rio Arriba County, New Mexico, and was a keen hunter, especially fond of the chase of cougar, bear, and elk. One day while riding a stony mountain trail he saw a grisly cub watching him from the chaparral above, and he dismounted to try to capture it; his rifle was a 40-90 Sharp's. Just as he neared the cub, he heard a growl and caught a glimpse of the old she, and he at once turned up-hill, and stood under some tall, quaking aspens. From this spot he fired at and wounded the she, then seventy yards off; and she charged furiously. He hit her again, but as she kept coming like a thunderbolt he climbed hastily up the aspen, dragging his gun with him, as it had a strap. When the bear reached the foot of the aspen she reared, and bit and clawed the slender trunk, shaking it for a moment, and he shot her through the eye. Off she sprang for a few yards, and then spun round a dozen times, as if dazed or partially stunned; for the bullet had not touched the brain. Then the vindictive and resolute beast came back to the tree and again reared up against it; this time to receive a bullet that dropped her lifeless. Mr. Whitney then climbed down and walked to where the cub had been sitting as a looker-on. The little animal did not move until he reached out his hand; when it suddenly struck at him like an angry cat, dove into the bushes, and was seen no more.

In the summer of 1888 an old-time trapper, named Charley Norton, while on Loon Creek, of the middle fork of the Salmon, meddled with a she and her cubs. She ran at him and with one blow of her paw almost knocked off his lower jaw; yet he recovered, and was alive when I last heard of him.

Yet the very next spring the cowboys with my own wagon on the Little Missouri round-up killed a mother bear which made but little more fight than a coyote. She had two cubs, and was surprised in the early morning on the prairie far from cover. There were eight or ten cowboys together at the time, just starting off on a long circle, and of course they all got down their ropes in a second, and putting spurs to their fiery little horses started toward the bears at a run, shouting and swinging their loops round their heads. For a moment the old she tried to bluster and made a half-hearted threat of charging; but her courage failed before the rapid onslaught of her yelling, rope-swinging assailants; and she took to her heels and galloped off, leaving the cubs to shift for themselves. The cowboys were close behind, however, and after half a mile's run she bolted into a shallow cave or hole in the side of a butte, where she stayed cowering and growling, until one of the men leaped off his horse, ran up to the edge of the hole, and killed her with a single bullet from his revolver, fired so close that the powder burned her hair. The unfortunate cubs were roped, and then so dragged about that they were speedily killed instead of being brought alive to camp, as ought to have been done.

In the cases mentioned above the grisly attacked only after having been itself assailed, or because it feared an assault, for itself or for its young. In the old days, however, it may almost be said that a grisly was more apt to attack than to flee. Lewis and Clarke and the early explorers who immediately succeeded them, as well as the first hunters and trappers, the "Rocky Mountain men" of the early decades of the present century, were repeatedly assailed in this manner; and not a few of the bear hunters of that period found that it was unnecessary to take much trouble about approaching their quarry, as the grisly was usually prompt to accept the challenge and to advance of its own accord, as soon as it discovered the foe. All this is changed now. Yet even at the present day an occasional vicious old bear may be found, in some far-off and little-trod fastness, which still keeps up the former habit of its kind. All old hunters have tales of this sort to relate, the prowess, cunning, strength, and ferocity of the grisly being favorite topics for camp-fire talk throughout the Rockies; but in most cases it is not safe to accept these stories without careful sifting.

Still it is just as unsafe to reject them all. One of my own cowboys was once attacked by a grisly, seemingly in pure wantonness. He was riding up a creek bottom and had just passed a clump of rose and bullberry bushes when his horse gave such a leap as almost to unseat him, and then darted madly forward. Turning round in the saddle to his utter astonishment he saw a large bear galloping after him, at the horse's heels. For a few jumps the race was close, then the horse drew away and the bear wheeled and went into a thicket of wild plums. The amazed and indignant cowboy, as soon as he could rein in his steed, drew his revolver and rode back to and around the thicket, endeavoring to provoke his late pursuer to come out and try conclusions on more equal terms; but prudent Ephraim had apparently repented of his freak of ferocious bravado, and declined to leave the secure shelter of the jungle.

Other attacks are of a much more explicable nature. Mr. Huffman, the photographer of Miles City, informed me once when butchering some slaughtered elk he was charged twice by a she-bear and two well-grown cubs. This was a piece of sheer bullying, undertaken solely with the purpose of driving away the man and feasting on the carcasses; for in each charge the three bears, after advancing with much blustering, roaring, and growling, halted just before coming to close quarters. In another instance a gentleman I once knew, a Mr. S. Carr was charged by a grisly from mere ill temper at being disturbed at mealtime. The man was riding up a valley; and the bear was at an elk carcass, near a clump of firs. As soon as it became aware of the approach of the horseman, while he was yet over a hundred yards distant, it jumped on the carcass, looked at him a moment, and then ran straight for him. There was no particular reason why it should have charged, for it was fat and in good trim, though when killed its head showed scars made by the teeth of rival grislies. Apparently it had been living so well, principally on flesh, that it had become quarrelsome; and perhaps its not over sweet disposition had been soured by combats with others of its own kind. In yet another case, a grisly charged with even less excuse. An old trapper, from whom I occasionally bought fur, was toiling up a mountain pass when he spied a big bear sitting on his haunches on the hill-side above. The trapper shouted and waved his cap; whereupon, to his amazement, the bear uttered a loud "wough" and charged straight down on him—only to fall a victim to misplaced boldness.

I am even inclined to think that there have been wholly exceptional occasions when a grisly has attacked a man with the deliberate purpose of making a meal of him; when, in other words, it has started on the career of a man-eater. At least, on any other theory I find it difficult to account for an attack which once came to my knowledge. I was at Sand Point, on Pend'Oreille Lake, and met some French and Meti trappers, then in town with their bales of beaver, otter, and sable. One of them, who gave his name as Baptiste Lamoche, had his head twisted over to one side, the result of the bite of a bear. When the accident occurred he was out on a trapping trip with two companions. They had pitched camp right on the shore of a cove in a little lake, and his comrades were off fishing in a dug-out or pirogue. He himself was sitting near the shore, by a little lean-to, watching some beaver meat which was sizzling over the dying embers. Suddenly, and without warning, a great bear, which had crept silently up beneath the shadows of the tall evergreens, rushed at him, with a guttural roar, and seized him before he could rise to his feet. It grasped him with its jaws at the junction of the neck and shoulder, making the teeth meet through bone, sinew, and muscle; and turning, tracked off towards the forest, dragging with it the helpless and paralyzed victim. Luckily the two men in the canoe had just paddled round the point, in sight of, and close to, camp. The man in the bow, seeing the plight of their comrade, seized his rifle and fired at the bear. The bullet went through the beast's lungs, and it forthwith dropped its prey, and running off some two hundred yards, lay down on its side and died. The rescued man recovered full health and strength, but never again carried his head straight.

Old hunters and mountain-men tell many stories, not only of malicious grislies thus attacking men in camp, but also of their even dogging the footsteps of some solitary hunter and killing him when the favorable opportunity occurs. Most of these tales are mere fables; but it is possible that in altogether exceptional instances they rest on a foundation of fact. One old hunter whom I knew told me such a story. He was a truthful old fellow and there was no doubt that he believed what he said, and that his companion was actually killed by a bear; but it is probable that he was mistaken in reading the signs of his comrade's fate, and that the latter was not dogged by the bear at all, but stumbled on him and was slain in the surprise of the moment.

At any rate, cases of wanton assaults by grislies are altogether out of the common. The ordinary hunter may live out his whole life in the wilderness and never know aught of a bear attacking a man unprovoked; and the great majority of bears are shot under circumstances of no special excitement, as they either make no fight at all, or, if they do fight, are killed before there is any risk of their doing damage. If surprised on the plains, at some distance from timber or from badly broken ground, it is no uncommon feat for a single horseman to kill them with a revolver. Twice of late years it has been performed in the neighborhood of my ranch. In both instances the men were not hunters out after game, but simply cowboys, riding over the range in early morning in pursuance of their ordinary duties among the cattle. I knew both men and have worked with them on the round-up. Like most cowboys, they carried 44-calibre Colt revolvers, and were accustomed to and fairly expert in their use, and they were mounted on ordinary cow-ponies—quick, wiry, plucky little beasts. In one case the bear was seen from quite a distance, lounging across a broad table-land. The cowboy, by taking advantage of a winding and rather shallow coulie, got quite close to him. He then scrambled out of the coulie, put spurs to his pony, and raced up to within fifty yards of the astonished bear ere the latter quite understood what it was that was running at him through the gray dawn. He made no attempt at fight, but ran at top speed towards a clump of brush not far off at the head of a creek. Before he could reach it, however, the galloping horsemen was alongside, and fired three shots into his broad back. He did not turn, but ran on into the bushes and then fell over and died.

In the other case the cowboy, a Texan, was mounted on a good cutting pony, a spirited, handy, agile little animal, but excitable, and with a habit of dancing, which rendered it difficult to shoot from its back. The man was with the round-up wagon, and had been sent off by himself to make a circle through some low, barren buttes, where it was not thought more than a few head of stock would be found. On rounding the corner of a small washout he almost ran over a bear which was feeding on the carcass of a steer that had died in an alkali hole. After a moment of stunned surprise the bear hurled himself at the intruder with furious impetuosity; while the cowboy, wheeling his horse on its haunches and dashing in the spurs, carried it just clear of his assailant's headlong rush. After a few springs he reined in and once more wheeled half round, having drawn his revolver, only to find the bear again charging and almost on him. This time he fired into it, near the joining of the neck and shoulder, the bullet going downwards into the chest hollow; and again by a quick dash to one side he just avoided the rush of the beast and the sweep of its mighty forepaw. The bear then halted for a minute, and he rode close by it at a run, firing a couple of shots, which brought on another resolute charge. The ground was somewhat rugged and broken, but his pony was as quick on its feet as a cat, and never stumbled, even when going at full speed to avoid the bear's first mad rushes. It speedily became so excited, however, as to render it almost impossible for the rider to take aim. Sometimes he would come up close to the bear and wait for it to charge, which it would do, first at a trot, or rather rack, and then at a lumbering but swift gallop; and he would fire one or two shots before being forced to run. At other times, if the bear stood still in a good place, he would run by it, firing as he rode. He spent many cartridges, and though most of them were wasted occasionally a bullet went home. The bear fought with the most savage courage, champing its bloody jaws, roaring with rage, and looking the very incarnation of evil fury. For some minutes it made no effort to flee, either charging or standing at bay. Then it began to move slowly towards a patch of ash and wild plums in the head of a coulie, some distance off. Its pursuer rode after it, and when close enough would push by it and fire, while the bear would spin quickly round and charge as fiercely as ever, though evidently beginning to grow weak. At last, when still a couple of hundred yards from cover the man found he had used up all his cartridges, and then merely followed at a safe dis-tance. The bear no longer paid heed to him, but walked slowly forwards, swaying its great head from side to side, while the blood streamed from between its half-opened jaws. On reaching the cover he could tell by the waving of the bushes that it walked to the middle and then halted. A few minutes afterwards some of the other cowboys rode up, having been attracted by the incessant firing. They surrounded the thicket, firing and throwing stones into the bushes. Finally, as nothing moved, they ventured in and found the indomitable grisly warrior lying dead.

Cowboys delight in nothing so much as the chance to show their skill as riders and ropers; and they always try to ride down and rope any wild animal they come across in favorable ground and close enough up. If a party of them meets a bear in the open they have great fun; and the struggle between the shouting, galloping, rough-riders and their shaggy quarry is full of wild excitement and not unaccompanied by danger. The bear often throws the noose from his head so rapidly that it is a difficult matter to catch him; and his frequent charges scatter his tormentors in every direction while the horses become wild with fright over the roaring, bristling beast—for horses seem to dread a bear more than any other animal. If the bear cannot reach cover, however, his fate is sealed. Sooner or later, the noose tightens over one leg, or perchance over the neck and fore-paw, and as the rope straightens with a "plunk," the horse braces itself desperately and the bear tumbles over. Whether he regains his feet or not the cowboy keeps the rope taut; soon another noose tightens over a leg, and the bear is speedily rendered helpless.

I have known of these feats being performed several times in northern Wyoming, although never in the immediate neighborhood of my ranch. Mr. Archibald Roger's cowhands have in this manner caught several bears, on or near his ranch on the Gray Bull, which flows into the Bighorn; and those of Mr. G. B. Grinnell have also occasionally done so. Any set of moderately good ropers and riders, who are accustomed to back one another up and act together, can accomplish the feat if they have smooth ground and plenty of room. It is, however, indeed a feat of skill and daring for a single man; and yet I have known of more than one instance in which it has been accomplished by some reckless knight of the rope and the saddle. One such occurred in 1887 on the Flathead Reservation, the hero being an Indian; and another in 1890 at the mouth of the Bighorn, where a cowboy roped, bound, and killed a large bear single-handed.

My friend General "Red" Jackson, of Bellemeade, in the pleasant mid-county of Tennessee, once did a feat which casts into the shade even the feats of the men of the lariat. General Jackson, who afterwards became one of the ablest and most renowned of the Confederate cavalry leaders, was at the time a young officer in the Mounted Rifle Regiment, now known as the 3rd United States Cavalry. It was some years before the Civil War, and the regiment was on duty in the Southwest, then the debatable land of Comanche and Apache. While on a scout after hostile Indians, the troops in their march roused a large grisly which sped off across the plain in front of them. Strict orders had been issued against firing at game, because of the nearness of the Indians. Young Jackson was a man of great strength, a keen swordsman, who always kept the finest edge on his blade, and he was on a swift and mettled Kentucky horse, which luckily had but one eye. Riding at full speed he soon overtook the quarry. As the horse hoofs sounded nearer, the grim bear ceased its flight, and whirling round stood at bay, raising itself on its hind-legs and threatening its pursuer with bared fangs and spread claws. Carefully riding his horse so that its blind side should be towards the monster, the cavalryman swept by at a run, handling his steed with such daring skill that he just cleared the blow of the dreaded fore-paw, while with one mighty sabre stroke he cleft the bear's skull, slaying the grinning beast as it stood upright

16

Bob White, Down 't Aberdeen

by Nash Buckingham

Despite the great number of collections of Nash Buckingham stories, and reprints of those collections, this is a tale many readers have never seen. At least as it reads here. Published in September 1913 in Field & Stream, *this Buckingham account of quail hunting with his Vermont buddy, Col. Harold P. Sheldon, later formed the basis of the story "Bobwhite Blue! Bobwhite Gray!" included in* De Shootinest Gent'man & Other Tails *when that book was first published in 1934. This earlier version stands on its own as a wonderful read, quite different from the later version and an engrossing look at quail hunting during the long-ago days of multitudinous coveys. It was included (with the two-word Bob White spelling) in* The Field & Stream Treasury, *now out of print and fairly hard to come by.*

No writer has ever captured the halcyon days of waterfowling and quail hunting with the volume of engaging prose written by Nash Buckingham. He saw and wrote about the very best shotgunning ever seen in America, the first thirty years of the 1900s. I have read Buckingham so much that I can see him in my mind as if I had been alongside him, watching as he waded the flooded tall timber with his duck call in one hand and in the other his ten-pound, thirty-two-inch, 12-gauge magnum overbored by the master, Burt Becker. Or followed a pair of pointers with his best buddy, Hal Bowen Howard, on a ten-covey afternoon of quail hunting.

One aspect of Buckingham's writing that I have always appre-
ciated, and never seen discussed in print, was his delight in food and
his descriptions of the grub as it is being laid on the groaning boards.
Meals are always a big part of Mr. Nash's sporting days, and his prose
leaves no doubt that he was a trencherman of the first rank.

ANDREW'S LETTER WAS CHARACTERISTIC. "ENTIRELY ALL RIGHT AND welcome to include the Gentleman from Boston. Never mind the Yankee strain in his breeding. If he proves a good shot and able to negotiate a few of Colonel Lauderdale's 75–90 h.p. toddies, the Rebels will stand for his pedigree, and even though it leaks out that he's a Republican, why our game laws will protect him. I know a place where the birds are holding a convention. Down across the river, about eight miles from here, in a sandy-loam and pine-hill country full of sedge, pea patches and sorghum. I have a fine old friend there. He runs a water mill, but the last man he killed was a Prohibitionist. Grinds his own flour and believe me, boy, he is a biscuit maker. If you don't choose goggle-eyed hen eggs (from contented hens) about twice the size of fifty-dollar gold pieces, and can't choke down real all-pork sausage and baked hams, why bring along your own sum'p'n t'eat. The plug gets in so late that you all may have to go to the hotel for the night but Johnny'll move your outfit out to the house next day. Couldn't do much with Johnny after dark anyhow. There's a ghost scare on down here. A phantom called Mother Hubbard is working around the streets and Johnny claims that she 'done run sev-ul uv his frens' right on to degradation.' Fat chance to get him to hang around till midnight!"

How pleasant the recollection that drifted back a twelvemonth in prospective enjoyment of another visit! We were sitting again in comfort-able cane-bottomed rockers on the wide veranda of the High Private's ancestral home. From crevices of the lofty, iron-capped columns clung villages of nests, in and out of which twittered the sparrows, bent either upon warlike sally against shrill encroaching jays or engaged in pierc-ing squabbles relating to matters of domestic retention. It was Sunday afternoon on the Old Home Place, in the sweet purpling of a brave autumnal day. From down Matubba road the puffity-pant of the cotton gin was hushed. No crop wagons creaked past in swirls of Indian summer dust with their sputtering crackle of long blacksnake whips, uncoiling over the sodgerin' back and along sleek ribs of "jughaids." There was no jocose lingo of the mule curse; no bare-fanged country dogs, entrenched beneath the wagons. It was the time of year when flashing dawns melted away the tinge of frost scrolls from russet woodland; when gaud and arrogance of capricious color gave riotous defiance to the approach of sombrous winter. Doomed by ripe fatness and assaults with stick and stone, luscious persimmons plumped to earth and schoolboy stomachs. "Egg-bustin'" puppies raced abroad, causing Brer Rabbit to hoist subject-to-change-without-notice signs. Canvas-coated hunters rode afield; lithe pointers and setters searched hill and dale for Bob Whites that leaped roaring from embrowning covert. And then—I glanced mournfully through an office window into the forbidding bleakness of our latest cold snap. Surely, I reflected, it was a fine day for a murder or to set a hen. But, to the Gentleman from Boston, languishing at his hotel, I broke the glad tidings of our invitation, and grouchily set about waiting a squarer deal from the elements. Next day dawned clear as a bell. I had just spread the sporting section when Andrew called over Long Distance. At five that afternoon we cast off, aboard the "Plug," an abused little red-in-the-face train with a seven-hour-or-more-trip staring us straight in the stomach. Fast trains chased us into sidings and burly freights hooted us into submission, leaving the poor Plug to scramble home out of breath, practically discouraged and ready to give up. It was past midnight when we finally boomed across the Tombigbee, did a "gran' right an' left" in the switching line and bumped into the silent and aristocratic town of Aberdeen, Mississippi.

We hastened uptown, registered at the comfortable Clopton House and dug far into our warm beds.

Morning came with reverse English on the fair weather. Leaden, blowy skies, an icy wind that promised chilly creeps and deeply gashed gumbo roads frozen into treacherous depths. Andrew was on hand early and regretted that it would be practically impossible to reach his selected territory. "But," said he, "we'll take in some ground I shot over last week and find all the birds we're lookin' for."

Breakfast over, the steeds were led up; Andrew whistled for Flash and Jim and we were off. The horse allotted the Gentleman from Boston was of dignified personality and winning ways, but the brute I drew was a "low-life" pure and simple. Scarcely had I a leg up, when, for the edification of a morbidly curious public, the wretch came undone right there on Main street. The idea of a regular, everyday Southern horse trying to sunfish and timberline rather surprised me, to say the least, and for a moment, just a moment, I had a good notion to hang my spurs in him and accompany the scratching with a tremendous beating over the head with my hat and a lot of yelling thrown in or off. But I had no spurs, so kept my hat out of the ring, clung to my weapon and pulled leather until Seldom-Fed quit hogging.

Our trek led through the stately old burg past the huge courthouse, crumbly with its struggle against the years, reminiscent of impassioned oratory and bitter but courtly legal battles. At intervals we glimpsed through spacious boundaries of wintered cedar hedge, oak, and locust, old-fashioned homes of singular and comforting beauty. Some, with their broad porches and superb lines of colonial paneling drooping into an almost sagging dilapidation of wartime impoverishment; others bespeaking an eloquent survival and defiance of time.

Leaving town we struck off into a bottom land of down corn and thicket. Out of the north a freezing, stinging wind wrung tears from our eyes with its biting whip. At the first ditch Andrew broke ice, wet our dogs' feet and applied a coating of tannic acid. A moment later, when cast off, they headed up through a corn field. Almost in the same breath it seemed, they froze on a point at an impenetrable thicket bordering a wide pond. We were more than glad to dismount and hurry toward the find. Approaching, we saw the birds flush wild and sweep across the pond into some briar tangles. We skirted the marsh, and, shooting in turn, managed to start the ball rolling with five singles. Leading our mounts, for walking proved far more preferable than facing the wind, we plugged through a creek bottom. We were joined here by a strange pointer belonging, Andrew said, to a gentleman in Aberdeen. "Flight" had evidently observed the departure of our safari, and being of congenial trend, had taken up the trail. Rounding a thicket clump we discovered Jimmy holding staunchly, with Flash backing as though his very life depended upon it. The new dog celebrated his arrival by pausing a second, as though to contemplate the picture, then dashed in, sending birds in every direction. The Gentleman from Boston accomplished a neat double, Andrew singled, but I was too far away to do much of anything save cuss and watch down a single or two. Andrew had Flash and Jim retrieve, then turned and eyed the guilt-stricken Flight with narrowed lids. Placing his gun against a convenient bush, he ripped a substantial switch from a sapling and grittingly invited the hapless one approach. This he did, in fawning, contrite hesitation, while the other dogs loafed in to enjoy the circus and give him the laugh. A moment later his cries rent the air, but the whaling had its effect—he flushed no more that day and attended strictly to business. At the horses we found Joe Howard, Andrew's cousin, who brought with him his good pointer, Ticket. Joe had ridden from his home two miles beyond town and reported tough sledding.

Fording a slushy bayou, we rode a short distance before seeing Flash, rigid as a poker, pointing in a ravine. Tick and Jim flattened on sight and Flight, with vivid memory of his recent dressing down, sprawled when Andrew's sharp warning reached him. A huge bevy buzzed from the sedge. "Blam-blam and blooie-blooie" ensued, with the result that each man tucked away a pair of birds in his coat. The singles went "home-free" by winging it across an ice-gorged back water. Farther on, Flight re-established himself somewhat in our good graces by a ripping find. It was ludicrous to see the fellow roll his protruding eyes and warn off the covetous Ticket who wormed a bit too near in an effort to assist. But best of all a glorious sun burned a blazing way through the clouds and cheered up everything.

In higher country, following the direction taken by some split-covey singles we saw Flight and Flash standing perhaps forty feet apart at the edge of a dense timber bottom. Thinking they had spotted some truants we separated; the Boston Boy and I going to Flash while Joe and Andrew pinned their faith to Flight's fancy. To our amazement two clustrous bevies roared from the clover almost simultaneously. Ed and I dropped four from our rise, while Joe and Andrew drew equal toll from theirs. For the next half hour we enjoyed the most magnificent of all shooting—single birds scattered in hedge boundaries and along the leaf-strewn files of the timber. We kicked about here and there, joking, laughing, betting on shots, taking turns as the dogs ranged stealthily ahead, pointing, it seemed, almost every moment. Occasionally, when a bird lay low or flushed wild some smooth chap, made a getaway, but we begrudged not one of these his escape. Finally, with bulging pockets we returned to the horses.

At a free-flowing artesian well Joe and Andrew produced capacious saddle pockets and unwound savory bundles. Their contents would have made the weariest Fletcherite drool at the mouth and forget his number of chews. There was cold quail and crisp "beat" biscuit. Then came "hog-haid" sandwiches and meaty spareribs, home-made pickles and hard-boiled eggs. And to top off came a jam cake and a chocolate one, the latter inlaid with marshmallow sauce and studded with walnut and pecan hearts.

Nothing disturbed the noon stillness save grunts of purest satisfaction serene and an occasional yell of "Aw, git away f'um here, dawg."

Climbing into our saddles we rode down through the spongy accretions of the bottoms, across a wide slough and out into a vast section of waste or "ole po' land" as Andrew termed it. A short way on Jim was discovered gazing rapturously into a plum thicket. We saw the birds go up and wing past, settling across a drainage ditch. One of the dogs had evidently come along down wind and frisked Jim out of a point, for he was very much embarrased. Then in rapid succession the dogs found birds seemingly right and left. Three big gangs were turned up within a radius of ten acres. It was glorious sport and the afternoon wore away almost without our knowledge. What with a puffy kill here, a miss there and the ever-recurring thrill when some tireless dog whirled into discovery, we were almost glad to gather up our reins and hit off toward the line of greening hills that marked the direction of our circle home.

In a short while we splashed across an expanse of meadow and began climbing through sedge-strewn valleys and steep ridges of pine forest. Shadows were lengthening among the trees and our horses' steps were muffled in the needle bedding underfoot. In an opening we halted and look away across the lowlands of our morning to where Aberdeen lay brooding in the peace and quiet of tranquil, fading sunshine. The piercing blast had softened with the chill of falling night. It seemed a thousand miles to the warmth of indoors and the delight of complete well-fed weariness. The faithful dogs had as yet evinced no signs of fatigue, in fact they were splitting the grass at top speed. Just as we reached the Gillespie place boundary fence Jimmy paused at a dry ditch along the road, sniffed, and then with head in air, walked forward as though treading on eggs.

"He's got his Sunday clothes on ag'in, ain't he?" asked Andrew, his face lighting with pardonable pride and a lean expansive grin. "But I believe we've all got pretty durn near the limit."

"Les'try 'em jus' one mo' fair fall," replied Joe, "it would be a shame to put one over on Jim dog after all his trouble."

"Satisfactory to me," pronounced Andrew. "Light down, gents, and bust a few night caps"—shoving two shells into his stubby Parker. Here Jimmy broke his point and tiptoed gingerly after the running birds. Then, out over the brink boiled a veritable beehive of quail. Ensued a miniature sham battle, followed by shouts of "I got two" and counter claims of "I killed that one" and "Fetch daid, suh." Discipline was forgotten for the nonce, but matters were adjusted when the dogs brought in enough birds to credit each man with a clean, undisputed double. "Better count up here," said Joe, "I've gotta leave you lads at the nex' gate." So the tally began, with low murmurings as each chap pulled bird after bird from his multipocketed coat.

"The limit here," announced Andrew, finishing first.

"For the first time in my young life a limit," chortled the Boston Boy.

"Another victory for the untrammeled Democracy," said Joe.

"Sufficiency here," I confessed.

At a padlocked gate, down the road, Joe took leave of us with a parting shout of "See you in the morning, boys, at the Houston place gate." The sun was glowing faintly behind its borderland of western ridge spires. Our dogs, seeming to realize that their day's work was done, leaped gladly along to keep our pace. Through field and brake we trotted, and at length, swinging into a black buckshot road, straightened out for the home stretch down Life Boat Chapel lane. It was to me a familiar way, past homely daubed shacks and cabins, ashine with the gleam of lowly lamplight, redolent of wood fires, frying bacon and contentment.

And how the dogs did bark when we swung into the grounds of our host! What is there better in life than an evening spent within the domain of Sweet Hospitality? What is more delightful than when, clothed in the refreshened garb of citizenry, one lies at ease in a deep armchair or sits down to such a dinner as only an "Auntie" can dish up? And surely out upon the sea of night there rides no fairer craft than a towering four-poster.

It was past seven o'clock when we found ourselves at family break-fast. You have, no doubt, often begun the morning meal with a luscious orange. But listen! You may suit yourself about the spiced aromatic spirits of little pigs, or slices of float-away omelette, but personally I prefer to rather economize on space until the waffles start flocking in in droves. Did you ever tenderly smear a pair of round, crisp, eat-me-quick-for-the-love-of-Mike members of the waffle family; watching the molten country butter search out the receptive crevices and overflow each hollow? Then slathered the twain with a ruddy coating of home-kettled, right-from-the-heart, ribbon cane molasses? But at length Pud sounded retreat by announcing the horses. Scabbards and saddle pockets were tied on and we were off in the bright sunshine of a perfect day.

At the Houston place gate we found Joe waiting with the ever ready Ticket and Lady, the latter a Marse Ben-Bragg-Gladstone pup. Within two hours we had raised six bevies. Ticket was the first to make birds, stiffening in a clover patch along a railroad cut. Then little Lady raced away across a hill and made a neat find on the cast. Flash and Jim were old stagers on these grounds. Jim nailed a gang for Andrew near a black-jack stretch and Flash, after handling some of the singles, delved far into the interior and fastened upon a covey. For some time we had royal sport trying to make respectable averages in the dense tangle and the dogs tried hard to overlook the messy work their masters were doing when brown bullets would whir from the dead leaves and top the blackjacks in whizzing farewell.

After lunch we rode the hill crests, letting the dogs cut up the sides and valleys. On an opposite ridge we saw Andrew approach the top with Lady and Jim flagging ahead. Down went the pair on a clean-cut point.

"It's a shame to take the money," shouted Andrew, and, sure enough, he whirled two of the crowd into bird paradise. Midafternoon is the ideal time for bird finding and it was a treat to see the Boston Boy's eyes widen in wonderment when the dogs picked up bunch after bunch.

"By the gills of the sacred codfish," he exclaimed, feverishly ripping open a fresh box of shells, "I never knew there were this many birds in existence." But at length it again neared knocking-off time, so we spurred through the fields hoping for just one more find to make the day complete.

"There they are," called Joe, rising in his stirrups, pointing to Flash and Jim. And, sure enough, they were at it again, and such a whopper the covey proved! We were actually too amazed to shoot on the rise, but watched the fugitives settle in a marshy strip of iron weed bordering a willow "dreen." Suffice to say that we gave them our personal attention and when the war was over the result proved a fitting climax to another red-letter day. Twenty or twenty-five birds doesn't sound so many to a game hog, perhaps, but shooting four in a party, turn about or shooting alone, when a man has spent the hours afield with nature and taken from her cherished stores the satisfaction of twenty clean kills and the vagrant clinging pangs of many misses, he has done pretty much all that an unselfish heart could ever crave.

"Well," questioned Andrew, when our horses' heads were set toward home, "how does the Minute Man from ye Boston Towne like an every-day, Down-in-Dixie bird hunt, with a little Rebel Yell stuff on the side?"

The Gentleman from Boston sighed a sigh of rich content and stretched wearily in his saddle.

"You are now speaking," said he, with that methodical diction characteristic of the ultra-grammatical Bostonian, "of the very best thing in the universe."

"D'm'f'taint," I echoed softly.

And Andrew triple-plated this confirmation in the tongue of our Fatherland.

"Sho' is!"

17

The White Goat and His Country

by Owen Wister

The author of the first popular western novel, The Virginian, *shows his prose skills in this portrait of early mountain goat hunting. From* The Virginian, *Mr. Wister (1860–1938) is famous for the expression, "When you call me that, smile!" Also in* The Virginian, *he wrote, "When a man ain't got no ideas of his own, he'd ought to be kind o' careful who he borrows 'em from." He was a good friend of Theodore Roosevelt and shared hunting adventures with him, and he was a friend of Ernest Hemingway.*

IN A CORNER OF WHAT IS OCCASIONALLY TERMED "OUR EMPIRE OF THE Northwest," there lies a country of mountains and valleys where, until recently, citizens have been few. At the present time certain mines, and uncertain hopes, have gathered an eccentric population and evoked some sudden towns. The names which several of these bear are tolerably sumptuous: Golden, Oro, and Ruby, for instance; and in them dwell many colonels and judges, and people who own one suit of clothes and half a name (colored by adjuncts, such as Hurry Up Ed), and who sleep almost anywhere. These communities are brisk, sanguine, and nomadic, full of good will and crime; and in each of them you will be likely to find a weekly newspaper, and an editor who is busy writing things about the neighboring editors. The flume slants down the hill bearing water to the concentrator; buckets unexpectedly swing out from the steep pines into mid-air, sailing along their wire to the mill; little new staring shanties appear daily; somebody having trouble in a saloon upsets a lamp, and half the town goes to ashes, while the colonels and Hurry Up Eds carouse over the fireworks till morning. In a short while there are more little shanties than ever, and the burnt district is forgotten. All this is going on not far from the mountain goat, but it is a forlorn distance from the railroad; and except for the stage line which the recent mining towns have necessitated, my route to the goat country might have been too prolonged and uncertain to attempt.

I stepped down one evening from the stage, the last public conveyance I was to see, after a journey that certainly has one good side. It is completely odious; and the breed of sportsmen that takes into camp every luxury excepting, perhaps, cracked ice, will not be tempted to infest the region until civilization has smoothed its path. The path, to be sure, does not roughen until one has gone along it for twenty-eight hundred miles. You may leave New York in the afternoon, and arrive very early indeed on the fifth day at Spokane. Here the luxuries begin to lessen, and a mean once-a-day train trundles you away on a branch west of Spokane at six in the morning into a landscape that wastes into a galloping consumption. Before noon the last sick tree, the ultimate starved blade of wheat, has perished from sight, and you come to the end of all things, it would seem; a domain of wretchedness unspeakable. Not even a warm, brilliant sun can galvanize the corpse of the bare ungainly earth. The railroad goes no further,—it is not surprising,—and the stage arranges to leave before the train arrives. Thus you spend sunset and sunrise in the moribund terminal town, the inhabitants of which frankly confess that they are not staying from choice. They were floated here by a boom-wave, which left them stranded. Kindly they were, and anxious to provide the stranger with what comforts existed.

Geographically I was in the "Big Bend" country, a bulk of land looped in by the Columbia River, and highly advertised by railroads for the benefit of "those seeking homes." Fruit and grain no doubt grow somewhere in it. What I saw was a desert cracked in two by a chasm sixty-five miles long. It rained in the night, and at seven next morning, bound for Port Columbia, we wallowed northward out of town in the sweating canvas-covered stage through primeval mud. After some eighteen miles we drew out of the rain area, and from around the wheels there immediately arose and came among us a primeval dust, monstrous, shapeless, and blind. First your power of speech deserted you, then your eyesight went, and at length you became uncertain whether you were alive. Then hilarity at the sheer discomfort overtook me, and I was joined in it by a brother American; but two Jew drummers on the back seat could not understand, and seemed on the verge of tears. The landscape was entirely blotted out by the dust. Often you could not see the roadside,—if the road had any side. We may have been passing homes and fruit-trees, but I think not. I remember wondering if getting goat after all—But they proved well worth it.

Toward evening we descended into the sullen valley of the Columbia, which rushes along, sunk below the level of the desert we had crossed. High sterile hills flank its course, and with the sweeping, unfriendly speed of the stream, its bleak shores seemed a chilly place for home-seekers. Yet I blessed the change. A sight of running water once more, even of this overbearing flood, and of hills however dreary, was exhilaration after the degraded, stingy monotony of the Big Bend. The alkali trails in Wyoming do not seem paradises till you bring your memory of them here. Nor am I alone in my estimate of this impossible hole. There is a sign-post sticking up in the middle of it, that originally told the traveler it was thirty-five miles to Central Ferry. But now the traveler has retorted; and three different hand-writings on this sign-post reveal to you that you have had predecessors in your thought, comrades who shared your sorrows:

Forty-five miles to water.
Seventy-five miles to wood.

And then the last word:

Two and one-half miles to hell.

Perhaps they were home-seekers.

We halted a moment at the town of Bridgeport, identified by one wooden store and an inchoate hotel. The rest may be seen upon blue-print maps, where you would suppose Bridgeport was a teeming metropolis. At Port Columbia, which we reached by a land-slide sort of road that slanted the stage over and put the twin Jew drummers in mortal fear, we slept in one of the two buildings which indicate that town. It is another important center,—in blue print,—but invisible to the naked eye. In the morning, a rope ferry floated the new stage and us travelers across the river. The Okanagon flows south from lakes and waters above the British line, and joins the Columbia here. We entered its valley at once, crossed it soon by another rope ferry, and keeping northward, with the river to the east between us and the Colville Reservation, had one good meal at noon, and entering a smaller valley, reached Ruby that evening. Here the stage left me to continue its way to Conconally, six miles further on. With the friends who had come to meet me, I ascended out of Ruby the next day over the abrupt hill westward, and passing one night out in my blankets near a hospitable but limited cabin (its flowing-haired host fed us, played us the fiddle, and would have had us sleep inside), arrived bag and baggage the fourth day from the railroad at the forks of the Methow River—the next tributary of the Columbia below the Okanagon. Here was a smiling country, winning the heart at sight. An ample beauty was over everything Nature had accomplished in this place; the pleasant trees and clear course of the stream, a fertile soil on the levels, the slopes of the foot-hills varied and gentle, unencumbered by woods, the purple cloak of forest above these on the mountains, and rising from the valley's head a crown of white, clean frozen peaks. These are known to some as the Isabella Range and Mount Gardner, though the maps do not name them. Moreover, I heard that now I was within twenty-five miles of goats; and definite ridges were pointed out as the promised land.

Many things were said to me, first and last. I remember a ragged old trapper, lately come over the mountains from the Skagit River. Goats, did I say? On top there the goats had tangled your feet walking in the trail. He had shot two in camp for staring at him. Another accurate observer had seen three hundred on a hill just above Early Winter as he was passing by. The cabined dwellers on the Methow tied their horses to the fence and talked to me—so I had come from the East after goats, had I?—and in the store of the Man at the Forks I became something of a curiosity.

Day by day I sat on the kegs of nails, or lay along the counter devoted to his dry-goods, and heard what passed. Citizens and denizens—for the Siwash with his women and horses was having his autumn hunt in the valley—knocked at the door to get their mail, or buy tobacco, or sell horns and fur, or stare for an hour and depart with a grunt; and the grave Man at the Forks stood behind one counter while I lay on the other, acquiring a miscellaneous knowledge. One old medical gentleman had slain all wild animals without weapons, and had been the personal friend of so many distinguished historical characters that we computed he was nineteen about the time of Bunker Hill. They were hospitable with their information, and I followed my rule of believing everything that I hear. And they were also hospitable with whatever they possessed. The memory of those distant dwellers among the mountains, young and old, is a friendly one, like the others I carry, whether of Wind or Powder Rivers, or the Yellowstone, or wherever Western trails have led me.

Yet disappointment and failure were the first things. There was all the zeal you could wish. We had wedged painfully into a severe country—twelve miles in two days, and trail-cutting between—when sickness turned us back, goatless. By this time October was almost gone, and the last three days of it went in patching up our disintegrated outfit. We needed other men and other horses; and while these were being sought, nothing was more usual than to hear "if we'd only been along with So-and-So, he saw goats" here and there, and apparently everywhere. We had, it would seem, ingeniously selected the only place where there were none. But somehow the services of So-and-So could not be procured. He had gone to town; or was busy getting his winter's meat; or his married daughter had just come to visit him, or he had married somebody else's daughter. I cannot remember the number of obstacles always lying between ourselves and So-and-So.

At length we were once more in camp on a stream named the Twispt. In the morning—new stroke of misfortune—one of us was threatened with illness, and returned to the Forks. We three, the guide, the cook, and myself, went on, finally leaving the narrow valley, and climbing four hours up a mountain at the rate of about a mile an hour. The question was, had winter come in the park above, for which we were heading?

On top, we skirted a bare ridge from which everything fell precipitously away, and curving round along a steep hollow of the hill, came to an edge and saw the snow lying plentifully among the pines through which we must go down into the bottom of the park. But on the other side, where the sun came, there was little or none, and it was a most beautiful place. At the head of it was a little frozen lake fringed with tamarack, and a stream flowed down from this through scattered birches and pines, with good pasture for the horses between. The park sank at its outlet into a tall impassable cañon through which the stream joined the Twispt, miles below. It was a little lap of land clear at the top of the mountains, the final peaks and ridges of which rose all around, walling it in completely. You must climb these to be able to see into it, and the only possible approach for pack-horses was the pine-tree slant, down which we came. Of course there was no trail.

We prospected before venturing, and T——, the guide, shook his head. It was only a question of days—possibly of hours—when snow must shut the place off from the world until spring. But T—— appreciated the three thousand miles I had come for goats; and if the worst came to the worst, said he, we could "make it in" to the Forks on foot, leading the horses, and leaving behind all baggage that weighed anything. So we went down. Our animals slipped a little, the snow balling their feet; but nothing happened, and we reached the bottom and chose a camp in a clump of tamarack and pine. The little stream, passing through shadows here, ran under a lid of frozen snow easily broken, and there was plenty of wood, and on the ground only such siftings of snow as could be swept clean for the tent. The saddles were piled handily under a tree, a good fireplace was dug, we had a comfortable supper; and nothing remained but that the goats should be where they ought to be—on the ridges above the park.

I have slept more soundly; doubt and hope kept my thoughts active. Yet even so, it was pleasant to wake in the quiet and hear the bell on our horse, Duster, occasionally tankle somewhere on the hill. My watch I had forgotten to place at T——'s disposal, so he was reduced to getting the time of day from the stars. He consulted the Great Bear, and seeing this constellation at an angle he judged to indicate five o'clock, he came back into the tent, and I heard him wake the cook, who crawled out of his blankets.

"Why, it's plumb night," the cook whined.

"Make the breakfast," said T——.

I opened my eyes, and shut them immediately in despair at the darkness that I saw. Presently I heard the fire and the pans, and knew that the inevitable had come. So I got my clothes on, and we looked at my watch. It was only 4.30 A. M. T—— and the Great Bear had made half an hour's miscalculation, and the face of the cook was so grievous that I secretly laughed myself entirely awake. "Plumb night" lasted some time longer. I had leisure to eat two plates of oatmeal and maple syrup, some potato-and-onion soup, bacon, and coffee, and digest these, before dawn showed.

T—— and I left camp at 6.40 A. M. The day was a dark one. On the high peaks behind camp great mounds of cloud moved and swung, and the sky was entirely overcast. We climbed one of the lower ridges, not a hard climb nor long, but very sliding, and often requiring hands and feet to work round a ledge. From the top we could see the open country lying comfortably below and out of reach of the howling wind that cut across the top of the mountain, straight from Puget Sound, bringing all that it could carry of the damp of the Pacific. The ridges and summits that surrounded our park continually came into sight and disappeared again among the dense vapors which bore down upon them.

We went cautiously along the narrow top of crumbling slate, where the pines were scarce and stunted, and had twisted themselves into corkscrews so they might grip the ground against the tearing force of storms. We came on a number of fresh goat-tracks in the snow or the soft shale. These are the reverse of those of the mountain sheep, the V which the hoofs make having its open end in the direction the animal is going. There seemed to be several, large and small; and the perverted animals invariably chose the sharpest slant they could find to walk on, often with a decent level just beside it that we were glad enough to have. If there were a precipice and a sound flat top, they took the precipice, and crossed its face on juts that did not look as if your hat would hang on them. In this I think they are worse than the mountain sheep, if that is possible.

Certainly they do not seem to come down into the high pastures and feed on the grass levels as the sheep will.

T—— and I hoped we should find a bunch, but that was not to be, in spite of the indications. As we continued, I saw a singular-looking stone lying on a little ledge some way down the mountain ahead. I decided it must be a stone, and was going to speak of it, when the stone moved, and we crouched in the slanting gravel. T—— had been making up his mind it was a stone. The goat turned his head our way, but did not rise. He was two hundred yards across a split in the mountain, and the wind blowing hard. T—— wanted me to shoot, but I did not dare to run such a chance. I have done a deal of missing at two hundred yards, and much nearer, too. So I climbed, or crawled, out of sight, keeping any stone or little bush between me and the goat, till I got myself where a buttress of rock hid me, and then I ran along the ridge and down and up the scoop in it made by the split of the mountain, and so came cautiously to where I could peer over and see the goat lying turned away from me, with his head commanding the valley. He was on a tiny shelf of snow, beside him was one small pine, and below that the rock fell away steeply into the gorge. Ought I to have bellowed at him, and at least have got him on his legs? I know it would have been more honorable. He looked white, and huge, and strange; and somehow I had a sense of personality about him more vivid than any since I watched my first silver-tip lift a rotten log, and, sitting on his hind legs, make a breakfast on beetles, picking them off the log with one paw.

I fired, aiming behind the goat's head. He did not rise, but turned his head round. The white bead of my Lyman sight had not showed well against the white animal, and I thought I had missed him. Then I fired again, and he rolled very little—six inches—and lay quiet. He could not have been more than fifty yards away, and my first shot had cut through the back of his neck and buried itself in mortal places, and the second in his head merely made death instantaneous. Shooting him after he had become alarmed might have lost him over the edge; even if a first shot had been fatal, it could not have been fatal soon enough. Two struggles on that snow would have sent him sliding through space. As it was, we had a steep, unsafe scramble down through the snow to where he lay stretched out on the little shelf by the tree.

He was a fair-sized billy, and very heavy. The little lifting and shoving we had to do in skinning him was hard work. The horns were black, slender, slightly spreading, curved backward, pointed, and smooth. They measured six inches round the base, and the distance from one point to the other, measured down one horn, along the skull, and up the other, was twenty-one and a half inches. The hoofs were also black and broad and large, wholly unlike a tame goat's. The hair was extraordinarily thick, long, and of a weather-beaten white; the eye large and deep-brown.

I had my invariable attack of remorse on looking closely at the poor harmless old gentleman, and wondered what achievement, after all, could be discerned in this sort of surprise and murder. We did not think of securing any of his plentiful fat, but with head and hide alone climbed back up the ticklish slant, hung the trophies on a tree in a gap on the camp side of the ridge, and continued our hunt. It was not ten o'clock yet, and we had taken one hour to skin the goat. We now hunted the higher ridges behind camp until 1 P. M., finding tracks that made it seem as if a number of goats must be somewhere near by. But the fog came down and shut everything out of sight; moreover, the wind on top blew so that we could not have seen had it been clear.

We returned to camp, and found it greatly improved. The cook had carpentered an important annex to the tent. By slanting pine-logs against a ridge-pole and nailing them, he had built a room, proof against wind and rain, and in it a table. One end was against the opening of the tent, the other at the fire. The arrangement was excellent, and timely also. The storm revived during the night, and it rained fitfully. The roar of the wind coming down from the mountain into our park sounded like a Niagara, and its approach was tremendous. We had built up a barrier of pine-brush, and this, with a clump of trees, sheltered us well enough; but there were wild moments when the gust struck us, and the tent shuddered and strained, until that particular breeze passed on with a diminishing roar down the cañon.

The next morning the rain kept us from making an early start, and we did not leave camp until eight. Now and then a drizzle fell from the mist, and the banks of clouds were still driving across the higher peaks, but during the day the sun slowly got the better of them. Again we saw a solitary goat, this time far below down the ridge we had chosen. Like the sheep, these animals watch the valley. There is no use in attempting to hunt them from there. Their eyes are watchful and keen, and the chances are that if you are working up from below and see a goat on the hill, he will have been looking at you for some time. Once he is alarmed, ten minutes will be enough for him to put a good many hours of climbing between himself and you. His favorite trick is to remain stock-still, watching you till you pass out of his sight behind something, and then he makes off so energetically that when you see him next he will be on some totally new mountain. But his intelligence does not seem to grasp more than the danger from below. While he is steadfastly on the alert against this, it apparently does not occur to him that anything can come down upon him. Consequently from above you may get very near before you are noticed. The chief difficulty is the noise of falling stones your descent is almost sure to make. The character of these mountain-sides is such that even with the greatest care in stepping we sent a shower rattling down from time to time. We had a viciously bad climb. We went down through tilted funnels of crag, avoiding jumping off places by crossing slides of brittle slate and shale, hailing a dead tree as an oasis. And then we lost count, and T—— came unexpectedly on the goat, which was up and away and was shot by T—— before I could get a sight of him. I had been behind some twenty yards, both of us supposing we had to go considerably further. T—— was highly disgusted. "To think of me managing such a botch as that," he said, "when you've come so far"; and he wanted me to tell the people that I had shot the goat myself. He really cared more than I did.

This goat was also a billy, and larger than the first. We sat skinning him where he had fallen at the edge of a grove of tamarack, and T—— conversed about the royal family of England. He remarked that he had always rather liked "that chap Lorne."

I explained to him that "that chap Lorne" had made himself ridiculous forever at the Queen's Jubilee. Then, as T—— did not know, I told him how the marquis had insisted on riding in the procession upon a horse, against which the Prince of Wales, aware of the tame extent of his horsemanship, had warned him. In the middle of the pageant, the Queen in her carriage, the crowned heads of Europe escorting her on horseback, and the whole world looking on—at this picturesque moment, Lorne fell off. I was not sure that T—— felt fully how inappropriate a time this was for a marquis to tumble from his steed.

"I believe the Queen sent somebody," I continued.

"Where?" said T——.

"To him. She probably called the nearest king and said: 'Frederick, Lorne's off. Go and see if he's hurt.'"

"'And if he ain't hurt, _hurt him_,'" said T——, completing her Majesty's thought.

This second billy seemed to me twice the size of a domestic goat. He was certainly twice the weight. His hide alone weighed thirty pounds, as far as one could determine by balancing it against weights that we knew, such as a sack of flour or sugar. But I distrust the measurements of wild animals made by guesswork on a mountain-top during the enthusiastic state of the hunter's mind which follows at once upon a lucky shot. Therefore, I can positively vouch for this only, that all the goats which I have seen struck me as being larger and heavier animals than the goat of civilization. After all, the comparison is one into which we are misled by the name. This is an antelope; and though, through certain details of his costume, he is able to masquerade as a goat, it must be remembered that he is of a species wholly distinct.

We took the web tallow, and the tallow of one kidney. The web was three quarters of an inch thick.

Neither elk, nor any animal I have seen, except bear, has such quantities of fat, and I do not think even a bear has a thicker hide. On the rump it was as thick as the sole of my boot, and the masses of hair are impenetrable to anything but modern firearms. An arrow might easily stick harmless; and I am told that carnivorous animals who prey upon the deer in these mountains respectfully let the goat alone. Besides his defensive armor, he is an ugly customer in attack. He understands the use of his thin, smooth horns, and, driving them securely into the belly of his enemy, jumps back and leaves him a useless, ripped-open sack. Male and female have horns of much the same size; and in taking a bite out of one of either sex, as T—— said, a mountain lion would get only a mouthful of hair.

But modern firearms have come to be appreciated by the wild animals; and those which were once unquestionably dangerous to pioneers, now retreat before the Winchester rifle. Only a bear with cubs to defend remains formidable.

I said this to T——, who told me a personal experience that tends to destroy even this last chance for the sportsman to be doughty. T—— came on a bear and cubs in the spring, and of course they made off, but his dog caught and held one little cub which cried out like a child—and its contemptible mama hurried straight on and away.

Not so a goat mama of which T—— also told me. Some prospectors came on a bunch of goats when the kids were young enough to be caught. One of the men captured a kid, and was walking off with it, when the mother took notice and charged furiously down on him. He flew by in ignominious sight of the whole camp with the goat after him, till he was obliged to drop the kid, which was then escorted back to its relatives by its most competent parent.

Yet no room for generalizing is here. We cannot conclude that the *Ursus* family fails to think blood as thick as other people do. These two incidents merely show that the race of bears is capable of producing unmaternal females, while, on the other hand, we may expect occasionally to find in a nanny-goat a Mother of the Gracchi.

I wished to help carry the heavy hide of the second billy; but T—— inflicted this upon himself, "every step to camp," he insisted, "for punishment at disappointing you." The descent this day had been bad enough, taking forty minutes for some four hundred yards. But now we were two hours getting up, a large part of the way on hands and knees. I carried the two rifles and the glass, going in front to stamp some sort of a trail in the sliding rocks, while T—— panted behind me, bearing the goat-hide on his back.

Our next hunt was from seven till four, up and down, in the presence of noble and lonely mountains. The straight peaks which marshal round the lake of Chelan were in our view near by, beyond the valley of the

Twispt, and the whole Cascade range rose endlessly, and seemed to fill the world. Except in Switzerland, I have never seen such an unbroken area of mountains. And all this beauty going begging, while each year our American citizens of the East, more ignorant of their own country and less identified with its soil than any race upon earth, herd across the sea to the tables d'hôte they know by heart! But this is wandering a long way from goats, of which this day we saw none.

A gale set in after sunset. This particular afternoon had been so mellow, the sun had shone so clear from a stable sky, that I had begun to believe the recent threats of winter were only threats, and that we had some open time before us still. Next morning we waked in midwinter, the flakes flying thick and furious over a park that was no longer a pasture, but a blind drift of snow. We lived in camp, perfectly comfortable. Down at the Forks I had had made a rough imitation of a Sibley stove. All that its forger had to go on was my unprofessional and inexpert description, and a lame sketch in pencil; but he succeeded so well that the hollow iron cone and joints of pipe he fitted together turned out most efficient. The sight of the apparatus packed on a horse with the panniers was whimsical, and until he saw it work I know that T—— despised it. After that, it commanded his respect. All this stormy day it roared and blazed, and sent a lusty heat throughout the tent. T—— cleaned the two goat-heads, and talked Shakspere and Thackeray to me. He quoted Henry the Fourth, and regretted that Thackeray had not more developed the character of George Warrington. Warrington was the *man* in the book. When night came the storm was gone.

By eight the next morning we had sighted another large solitary billy. But he had seen us down in the park from his ridge. He had come to the edge, and was evidently watching the horses. If not quick-witted, the goat is certainly wary; and the next time we saw him he had taken himself away down the other side of the mountain, along a spine of rocks where approach was almost impossible. We watched his slow movements through the glass, and were both reminded of a bear. He felt safe, and was stepping deliberately along, often stopping, often walking up some small point and surveying the scenery. He moved in an easy, rolling fashion, and turned his head importantly. Then he lay down in the sun, but saw us on our way to him, and bounced off. We came to the place where he had jumped down sheer twenty feet at least. His hoof-tracks were on the edge, and in the gravel below the heavy scatter he made in landing; and then,—hasty tracks round a corner of rock, and no more goat that day.

I had become uneasy about the weather. It was all sunshine again, and though our first goat was irretrievably gone, we had the afternoon before us. Nevertheless, when I suggested we should spend it in taking the shoes off the horses, so they might be able to walk homeward without falling in the snow, T—— thought it our best plan. We wanted to find a bunch of goats now, nannies and kids, as well as billies. It had been plain that these ridges here contained very few, and those all hermits; males who from age, or temperament, or disappointment in love, had retired from society, and were spending the remainder of their days in a quiet isolation and whatever is the goat equivalent for reading Horace. It was well enough to have begun with these philosophers, but I wanted new specimens.

We were not too soon. A new storm had set in by next morning, and the unshod horses made their journey down the mountain, a most odious descent for man and beast, in the sliding snow. But down on the Twispt it was yet only autumn, with no snow at all. This was a Monday, the 7th of November, and we made haste to the Forks, where I stopped a night to read a large, accumulated mail, and going on at once, overtook my outfit, which had preceded me on the day before.

Our new camp—and our last one—was up the Methow, twenty-three miles above the Forks, in a straight line. Here the valley split at right angles against a tall face of mountain, and each way the stream was reduced to a brook one could cross afoot. The new valley became steep and narrow almost at once, and so continued to the divide between Columbia water and tributaries of the Skagit. We lived comfortably in an old cabin built by prospectors. The rain filtered through the growing weeds and sand on the roof and dropped on my head in bed; but not much, and I was able to steer it off by a rubber blanket. And of course there was no glass in the windows; but to keep out wind and wet we hung gunny sacks across those small holes, and the big stone fireplace was magnificent.

By ten next morning T—— and I saw "three hundred" goats on the mountain opposite where we had climbed. Just here I will risk a generalization. When a trapper tells you he has seen so many hundred head of game, he has not counted them, but he believes what he says. The goats T—— and I now looked at were a mile away in an air-line, and they seemed numberless. The picture which the white, slightly moving dots made, like mites on a cheese, inclined one to a large estimate of them, since they covered the whole side of a hill. The more we looked the more we found; besides the main army there were groups, caucuses, families sitting apart over some discourse too intimate for the general public; and beyond these single animals could be discerned, moving, gazing, browsing, lying down.

"Megod and Begod," said T—— (he occasionally imitated a brogue for no hereditary reason), "there's a hundred thousand goats!"

"Let's count 'em," I suggested, and we took the glasses. There were thirty-five.

We found we had climbed the wrong hill, and the day was too short to repair this error. Our next excursion, however, was successful. The hill where the goats were was not two miles above camp,—you could have seen the animals from camp but for the curve in the cañon,—yet we were four hours and a half climbing the ridge, in order to put ourselves above them. It was a hard climb, entirely through snow after the first. On top the snow came at times considerably above the knees. But the judicious T—— (I have never hunted with a more careful and thorough man) was right in the route he had chosen, and after we had descended again to the edge of the snow, we looked over a rock, and saw, thirty yards below us, the nanny and kid for which we had been aiming. I should have said earlier that the gathering of yesterday had dispersed during the night, and now little bunches of three and four goats could be seen up and down the cañon. We were on the exact ground they had occupied, and their many tracks were plain. My first shot missed—thirty yards!—and as nanny and kid went bounding by on the hill below, I knocked her over with a more careful bullet, and T—— shot the kid. The little thing was not dead when we came up, and at the sight of us it gave a poor little thin bleat that turns me remorseful whenever I think of it. We had all the justification that any code exacts. We had no fresh meat, and among goats the kid alone is eatable; and I justly desired specimens of the entire family.

We carried the whole kid to camp, and later its flesh was excellent. The horns of the nanny, as has been said before, are but slightly different from those of the male. They are, perhaps, more slender, as is also the total makeup of the animal. In camp I said to T—— that I desired only one more of those thirty-five goats, a billy; and that if I secured him the next day, that should be the last. Fortune was for us. We surprised a bunch of several. They had seen me also, and I was obliged to be quick. This resulted in some shots missing, and in two, perhaps three, animals going over ledges with bullets in them, leaving safe behind the billy I wanted. His conduct is an interesting example of the goat's capacity to escape you and die uselessly, out of your reach.

I had seen him reel at my first shot, but he hurried around a corner, and my attention was given to others. As I went down, I heard a shot, and came round the corner on T——, who stood some hundred yards further along the ledge beside a goat. T—— had come on him lying down. He had jumped up and run apparently unhurt, and T—— had shot him just as he reached the end of the ledge. Beyond was a fall into inaccessible depths. Besides T——'s shot we found two of mine—one clean through from the shoulder—the goat had faced me when I fired first—to the ham, where the lead was flat against the bone. This goat was the handsomest we had, smaller than the other males, but with horns of a better shape, and with hair and beard very rich and white. Curiously enough, his lower jaw between the two front teeth had been broken a long time ago, probably from some fall. Yet this accident did not seem to have interfered with his feeding, for he was in excellent plump condition.

This completely satisfied me, and I willingly decided to molest no more goats. I set neither value nor respect on numerical slaughter. One cannot expect Englishmen to care whether American big game is exterminated or not; that Americans should not care is a disgrace. The pervading spirit of the far West as to game, as to timber, as to everything that a true American should feel it his right to use and his duty to preserve for those coming after, is—"What do I care, so long as it lasts my time?"

There remain a few observations to make, and then I have said the little that I know about goats. Their horns are not deciduous, so far at least as I could learn, and the books say this also. But I read a somewhat inaccurate account of the goat's habits in winter-time. It was stated that at that season, like mountain sheep, he descends and comes into the valleys. This does not seem to be the case. He does not depend upon grass, if indeed he eats grass at all. His food seems to be chiefly the short, almost lichen-like moss that grows on the faces and at the base of the rocks and between them in the crevices. The community of goats I watched was feeding; afterward, when on the spot where they had been, I found there was no grass growing anywhere near, and signs pointed to its having been the moss and rock plants that they had been eating. None of the people in the Methow country spoke of seeing goats come out of the mountains during winter. I have not sufficient data to make the assertion, but I am inclined to believe that the goat keeps consistently to the hills, whatever the season may be, and in this differs from the mountain sheep as he differs in appearance, temperament, and in all characteristics excepting the predilection for the inclined plane; and in this habit he is more vertical than the sheep.

Lest the region I hunted in may have remained vague to Eastern readers, it is as well to add that in an air-line I was probably some thirty miles below the British border, and some hundred and twenty east of Puget Sound.

18

Homebodies

by Tom Hennessey

For an old geezer like myself in his mid-80s, the loss of dear friends is inevitable. That does not make it any easier, and when Tom Hennessey passed my heart fell to the ground. A skilled writer and artist, and outdoor editor of the Bangor Daily News, *Tom always seemed indestructible to me. He was of the essence of Maine: strong-willed, capable in all weathers, and as Maine as birch bark, rock-rimmed mountains, ruffed grouse, brook trout, black bears, and salty ocean ledges. He was a dog man supreme, never without one, specifically Labrador retrievers and pointing dogs. Tom was a master of capturing powerful emotions in a few words. This piece is one of my favorites, and the second of three we are presenting in these pages. They are all excerpted from Tom's book* Feathers 'n Fins, *1989, Amwell Press. Here, Tom takes on one of the consistent and major questions in gun dog hunting: Can a dog be excellent in the field and a great companion at home?*

I'D BET THAT BY NOW SOMEONE WHO CAUGHT HIS FIRST AND ONLY salmon three years ago has gone out of his way to inform you that a salmon won't take a fly when the river is shrouded with mist. Don't believe it. I'd also wager that some sage observer who has never been behind a bird dog has made a point telling you that a woodcock, when flushed, always pauses at the top of its rise. I've always had a sneaking suspicion that this information was passed down by a woodcock. Here's another that could just as well have gone unsaid: You can't keep a hunting dog in the house because it will lose its sense of smell.

I've had the pleasure and privilege of owning a few hunting dogs. Some were kenneled, some took up residence in the house. Without hesitation I can say that my "house dogs" could hunt alongside my "kennel dogs" any day of the week. Misty, a Brittany spaniel who lived in my house and was as good a bird dog as I've seen, would tear the rugs off the floors whenever I put on my hunting hat or picked up a gun. One the same note, Sam and Jake, two birdy characters who occupied my kennel, turned themselves inside out whenever I appeared in hunting togs, or made the mistake of picking up a dog's bell.

Again, I have never been aware of a dog's physical hunting abilities being affected by its abode. If a pup's natural instincts are hones by training and hunting experience, the result is usually a dog stuffed full of desire to hunt. As long as the dog is well cared for, it wouldn't make any difference if it curled up to sleep in a kennel or the Waldorf Towers. Once instilled, that desire is there for the duration.

It is, of course, difficult to have several dogs living in a house. Packs of hounds obviously are kept in kennels. Reference here is to the bird dog, retriever, or perhaps, the rabbit hound whose owner prefers to make it a part of the family. Those who vacuum the floors and rugs will tell you that a dog in the house creates a lot of work. No question. At present I keep two hunting partners in the house and have to admit that life would often be easier if they were kenneled.

You're probably well aware that a hunting dog who shares your dwelling soon becomes a person disguised as a Brittany spaniel, English setter, beagle, or Labrador retriever. Directly, you'll discover that Duke has established his own schedule, which he must strictly adhere and attend to regardless of your plans or commitments.

Daylight is his signal to stop sleeping. And it won't make any difference if you're plastered into a body cast and have both legs in traction, he'll sit by the bed staring at you and making noises until, mumbling and grumbling, you arise and start the day shift. And try to explain to him, when daylight saving time rolls around, that even though it's light outside, its only 5 a.m. Doesn't mean a thing. You might as well get up. Sooner war, sooner peace.

A creature of habit. Duke's schedule dictates that he must "turn in" not too long after the supper dishes are dry. Don't, however, think that having a few friends in for the evening will change things. No, siree, bub. No way. Pretty soon you'll notice him pacing and casting you sidelong looks. When that fails, he'll sit in the hallway leading to the bedrooms and run through his repertoire of grunts, groans, whimpers, and whines, which he punctuates with a bark.

Barking. Now there's a subject you would never have become well versed in if ol' Duke were kenneled. There is a bark—"yip"—that, translated, means water. Another—usually a sharp "yap" often preceded by an attention-getting growl—that means food. An indignant "woof" means he wants the scraps on the sideboard, and a high-pitched "yelp" indicates that his ball is under the couch and you'd better get the hell over there and get it out.

The roaring bark that rattles windows, however, he reserves for the paperboy, trash man, UPS driver, Girl Scouts selling cookies, and things that go bump in the night. As you know, that midnight warning can be hazardous to your health. It will hit you straight up out of a sound sleep. Straighten your hair, stop your breathing, and leave you with palpitations of the heart. Not to mention that you'll have to break loose from your wife's headlock.

If you have a live-in Labrador retriever, it's no secret to you that this breed just naturally loves to lug things around. Seldom does a Lab go from one room to another without bringing a "present." Consequently, you spend a lot of time looking for the mates to shoes, boots, socks, slippers, and gloves. Exasperating as it is, it can also become embarrassing. Take, for instance, the time a few of my hunting pals and I were batting the breeze in my kitchen. Coke, my chocolate Lab, seized the opportunity to visit the laundry room and then sashay onto center stage dragging certain of my wife's unmentionables. Nancy, of course, was present. See what you miss by keeping your dogs kenneled?

A hunting dog that lives in the house learns quickly. Because Jill is in close contact with you she becomes sensitive to the inflections of your voice, your facial expressions, and reads, unerringly, your every change of attitude. Make no mistake about it, she knows your mood and mind set just by the way you pull on your pants. And I'm sure you've notices that she quietly leaves the room whenever you begin spouting exclamations beginning with "son-of . . ." and ending with names found in the Bible.

I regret that I had to keep some of my dogs in the kennel. For that reason I never got to fully know and understand them. Nor was I able to recognize many of their traits and characteristics. Sure, I had a great rapport with them, especially during hunting season. But other than that, I spent time with them only when I fed them or took them for a run each day. They never got to ride down to the post office or the hardware store, or up to the salmon club to listen to the fireside stories like Coke does. And it bothers me that there must have been nights when, after a day's hunting, my kenneled dogs were sore or lame. Often, I wouldn't become aware of it until the following day.

Can a hunting dog live in the house? You bet. Will ol' feather-finder "lose his nose"? You can't prove it by me. Again, the dogs that have slept curled on my den couch, and who got a portion of my pancakes in the morning, hunted just as hard and performed every bit as well as any dog I had quartered in the kennel. And all of them, insiders and outsiders, lived and hunted into their thirteenth and fourteenth years.

The only drawback of keeping a hunting a dog in the house is that you become ridiculously attached to it. So much, in fact, that you'll feel guilty when you tell your setter or retriever, "Stay!" as you leave the house to go deer hunting. It gets worse, especially if your wife is also addicted to dogs. Nancy has always admonished me for hunting alone. One morning, as Coke and I were getting into my pickup, she leaned out the back door and asked, "Who are you going hunting with?"

"I'm going alone," I answered.

Her pause and reply were as chilling as the pre-dawn darkness: "If something happens to you, how will that dog get home?"

19

The Forest and the Steppe

by Ivan Turgenev

The stories in Ivan Turgenev's A Hunter's Sketches *were written and published in installments between 1847 and 1851. (In some translations, the book is called* A Sportsman's Sketches.*) The complete book of twenty-two sketches was published in 1852, and twenty years later three additional chapters were added. Turgenev's fervent passion toward nature and the Russian countryside are evident throughout the book but reach a peak of atmosphere and beautiful descriptions in this piece, the book's final chapter. Ernest Hemingway was responsible for bringing* A Hunter's Sketches *to the attention of many readers by his occasional mentions of the book as a personal reading favorite.*

And slowly something began to draw him,
Back to the country, to the garden dark,
Where lime-trees are so huge, so full of shade,
And lilies of the valley, sweet as maids,
Where rounded willows o'er the water's edge
Lean from the dyke in rows, and where the oak
Sturdily grows above the sturdy field,
Amid the smell of hemp and nettles rank . . .
There, there, in meadows stretching wide,
Where rich and black as velvet is the earth,
Where the sweet rye, far as the eye can see,
Moves noiselessly in tender, billowing waves,
And where the heavy golden light is shed

From out of rounded, white, transparent clouds:
There it is good. . . .
(From a poem consigned to the flames)

The reader is, very likely, already weary of my sketches; I hasten to reassure him by promising to confine myself to the fragments already printed; but I cannot refrain from saying a few words at parting about a hunter's life.

Hunting with a dog and a gun is delightful in itself, *für sich,* as they used to say in old days; but let us suppose you were not born a hunter, but are fond of nature and freedom all the same; you cannot then help envying us hunters. . . . Listen.

Do you know, for instance, the delight of settling off before day-break in spring? You come out on to the steps. . . . In the dark-grey sky stars are twinkling here and there; a damp breeze in faint gusts flies to meet you now and then; there is heard the secret, vague whispering of the night; the trees faintly rustle, wrapt in darkness. And now they put a rug in the cart, and lay a box with the samovar at your feet. The trace-horses move restlessly, snort, and daintily paw the ground; a couple of white geese, only just awake, waddle slowly and silently across the road. On the other side of the hedge, in the garden, the watchman is snoring peacefully; every sound seems to stand still in the frozen air—suspended, not moving. You take your seat; the horses start at once; the cart rolls off with a loud rumble. You ride—ride past the church, downhill to the right, across the dyke. . . . The pond is just beginning to be covered with mist. You are rather chilly; you cover your face with the collar of your fur cloak; you doze. The horses' hoofs splash sonorously through the pud-dles; the coachman begins to whistle. But by now you have driven over four versts . . . the rim of the sky flushes crimson; the jackdaws are heard, fluttering clumsily in the birch-trees; sparrows are twittering about the dark hayricks. The air is clearer, the road more distinct, the sky brightens, the clouds look whiter, and the fields look greener. In the huts there is the red light of flaming chips; from behind gates comes the sound of sleepy voices. And meanwhile the glow of dawn is beginning; already streaks of gold are stretching across the sky; mists are gathering in clouds

over the ravines; the larks are singing musically; the breeze that ushers
in the dawn is blowing; and slowly the purple sun floats upward. There
is a perfect flood of light; your heart is fluttering like a bird. Everything
is fresh, gay, delightful! One can see a long way all round. That way, beyond the copse, a village; there, further, another, with a white church, and
there a birch-wood on the hill; behind it the marsh, for which you are
bound. . . . Quicker, horses, quicker! Forward at a good trot! . . . There are
three versts to go—not more. The sun mounts swiftly higher; the sky is
clear. It will be a glorious day. A herd of cattle comes straggling from the
village to meet you. You go up the hill. . . . What a view! The river winds
for ten versts, dimly blue through the mist; beyond it meadows of watery green; beyond the meadows sloping hills; in the distance the plovers
are wheeling with loud cries above the marsh; through the moist bril-
liance suffused in the air the distance stands out clearly . . . not as in the
summer. How freely one drinks in the air, how quickly the limbs move,
how strong is the whole man, clasped in the fresh breath of spring! . . .

And a summer morning—a morning in July! Who but the hunter
knows how soothing it is to wander at daybreak among the underwoods?
The print of your feet lies in a green line on the grass, white with dew. You
part the drenched bushes; you are met by a rush of the warm fragrance
stored up in the night; the air is saturated with the fresh bitterness of
wormwood, the honey sweetness of buckwheat and clover; in the distance
an oak wood stands like a wall, and glows and glistens in the sun; it is
still fresh, but already the approach of heat is felt. The head is faint and
dizzy from the excess of sweet scents. The copse stretches on endlessly.
Only in places there are yellow glimpses in the distance of ripening rye,
and narrow streaks of red buckwheat. Then there is the creak of cart
wheels; a peasant makes his way among the bushes at a walking pace,
and sets his horse in the shade before the heat of the day. You greet him,
and turn away; the musical swish of the scythe is heard behind you. The
sun rises higher and higher. The grass is speedily dry. And now it is quite
sultry. One hour passes, another. . . . The sky grows dark over the horizon; the still air is baked with prickly heat. "Where can one get a drink
here, brother?" you inquire of the mower. "Yonder, in the ravine's a well."
Through the thick hazel bushes, tangled by the clinging grass, you drop

down to the bottom of the ravine. Right under the cliff a little spring is hidden; an oak bush greedily spreads out its twigs like great fingers over the water; great silvery bubbles rise trembling from the bottom, covered with fine velvety moss. You fling yourself on the ground, you drink, but you are too lazy to stir. You are in the shade, you drink in the damp fragrance, you take your ease, while the bushes face you, glowing and, as it were, turning yellow in the sun. But what is that? There is a sudden flying gust of wind; the air is astir all about you: was not that thunder? Is it the heat thickening? Is a storm coming on? ... And now there is a faint flash of lightning. Yes, there will be a storm! The sun is still blazing; you can still go on hunting. But the storm-cloud grows; its front edge, drawn out like a long sleeve, bends over into an arch. Make haste! over there you think you catch sight of a hay-barn ... make haste! ... You run there, go in. ... What rain! What flashes of lightning! The water drips in through some hole in the thatch-roof on to the sweet-smelling hay. But now the sun is shining bright again. The storm is over; you come out. My God, the joyous sparkle of everything! the fresh, limpid air, the scent of raspberries and mushrooms! And then the evening comes on. There is the blaze of fire glowing and covering half the sky. The sun sets; the air near you has a peculiar transparency as of crystal; over the distance lies a soft, warm-looking haze; with the dew a crimson light is shed on the fields, lately plunged in floods of limpid gold; from trees and bushes and high stacks of hay run long shadows. The sun has set; a star gleams and quivers in the fiery sea of the sunset; and now it pales; the sky grows blue; the separate shadows vanish; the air is plunged in darkness. It is time to turn homewards to the village, to the hut, where you will stay the night. Shouldering your gun, you move briskly, in spite of fatigue. Meanwhile, the night comes on: now you cannot see twenty paces from you; the dogs show faintly white in the dark. Over there, above the black bushes, there is a vague brightness on the horizon. What is it?—a fire? ... No, it is the moon rising. And away below, to the right, the village lights are twinkling already. And here at last is your hut. Through the tiny window you see a table, with a white cloth, a candle burning, supper. ...

Another time you order the racing droshky to be got out, and set off to the forest to shoot woodcock. It is pleasant making your way along the narrow path between two high walls of rye. The ears softly strike you in the face; the corn-flowers cling round your legs; the quails call around; the horse moves along at a lazy trot. And here is the forest, all shade and silence. Graceful aspens rustle high above you; the long hanging branches of the birches scarcely stir; a mighty oak stands like a champion beside a lovely lime-tree. You go along the green path, streaked with shade; great yellow flies stay suspended, motionless, in the sunny air, and suddenly dart away; midges hover in a cloud, bright in the shade, dark in the sun; the birds are singing peacefully; the golden little voice of the warbler sings of innocent, babbling joyousness, in sweet accord with the scent of the lilies of the valley. Further, further, deeper into the forest . . . the forest grows more dense. . . . An unutterable stillness falls upon the soul within; without, too, all is still and dreamy. But now a wind has sprung up, and the tree-tops are booming like falling waves. Here and there, through last year's brown leaves, grow tall grasses; mushrooms stand apart under their wide-brimmed hats. All at once a hare skips out; the dog scurries after it with a resounding bark. . . .

And how fair is this same forest in late autumn, when the snipe are on the wing! They do not keep in the heart of the forest; one must look for them along the outskirts. There is no wind, and no sun, no light, no shade, no movement, no sound; the autumn perfume, like the perfume of wine, is diffused in the soft air; a delicate haze hangs over the yellow fields in the distance. The still sky is a peacefully untroubled white through the bare brown branches; in parts, on the limes, hang the last golden leaves. The damp earth is elastic under your feet; the high dry blades of grass do not stir; long threads lie shining on the blanched turf, white with dew. You breathe tranquilly; but there is a strange tremor in the soul. You walk along the forest's edge, look after your dog, and meanwhile loved forms, loved faces, dead and living, come to your mind; long, long slumbering impressions unexpectedly awaken; the fancy darts off and soars like a bird; and all moves so clearly and stands out before your eyes. The heart at one time throbs and beats, plunging passionately forward; at another it is drowned beyond recall in memories. Your whole life, as it were, unrolls lightly and rapidly before you; a man at such times possesses all his past,

all his feelings and his powers—all his soul; and there is nothing around
to hinder him—no sun, no wind, no sound. . . .

And a clear, rather cold autumn day, with a frost in the morning,
when the birch, all golden like some tree in a fairy-tale, stands out pic-
turesquely against the pale-blue sky; when the sun, standing low in the
sky, does not warm, but shines more brightly than in summer; the small
aspen copse is all a-sparkle through and through, as though it were glad
and at ease in its nakedness; the hoar-frost is still white at the bottom
of the hollows; while a fresh wind softly stirs up and drives before it the
falling, crumpled leaves; when blue ripples whisk gladly along the river,
lifting rhythmically the scattered geese and ducks; in the distance the
mill creaks, half hidden by the willows; and with changing colours in the
clear air the pigeons wheel in swift circles above it.

Sweet, too, are dull days in summer, though the hunters do not like
them. On such days one can't shoot the bird that flutters up from under
your very feet and vanishes at once in the whitish dark of the hanging fog.
But how peaceful, how unutterably peaceful it is everywhere! Everything
is awake, and everything is hushed. You pass by a tree: it does not stir a
leaf; it is musing in repose. Through the thin steamy mist, evenly diffused
in the air, there is a long streak of black before you. You take it for a
neighbouring copse close at hand; you go up—the copse is transformed
into a high row of wormwood in the boundary-ditch. Above you, around
you, on all sides—mist. . . . But now a breeze is faintly astir; a patch of
pale-blue sky peeps dimly out; through the thinning, as it were, steaming
mist, a ray of golden-yellow sunshine breaks out suddenly, flows in a long
stream, strikes on the fields and in the copse—and now everything is
overcast again. For long this struggle is drawn out, but how unutterably
brilliant and magnificent the day becomes when at last light triumphs
and the last waves of the warmed mist here unroll and are drawn out
over the plains, there wind away and vanish into the deep, softly shining
heights.

Again you set off into outlying country, to the steppe. For some
ten versts you make your way over cross-roads, and here at last is the
highroad. Past endless trains of waggons, past wayside taverns, with the
hissing samovar under a shed, wide-open gates and a well, from one ham-

let to another; across endless fields, alongside green hempfields, a long, long time you drive. The magpies flutter from willow to willow; peasant women with long rakes in their hands wander in the fields; a man in a threadbare nankin overcoat, with a wicker pannier over his shoulder, trudges along with weary step; a heavy country coach, harnessed with six tall, broken-winded horses, rolls to meet you. The corner of a cushion is sticking out of a window, and on a sack up behind, hanging on to a string, perches a groom in a fur cloak, splashed with mud to his very eyebrows. And here is the little district town with its crooked little wooden houses, its endless fences, its empty stone shops, its old-fashioned bridge over a deep ravine. On, on! . . . The steppe country is reached at last. You look from a hill-top; what a view! Round low hills, tilled and sown to their very tops, are seen in broad undulations; ravines, overgrown with bushes, wind coiling among them; small copses are scattered like oblong islands; from village to village run narrow paths; churches stand out white; between willow bushes glimmers a little river, in four places dammed up by dykes; far off, in a field, in a line, an old manor house, with its out-houses, orchard, and threshing-floor, huddles close up to a small pond. But on, on you go. The hills are smaller and ever smaller; there is scarcely a tree to be seen. Here it is at last—the boundless, untrodden steppe!

And on a winter day to walk over the high snowdrifts after hares; to breathe the keen frosty air, while half-closing the eyes involuntarily at the fine blinding sparkle of the soft snow; to admire the emerald sky above the reddish forest! . . . And the first spring day when everything is shining, and breaking up, when across the heavy streams, from the melting snow, there is already the scent of the thawing earth; when on the bare thawed places, under the slanting sunshine, the larks are singing confidingly, and, with glad splash and roar, the torrents roll from ravine to ravine.

But it is time to end. By the way, I have spoken of spring: in spring it is easy to part; in spring even the happy are drawn away to the distance. . . . Farewell, reader! I wish you unbroken prosperity.

20

The Last Buffalo

by George Bird Grinnell

According to Wikipedia, George Bird Grinnell (1849–1938) was an American anthropologist, historian, naturalist, and writer. Grinnell was prominent in movements to preserve wildlife and conservation in the American West. Grinnell wrote articles to help spread the awareness of the conservation of buffalo. For many years, he published articles and lobbied for congressional support for the endangered American buffalo. In 1887, Grinnell was a founding member, with Theodore Roosevelt, of the Boone and Crockett Club, dedicated to the restoration of America's wildlands.

ON THE FLOOR, ON EITHER SIDE OF MY FIREPLACE, LIE TWO BUFFALO skulls. They are white and weathered, the horns cracked and bleached by the snows and frosts and the rains and heats of many winters and summers. Often, late at night, when the house is quiet, I sit before the fire, and muse and dream of the old days; and as I gaze at these relics of the past, they take life before my eyes. The matted brown hair again clothes the dry bone, and in the empty orbits the wild eyes gleam. Above me curves the blue arch; away on every hand stretches the yellow prairie, and scattered near and far are the dark forms of buffalo. They dot the rolling hills, quietly feeding like tame cattle, or lie at ease on the slopes, chewing the cud and half asleep. The yellow calves are close by their mothers; on little eminences the great bulls paw the dust, and mutter and moan, while those whose horns have grown one, two, and three winters are mingled with their elders.

Not less peaceful is the scene near some river-bank, when the herds come down to water. From the high prairie on every side they stream into the valley, stringing along in single file, each band following the deep trail worn in the parched soil by the tireless feet of generations of their kind. At a quick walk they swing along, their heads held low. The long beards of the bulls sweep the ground; the shuffling tread of many hoofs marks their passing, and above each long line rises a cloud of dust that sometimes obscures the westering sun.

Life, activity, excitement, mark another memory as vivid as these. From behind a near hill mounted men ride out and charge down toward the herd. For an instant the buffalo pause to stare, and then crowd together in a close throng, jostling and pushing one another, a confused mass of horns, hair, and hoofs. Heads down and tails in air, they rush away from their pursuers, and as they race along herd joins herd, till the black mass sweeping over the prairie numbers thousands. On its skirts hover the active, nimble horsemen, with twanging bowstrings and sharp arrows piercing many fat cows. The naked Indians cling to their naked horses as if the two were parts of one incomparable animal, and swing and yield to every motion of their steeds with the grace of perfect horsemanship. The ponies, as quick and skillful as the men, race up beside the fattest of the herd, swing off to avoid the charge of a maddened cow, and, returning, dart close to the victim, whirling hither and yon, like swallows on the wing. And their riders, with the unconscious skill, grace, and power of matchless archery, are drawing their bows to the arrow's head, and driving the feathered shaft deep through the bodies of the buffalo. Returning on their tracks, they skin the dead, then load the meat and robes on their horses, and with laughter and jest ride away.

After them, on the deserted prairie, come the wolves to tear at the carcasses. The rain and the snow wash the blood from the bones, and fade and bleach the hair. For a few months the skeleton holds together; then it falls apart, and the fox and the badger pull about the whitening bones and scatter them over the plain. So this cow and this bull of mine may have left their bones on the prairie, where I found them and picked them up to keep as mementos of the past, to dream over, and in such reverie to see again the swelling hosts which yesterday covered the plains, and to-day are but a dream.

So the buffalo passed into history. Once an inhabitant of this continent from the Arctic slope to Mexico, and from Virginia to Oregon, and, within the memory of men yet young, roaming the plains in such numbers that it seemed as if it could never be exterminated, it has now disappeared as utterly as has the bison from Europe. For it is probable that the existing herds of that practically extinct species, now carefully guarded in the forests of Grodno, about equal in numbers the buffalo in the Yellowstone Park; while the wild bison in the Caucasus may be compared with the "wood" buffalo which survive in the Peace River district. In view of the former abundance of our buffalo, this parallel is curious and interesting.

The early explorers were constantly astonished by the multitudinous herds which they met with, the regularity of their movements, and the deep roads which they made in traveling from place to place. Many of the earlier references are to territory east of the Mississippi, but even within the last fifteen years buffalo were to be seen on the Western plains in numbers so great that an entirely sober and truthful account seems like fable. Describing the abundance of buffalo in a certain region, an Indian once said to me, in the expressive sign-language of which all old frontiersmen have some knowledge: "The country was one robe."

Much has been written about their enormous abundance in the old days, but I have never read anything that I thought an exaggeration of their numbers as I have seen them. Only one who has actually spent months in traveling among them in those old days can credit the stories told about them. The trains of the Kansas Pacific Railroad used frequently to be detained by herds which were crossing the tracks in front of the engines; and in 1870, trains on which I was traveling were twice so held, in one case for three hours. When railroad travel first began on this road, the engineers tried the experiment of running through these passing herds; but after their engines had been thrown from the tracks they learned wisdom, and gave the buffalo the right of way. Two or three years later, in the country between the Platte and Republican rivers, I saw a closely massed herd of buffalo so vast that I dared not hazard a guess as to its numbers; and in later years I have traveled, for weeks at a time, in northern Montana without ever being out of sight of buffalo. These were not in close herds, except now and then when alarmed and running, but were usually scattered about, feeding or lying down on the prairie at a little distance from one another, much as domestic cattle distribute themselves in a pasture or on the range. As far as we could see on every side of the line of march, and ahead, the hillsides were dotted with dark forms, and the field-glass revealed yet others stretched out on every side, in one continuous host, to the most distant hills. Thus was gained a more just notion of their numbers than could be had in any other way, for the sight of this limitless territory occupied by these continuous herds was far more impressive than the spectacle of a surging, terrified mass of fleeing buffalo, even though the numbers which passed rapidly before the observer's gaze in a short time were very great.

The former range of the buffalo has been worked out with painstaking care by Dr. Allen, to whom we owe an admirable monograph on this species. He concludes that the northern limit of this range was north of the Great Slave Lake, in latitude about 63° N.; while to the south it extended into Mexico as far as latitude 25° N. To the west it ranged at least as far as the Blue Mountains of Oregon, while on the east it was abundant in the western portions of New York, Pennsylvania, Virginia, North and South Carolinas, and Georgia. In the interior the buffalo were very abundant, and occupied Ohio, Kentucky, West Virginia, Tennessee, West Georgia, Illinois, Indiana, and Iowa, parts of Michigan, Wisconsin, and Minnesota, the whole of the great plains, from southern Texas north to their northern limit, and much of the Rocky Mountains. In Montana, Idaho, Wyoming, and most of New Mexico they were abundant, and probably common over a large part of Utah, and perhaps in northern Nevada. So far as now known, their western limit was the Blue Mountains of Oregon and the eastern foot-hills of the Sierra Nevada.

Thus it will be seen that the buffalo once ranged over a large part of the American continent,—Dr. Allen says one third of it,—but it must not be imagined that they were always present at the same time in every part of their range. They were a wandering race, sometimes leaving a district and being long absent, and again returning and occupying it for a considerable period. What laws or what impulses governed these movements we cannot know. Their wandering habits were well understood by the Indians of the Western plains, who depended upon the buffalo for food. It was their custom to follow the herds about, and when, as sometimes occurred, these moved away and could not be found, the Indians were reduced to great straits for food, and sometimes even starved to death.

Under natural conditions the buffalo was an animal of rather sluggish habits, mild, inoffensive, and dull. In its ways of life and intelligence it closely resembled our domestic cattle. It was slow to learn by experience, and this lack of intelligence greatly hastened the destruction of the race. Until the very last years of its existence as a species, it did not appear to connect the report of firearms with any idea of danger to itself, and though constantly pursued, did not become wild. If he used skill and judgment in shooting, a hunter who had "got a stand" on a small bunch could kill them all before they had moved out of rifle-shot. It was my fortune, one summer, to hunt for a camp of soldiers, and more than once I have lain on a hill above a little herd of buffalo, shot down what young bulls I needed to supply the camp, and then walked down to the bunch and, by waving my hat and shouting, driven off the survivors, so that I could prepare the meat for transportation to camp. This slowness to take the alarm, or indeed to realize the presence of danger, was characteristic of the buffalo almost up to the very last. A time did come when they were alarmed readily enough, but this was not until all the large herds had been broken up and scattered, and the miserable survivors had been so chased and harried that at last they learned to start and run even at their own shadows.

Another peculiarity of the buffalo was its habit, when stampeded, of dashing blindly forward against, over, or through anything that might be in the way. When running, a herd of buffalo followed its leaders, and yet these leaders lost the power of stopping, or even of turning aside, because they were constantly crowded upon and pushed forward by those behind. This explains why herds would dash into mire or quicksands, as they often did, and thus perish by the thousand. Those in front could not stop, while those behind could not see the danger toward which they were rushing. So, too, they ran into rivers, or into traps made for them by the Indians, or against railroad cars, or even dashed into the rivers and swam blindly against the sides of steamboats. If an obstacle lay squarely across their path, they tried to go through it, but if it lay at an angle to their course, they would turn a little to follow it, as will be shown further on.

The buffalo calf is born from April to June, and at first is an awkward little creature, looking much like a domestic calf, but with a shorter neck. The hump at first is scarcely noticeable, but develops rapidly. They are odd-looking and very playful little animals. They are easily caught and tamed when quite young, but when a few months old they become as shy as the old buffalo, and are much more swift of foot.

Although apparently very sluggish, buffalo are really extremely active, and are able to go at headlong speed over a country where no man would dare to ride a horse. When alarmed they will throw themselves down the almost vertical side of a cañon and climb the opposite wall with cat-like agility. Sometimes they will descend cut banks by jumping from shelf to shelf of rock like the mountain sheep. To get at water when thirsty, they will climb down bluffs that seem altogether impracticable for such great animals. Many years ago, while descending the Missouri River in a flat-boat with two companions, I landed in a wide bottom to kill a mountain sheep. As we were bringing the meat to the boat, we saw on the opposite side of the river, about half-way down the bluffs, which were here about fifteen hundred feet high, a large buffalo bull. The bluffs were almost vertical, and this old fellow was having some difficulty in making his way down to the water. He went slowly and carefully, at times having pretty good going, and at others slipping and sliding for thirty or forty feet, sending the clay and stones rolling ahead of him in great quantities. We watched him for a little while, and then it occurred to some malicious spirit among us that it would be fun to see whether the bull could go up where he had come down. A shot was fired so as to strike near him,—for no one wanted to hurt the old fellow,—and as soon as the report reached his ears, he turned about and began to scramble up the bluffs. His first rush carried him, perhaps, a hundred feet vertically, and then he stopped and looked around. He seemed not to have the slightest difficulty in climbing up, nor did he use any caution, or appear to pick his way at all.

A second shot caused another rush up the steep ascent, but this time he went only half as far as before, and again stopped. Three or four other shots drove him by shorter and shorter rushes up the bluffs, until at length he would go no further, and subsequent shots only caused him to shake his head angrily. Plainly he had climbed until his wind had given out, and now he would stand and fight. Our fun was over, and looking back as we floated down the river, our last glimpse was of the old bull, still standing on his shelf, waiting with lowered head for the unknown enemy that he supposed was about to attack him.

It is not only under the stress of circumstances that the bison climbs. The mountain buffalo is almost as active as the mountain sheep, and was often found in places that tested the nerve and activity of a man to reach; and even the buffalo of the plains had a fondness for high places, and used to climb up on to broken buttes or high rocky points. In recent years I have often noticed the same habit among range cattle and horses.

The buffalo were fond of rolling in the dirt, and to this habit, practised when the ground was wet, are due the buffalo wallows which so frequently occur in the old ranges, and which often contain water after all other moisture, except that of the streams, is dried up. These wallows were formed by the rolling of a succession of buffalo in the same moist place, and were frequently quite deep. They have often been described. Less well known was the habit of scratching themselves against trees and rocks. Sometimes a solitary erratic boulder, five or six feet high, may be seen on the bare prairie, the ground immediately around it being worn down two or three feet below the level of the surrounding earth. This is where the buffalo have walked about the stone, rubbing against it, and, where they trod, loosening the soil, which has been blown away by the wind, so that in course of time a deep trench was worn about the rock. Often single trees along streams were worn quite smooth by the shoulders and sides of the buffalo.

When the first telegraph line was built across the continent, the poles used were light and small, for transportation over the plains was slow and expensive, and it was not thought necessary to raise the wires high above the ground. These poles were much resorted to by the buffalo to scratch against, and before long a great many of them were pushed over.

A story, now of considerable antiquity, is told of an ingenious employee of the telegraph company, who devised a plan for preventing the buffalo from disturbing the poles. This he expected to accomplish by driving into them spikes which should prick the animals when they rubbed against them. The result somewhat astonished the inventor, for it was discovered that where formerly one buffalo rubbed against the smooth telegraph poles, ten now struggled and fought for the chance to scratch themselves against the spiked poles, the iron furnishing just the irritation which their tough hides needed.

It was in spring, when its coat was being shed, that the buffalo, odd-looking enough at any time, presented its most grotesque appearance. The matted hair and wool of the shoulders and sides began to peel off in great sheets, and these sheets, clinging to the skin and flapping in the wind, gave it the appearance of being clad in rags.

The buffalo was a timid creature, but brought to bay would fight with ferocity. There were few sights more terrifying to the novice than the spectacle of an old bull at bay: his mighty bulk, a quivering mass of active, enraged muscle; the shining horns; the little, spiky tail; and the eyes half hidden beneath the shaggy frontlet, yet gleaming with rage, combined to render him an awe-inspiring object. Nevertheless, owing to their greater speed and activity, the cows were much more to be feared than the bulls.

It was once thought that the buffalo performed annually extensive migrations, and it was even said that those which spent the summer on the banks of the Saskatchewan wintered in Texas. There is no reason for believing this to have been true. Undoubtedly there were slight general movements north and south, and east and west, at certain seasons of the year; but many of the accounts of these movements are entirely misleading, because greatly exaggerated. In one portion of the northern country I know that there was a decided east and west seasonal migration, the herds tending in spring away from the mountains, while in the autumn they worked back again, seeking shelter in the rough, broken country of the foot-hills from the cold west winds of the winter.

The buffalo is easily tamed when caught as a calf, and in all its ways of life resembles the domestic cattle. It at once learns to respect a fence, and, even if at large, manifests no disposition to wander.

Three years ago there were in this country about two hundred and fifty domesticated buffalo, in the possession of about a dozen individuals. Of these the most important herd was that of Hon. C. J. Jones, of Garden City, Kansas, which, besides about fifty animals captured and reared by himself, included also the Bedson herd of over eighty, purchased in Manitoba. The Jones herd at one time consisted of about one hundred and fifty head. Next came that of Charles Allard and Michel Pablo, of the Flathead Agency in Montana, which in 1888 numbered thirty-five, and has now increased to about ninety. Mr. Jones's herd has been broken up, and he now retains only about forty-five head, of which fifteen are breeding cows. He tells me that within the past year or two he has sold over sixty pure buffalo, and that nearly as many more have died through injuries received in transporting them by rail.

Mr. Jones is the only individual who, of recent years, has made any systematic effort to cross the buffalo with our own domestic cattle. As far back as the beginning of the present century, this was successfully done in the West and Northwest; and in Audubon and Bachman's "Quadrupeds of America" may be found an extremely interesting account, written by Robert Wickliffe, of Lexington, Kentucky, giving the results of a series of careful and successful experiments which he carried on for more than thirty years. These experiments showed that the cross for certain purposes was a very valuable one, but no systematic efforts to establish and perpetuate a breed of buffalo cattle were afterward made until within the past ten years. Mr. Jones has bred buffalo bulls to Galloway, Polled Angus, and ordinary range cows, and has succeeded in obtaining calves from all. Such hybrids are of very large size, extremely hardy, and, as a farmer would say, "easy keepers." They are fertile among themselves or with either parent. A hybrid cow of Mr. Jones's that I examined was fully as large as an ordinary work-ox, and in spring, while nursing a calf, was fat on grass. She lacked the buffalo hump, but her hide would have made a good robe. The great size and tremendous frame of these crossbred cattle should make them very valuable for beef, while their hardiness would exempt them from the dangers of winter,—so often fatal to domestic range cattle,—and they produce a robe which is quite as valuable as that of the buffalo, and more beautiful because more even all over. If continued, these attempts at cross-breeding may do much to improve our Western range cattle.

Mr. Jones has sold a number of buffalo to persons in Europe, where there is a considerable demand for them. It is to be hoped that no more of these domesticated buffalo will be allowed to leave the country where they were born. Indeed, it would seem quite within the lines of the work now being carried on by the Agricultural Department, for the government to purchase all the domesticated American buffalo that can be had, and to start, in some one of the Western States, an experimental farm for buffalo breeding and buffalo crossing. With a herd of fifty pure-bred buffalo cows and a sufficient number of bulls, a series of experiments could be carried on which might be of great value to the cattle-growers of our western country. The stock of pure buffalo could be kept up and increased; surplus bulls, pure and half bred, could be sold to farmers; and, in time, the new race of buffalo cattle might become so firmly established that it would endure.

To undertake this with any prospect of success, such a farm would have to be managed by a man of intelligence and of wide experience in this particular field; otherwise all the money invested would be wasted. Mr. Jones is perhaps the only man living who knows enough of this subject to carry on an experimental farm with success.

Although only one species of buffalo is known to science, old mountaineers and Indians tell of four kinds. These are, besides the ordinary animal of the plains, the "mountain buffalo," sometimes called "bison," which is found in the timbered Rocky Mountains; the "wood buffalo" of the Northwest, which inhabits the timbered country to the west and north of Athabasca Lake; and the "beaver buffalo." The last named has been vaguely described to me by northern Indians as small and having a very curly coat. I know of only one printed account of it, and this says that it had "short, sharp horns which were small at the root and curiously turned up and bent backward, not unlike a ram's, but quite unlike the bend of the horn in the common buffalo." It is possible that this description may refer to the musk-ox, and not to a buffalo. The "mountain" and "wood" buffalo seem to be very much alike in habit and appearance. They are larger, darker, and heavier than the animal of the plains, but there is no reason for thinking them specifically distinct from it. Such differences as exist are due to conditions of environment.

The color of the buffalo in its new coat is a dark liver-brown. This soon changes, however, and the hides, which are at their best in November and early December, begin to grow paler toward spring; and when the coat is shed, the hair and wool from young animals is almost a dark smoky-gray. The calf when just born is of a bright yellow color, almost a pale red on the line of the back. As it grows older it becomes darker, and by late autumn is almost as dark as the adults. Variations from the normal color are very rare, but pied, spotted, and roan animals are sometimes killed. Blue or mouse-colored buffalo were occasionally seen, and a bull of this color was observed in the National Park last January. White buffalo—though often referred to as mythical—sometimes occurred. These varied from gray to cream-white. The rare and valuable "silk" or "beaver" robe owes its name to its dark color and its peculiar sheen or gloss. White or spotted robes were highly valued by the Indians. Among the Blackfeet they were presented to the Sun as votive offerings. Other tribes kept them in their sacred bundles.

Apart from man, the buffalo had but few natural enemies. Of these the most destructive were the wolves, which killed a great many of them. These, however, were principally old, straggling bulls, for the calves were protected by their mothers, and the females and young stock were so vigorous and so gregarious that they had but little to fear from this danger. It is probable that, notwithstanding the destruction which they wrought, the wolves performed an important service for the buffalo race, keeping it vigorous and healthy by killing weak, disabled, and superannuated animals, which could no longer serve any useful purpose in the herd, and yet consumed the grass which would support a healthy breeding animal. It is certainly true that sick buffalo, or those out of condition, were rarely seen.

The grizzly bear fed to some extent on the carcasses of buffalo drowned in the rivers or caught in the quicksands, and occasionally they caught living buffalo and killed them. A Blackfoot Indian told me of an attempt of this kind which he witnessed. He was lying hidden by a buffalo trail in the Bad Lands, near a little creek, waiting for a small bunch to come down to water, so that he might kill one. The buffalo came on in single file as usual, the leading animal being a young heifer. When they had nearly reached the water, and were passing under a vertical clay wall, a grizzly bear, lying hid on a shelf of this wall, reached down, and with both paws caught the heifer about the neck and threw himself upon her. The others at once ran off, and a short struggle ensued, the bear trying to kill the heifer, and she to escape. Almost at once, however, the Indian saw a splendid young bull come rushing down the trail toward the scene of conflict, and charge the bear, knocking him down. A fierce combat ensued. The bull would charge the bear, and when he struck him fairly would knock him off his feet, often inflicting severe wounds with his sharp horns. The bear struck at the bull, and tried to catch him by the head or shoulders, and to hold him, but this he could not do. After fifteen or twenty minutes of fierce and active fighting, the bear had received all the punishment he cared for, and tried to escape, but the bull would not let him go, and kept up the attack until he had killed his adversary. Even after the bear was dead the bull would gore the carcass and sometimes lift it clear of the ground on his horns. He seemed insane with rage, and, notwithstanding the fact that most of the skin was torn from his head and shoulders, appeared to be looking about for something else to fight. The Indian was very much afraid lest the bull should discover and kill him, and was greatly relieved when he finally left the bear and went off to join his band. This Blackfoot had never heard of Uncle Remus's tales, but he imitated Brer Rabbit—laid low and said nothing.

To the Indians the buffalo was the staff of life. It was their food, clothing, dwellings, tools. The needs of a savage people are not many, perhaps, but whatever the Indians of the plains had, that the buffalo gave them. It is not strange, then, that this animal was reverenced by most plains tribes, nor that it entered largely into their sacred ceremonies, and was in a sense worshiped by them. The Pawnees, in explaining their religious customs, say, "Through the corn and the buffalo we worship the Father." The Blackfeet ask, "What one of all the animals is most sacred?" and the reply given is, "The buffalo."

The robe was the Indian's winter covering and his bed, while the skin, freed from the hair and dressed, constituted his summer sheet or blanket. The dressed hide was used for moccasins, leggings, shirts, and women's dresses. Dressed cow-skins formed the lodges, the warmest and most comfortable portable shelters ever devised. Braided strands of rawhide furnished them with ropes and lines, and these were made also from the twisted hair. The green hide was sometimes used as a kettle, in which to boil meat, or, stretched over a frame of boughs, gave them coracles, or boats, for crossing rivers. The tough, thick hide of the bull's neck, allowed to shrink smooth, made a shield which would turn a lance-thrust, an arrow, or even the ball from an old-fashioned smooth-bore gun. From the rawhide, the hair having been shaved off, were made parfleches— envelop-like cases which served for trunks or boxes—useful to contain small articles. The cannon-bones and ribs were used to make implements for dressing hides; the shoulder-blades lashed to sticks made hoes and axes, and the ribs runners for small sledges drawn by dogs. The hoofs were boiled to make a glue for fastening the feathers and heads on their arrows, the hair used to stuff cushions, and later saddles, strands of the long black beard to ornament articles of wearing-apparel and implements of war, such as shields and quivers. The sinews lying along the back gave them thread and bowstrings, and backed their bows. The horns furnished spoons and ladles, and ornamented their war-bonnets. Water-buckets were made from the lining of the paunch. The skin of the hind leg cut off above the pastern, and again a short distance above the hock, was once used for a moccasin or boot. Fly-brushes were made from the skin of the tail dried on sticks. Knife-sheaths, quivers, bow-cases, gun-covers, saddle-cloths, and a hundred other useful and necessary articles, all were furnished by the buffalo.

The Indians killed some smaller game, as elk, deer, and antelope, but for food their dependence was on the buffalo. But before the coming of the whites their knives and arrowheads were merely sharpened stones, weapons which would be inefficient against such great, thick-skinned beasts. Even under the most favorable circumstances, with these primitive implements, they could not kill food in quantities sufficient to supply their needs. There must be some means of taking the buffalo in considerable numbers. Such wholesale capture was accomplished by means of traps or surrounds, which all depended for success on one characteristic of the animal, its curiosity.

The Blackfeet, Plains Crees, Gros Ventres of the Prairie, Sarcees, some bands of the Dakotas, Snakes, Crows, and some others, drove the herds of buffalo into pens from above, or over high cliffs, where the fall killed or crippled a large majority of the herd. The Cheyennes and Arapahoes drove them into pens on level ground; the Blackfeet, Aricaras, Mandans, Gros Ventres of the Village, Pawnees, Omahas, Otoes, and others, surrounded the herds in great circles on the prairie, and then, frightening them so that they started running, kept them from breaking through the line of men, and made them race round and round in a circle, until they were so exhausted that they could not run away, and were easily killed.

These primitive modes of slaughter have been described by earlier writers, and frequently quoted in recent years; yet, in all that has been written on this subject, I fail to find a single account which gives at all a true notion of the methods employed, or the means by which the buffalo were brought into the inclosures. Eye-witnesses have been careless observers, and have taken many things for granted. My understanding of this matter is derived from men who from childhood have been familiar with these things, and from them, during years of close association, I have again and again heard the story of these old hunting methods.

The Blackfoot trap was called the *piskun*. It was an inclosure, one side of which was formed by the vertical wall of a cut bank, the others being built of rocks, logs, poles, and brush six or eight feet high. It was not necessary that these walls should be very strong, but they had to be tight, so that the buffalo could not see through them. From a point on the cut bank above this inclosure, in two diverging lines stretching far out into the prairie, piles of rock were heaped up at short intervals, or bushes were stuck in the ground, forming the wings of a V-shaped chute, which would guide any animals running down the chute to its angle above the piskun. When a herd of buffalo were feeding near at hand, the people prepared for the hunt, in which almost the whole camp took part. It is commonly stated that the buffalo were driven into the piskun by mounted men, but this was not the case. They were not driven, but led, and they were led by an appeal to their curiosity. The man who brought them was usually the possessor of a "buffalo rock," a talisman which was believed to give him greater power to call the buffalo than was had by others. The previous night was spent by this man in praying for success in the enterprise of the morrow. The help of the Sun, *Napi*, and all Above People was asked for, and sweet-grass was burned to them. Early in the morning, without eating or drinking, the man started away from the camp and went up on the prairie. Before he left the lodge, he told his wives that they must not go out, or even look out, of the lodge during his absence. They should stay there, and pray to the Sun for his success, and burn sweet-grass until he returned. When he left the camp and went up on to the prairie toward the buffalo, all the people followed him, and distributed themselves along the wings of the chute, hiding behind the piles of rock or brush. The caller sometimes wore a robe and a bull's-head bonnet, or at times was naked. When he had approached close to the buffalo, he endeavored to attract their attention by moving about, wheeling round and round, and alternately appearing and disappearing. The feeding buffalo soon began to raise their heads and stare at him, and presently the nearest ones would walk toward him to discover what this strange creature might be, and the others would follow. As they began to approach, the man withdrew toward the entrance of the chute. If the buffalo began to trot, he increased his speed, and before very long he had the herd well within the wings. As soon as they had passed the first piles of rock, behind which some of the people were concealed, the Indians sprang into view, and by yelling and waving robes frightened the hind-most of the buffalo, which then began to run down the chute. As they passed along, more and more people showed themselves and added to their terror, and in a very short time the herd was in a headlong stampede, guided toward the angle above the piskun by the piles of rock on either side.

About the walls of the piskun, now full of buffalo, were distributed the women and children of the camp, who, leaning over the inclosure, waving their arms and calling out, did all they could to frighten the penned-in animals, and to keep them from pushing against the walls or trying to jump or climb over them. As a rule the buffalo raced round within the inclosure, and the men shot them down as they passed, until all were killed. After this the people all entered the piskun and cut up the dead, transporting the meat to camp. The skulls, bones, and less perishable offal were removed from the inclosure, and the wolves, coyotes, foxes, and badgers devoured what was left.

It occasionally happened that something occurred to turn the buffalo, so that they passed through the guiding arms and escaped. Usually they went on straight to the angle and jumped over the cliff into the inclosure below. In winter, when snow was on the ground, their straight course was made additionally certain by placing on, or just above, the snow a line of buffalo-chips leading from the angle of the V, midway between its arms, out on to the prairie. These dark objects, only twenty or thirty feet apart, were easily seen against the white snow, and the buffalo always followed them, no doubt thinking this a trail where another herd had passed.

By the *Siksikau* tribe of the Blackfoot nation and the Plains Crees, the piskun was built in a somewhat different way, but the methods employed were similar. With these people, who inhabited a flat country, the inclosure was built of logs and near a timbered stream. Its circular wall was complete; that is, there was no opening or gateway in it, but at one point this wall, elsewhere eight feet high, was cut away so that its height was only four feet. From this point a bridge or causeway of logs, covered with dirt, sloped by a gradual descent down to the level of the prairie. This bridge was fenced on either side with logs, and the arms of the V came together at the point where the bridge reached the ground. The buffalo were driven down the chute as before, ran up on this bridge, and were forced to leap into the pen. As soon as all had entered, Indians who had been concealed near by ran up and put poles across the opening through which the buffalo had passed, and over these poles hung robes so as entirely to conceal the outer world. Then the butchering of the animals took place.

Further to the south, out on the prairie, where timber and rocks and brush were not obtainable for making traps like these, simpler but less effective methods were adopted. The people would go out on the prairie and conceal themselves in a great circle, open on one side. Then some man would approach the buffalo, and decoy them into the circle. Men would now show themselves at different points and start the buffalo running in a circle, yelling and waving robes to keep them from approaching or trying to break through the ring of men. This had to be done with great judgment, however; for often if the herd got started in one direction it was impossible to turn it, and it would rush through the ring and none would be secured. Sometimes, if a herd was found in a favorable position, and there was no wind, a large camp of people would set up their lodges all about the buffalo, in which case the chances of success in the surround were greatly increased.

The tribes which used the piskun also practised driving the buffalo over high, rough cliffs, where the fall crippled or killed most of the animals which went over. In such situations, no inclosure was built at the foot of the precipice.

In the later days of the piskun in the north, the man who brought the buffalo often went to them on horseback, riding a white horse. He would ride backward and forward before them, zigzagging this way and that, and after a little they would follow him. He never attempted to drive, but always led them. The driving began only after the herd had passed the outer rock piles, and the people had begun to rise up and frighten them.

This method of securing meat has been practised in Montana within thirty years, and even more recently among the Plains Crees of the north. I have seen the remains of old piskuns, and the guiding wings of the chute, and have talked with many men who have taken part in such killings.

All this had to do, of course, with the primitive methods of buffalo killing. As soon as horses became abundant, and sheet-iron arrow-heads and, later, guns were secured by the Indians, these old practices began to give way to the more exciting pursuit of running buffalo and of surrounding them on horseback. Of this modern method, as practiced twenty years ago, and exclusively with the bow and arrow, I have already written at some length in another place.

To the white travelers on the plains in early days the buffalo furnished support and sustenance. Their abundance made fresh meat easily obtainable, and the early travelers usually carried with them bundles of dried meat, or sacks of pemmican, food made from the flesh of the buffalo, that contained a great deal of nutriment in very small bulk. Robes were used for bedding, and in winter buffalo moccasins were worn for warmth, the hair side within. Coats of buffalo-skin are the warmest covering known, the only garment which will present an effective barrier to the bitter blasts that sweep over the plains of the Northwest.

Perhaps as useful to early travelers as any product of the buffalo, was the "buffalo chip," or dried dung. This, being composed of comminuted woody fiber of the grass, made an excellent fuel, and in many parts of the treeless plains was the only substance which could be used to cook with.

The dismal story of the extermination of the buffalo for its hides has been so often told, that I may be spared the sickening details of the butchery which was carried on from the Mexican to the British boundary line in the struggle to obtain a few dollars by a most ignoble means. As soon as railroads penetrated the buffalo country, a market was opened for the hides. Men too lazy to work were not too lazy to hunt, and a good hunter could kill in the early days from thirty to seventy-five buffalo a day, the hides of which were worth from $1.50 to $4 each. This seemed an easy way to make money, and the market for hides was unlimited. Up to this time the trade in robes had been mainly confined to those dressed by the Indians, and these were for the most part taken from cows. The coming of the railroad made hides of all sorts marketable, and even those taken from naked old bulls found a sale at some price. The butchery of buffalo was now something stupendous. Thousands of hunters followed millions of buffalo and destroyed them wherever found and at all seasons of the year. They pursued them during the day, and at night camped at the watering-places, and built lines of fires along the streams, to drive the buffalo back so that they could not drink. It took less than six years to destroy all the buffalo in Kansas, Nebraska, Indian Territory, and northern Texas. The few that were left of the southern herd retreated to the waterless plains of Texas, and there for a while had a brief respite. Even here the hunters followed them, but as the animals were few and the territory in which they ranged vast, they held out here for some years. It was in this country, and against the last survivors of this southern herd, that "Buffalo Jones" made his successful trips to capture calves.

The extirpation of the northern herd was longer delayed. No very terrible slaughter occurred until the completion of the Northern Pacific Railroad; then, however, the same scenes of butchery were enacted.

Buffalo were shot down by tens of thousands, their hides stripped off, and the meat left to the wolves. The result of the crusade was soon seen, and the last buffalo were killed in the Northwest near the boundary line in 1883, and that year may be said to have finished up the species, though some few were killed in 1884 to 1885.

After the slaughter had been begun, but years before it had been accomplished, the subject was brought to the attention of Congress, and legislation looking to the preservation of the species was urged upon that body. Little general interest was taken in the subject, but in 1874, after much discussion, Congress did pass an act providing for the protection of the buffalo. The bill, however, was never signed by the President.

During the last days of the buffalo, a remarkable change took place in its form, and this change is worthy of consideration by naturalists, for it is an example of specialization—of development in one particular direction—which was due to a change in the environment of the species, and is interesting because it was brought about in a very few years, and indicates how rapidly, under favoring conditions, such specialization may sometimes take place.

This change was noticed and commented on by hunters who followed the northern buffalo, as well as by those who assisted in the extermination of the southern herd. The southern hunters, however, averred that the "regular" buffalo had disappeared—gone off somewhere—and that their place had been taken by what they called the southern buffalo, a race said to have come up from Mexico, and characterized by longer legs and a longer, lighter body than the buffalo of earlier years, and which was also peculiar in that the animals never became fat. Intelligent hunters of the northern herd, however, recognized the true state of the case, which was that the buffalo, during the last years of their existence, were so constantly pursued and driven from place to place that they never had time to lay on fat as in earlier years, and that, as a consequence of this continual running, the animal's form changed, and instead of a fat, short-backed, short-legged animal, it became a long-legged, light-bodied beast, formed for running.

This specialization in the direction of speed at first proceeded very slowly, but at last, as the dangers to which the animals were subjected became more and more pressing, it took place rapidly, and as a consequence the last buffalo killed on the plains were extremely long-legged and rangy, and were very different in appearance—as they were in their habits—from the animals of twenty years ago.

Buffalo running was not a sport that required much skill, yet it was not without its dangers. Occasionally a man was killed by the buffalo, but deaths from falls and from bursting guns were more common. Many curious stories of such accidents are told by the few surviving old-timers whose memory goes back fifty years, to the time when flint-lock guns were in use. A mere fall from a horse is lightly regarded by the practiced rider; the danger to be feared is that in such a fall the horse may roll on the man and crush him. Even more serious accidents occurred when a man fell upon some part of his equipment, which was driven through his body. Hunters have fallen in such a way that their whip-stocks, arrows, bows, and even guns, have been driven through their bodies. The old flint-lock guns, or "fukes," which were loaded on the run, with powder poured in from the horn by guess, and a ball from the mouth, used frequently to burst, causing the loss of hands, arms, and even lives.

While most of the deaths which occurred in the chase resulted from causes other than the resistance of the buffalo, these did occasionally kill a man. A curious accident happened in a camp of Red River Indians in the early seventies. The son of an Iroquois Indian, about twenty years old, went out one day with the rest of the camp to run buffalo. At night he did not return, and the next day all the men went out to search for him. They found the horse and the arms, but could not find the man, and could not imagine what had become of him. About a year later, as the Indians were hunting in another part of the country, a cow was seen which had something unusual on her head. They chased and killed her, and found that she had on her head the pelvis of a man, one of the horns having pierced the thin part of the bone, which was wedged on so tightly that they could hardly get it off. Much of the hair on the head, neck, and shoulders of the cow was worn off short, and on the side on which the bone was, down on the neck and shoulders, the hair was short, black, and looked new, as if it had been worn entirely off the skin, and was just beginning to grow out again. It is supposed that this bone was part of the missing young man, who had been hooked by the cow, and carried about on her head until his body fell to pieces.

My old and valued friend Charles Reynolds, for years chief of scouts at Fort Lincoln, Dakota, and who was killed by the Sioux in the Custer fight in 1876, told me of the death of a hunting partner of his, which shows how dangerous even a dying buffalo may be. The two men had started from the railroad to go south and bring in a load of meat. On finding a bunch of buffalo, they shot down by stalking what they required, and then on foot went up to the animals to skin them. One cow, lying on her side, was still moving a little convulsively, but dying. The man approached her as if about to cut her throat, but when he was within a few feet of her head, she sprang to her feet, rushed at him, struck him in the chest with her horns, and then fell dead. Charley ran up to his partner, and to his horror saw that the cow's horn had ripped him up from the belly to the throat, so that he could see the heart still expanding and contracting.

Charley buried his partner there, and returning to the town, told his story. He was at once arrested on the charge that he had murdered his companion, and was obliged to return to the place and to assist in digging up the body to satisfy the suspicious officials of the truth of his statements.

In the early days, when the game was plenty, buffalo-running was exhilarating sport. Given a good horse, the only other requisite to success was the ability to remain on his back till the end of the chase. No greater degree of skill was needed than this, and yet the quick motion of the horse, the rough ground to be traversed, and the feeling that there was something ahead that must be overtaken and stopped, made the ride attractive. There was the very slightest spice of danger; for while no one anticipated a serious accident, it was always possible that one's horse might step into a badger-hole, in which case his rider would get a fall that would make his bones ache.

The most exciting, and by far the most interesting, hunts in which I ever took part were those with the Indians of the plains. They were conducted almost noiselessly, and no ring of rifle-shot broke the stillness of the air, nor puff of smoke rose toward the still, gray autumn sky. The consummate grace and skill of the naked Indians, and the speed and quickness of their splendid ponies, were well displayed in such chases as these. More than one instance is recorded where an Indian sent an arrow entirely through the bodies of two buffalo. Sometimes such a hunt was signalized by some feat of daring bravado that, save in the seeing, was scarcely credible, as when the Cheyenne Big Ribs rode his horse close up to the side of a huge bull, and, springing on his back, rode the savage beast for some distance, and then with his knife gave him the death-stroke. Or a man might find himself in a position of comical danger, as did "The Trader" who was thrown from his horse on to the horns of a bull without being injured. One of the horns passed under his belt and supported him, and at the same time prevented the bull from tossing him. In this way he was carried for some distance on the animal's head, when the belt gave way and he fell to the ground unhurt, while the bull ran on. There were occasions when buffalo or horses fell in front of horsemen riding at full run, and when a fall was avoided only by leaping one's horse over the fallen animal. In the buffalo chase of old days it was well for a man to keep his wits about him; for, though he might run buffalo a thousand times without accident, the moment might come when only instant action would save him his life, or at least an ugly hurt.

In the early days of the first Pacific Railroad, and before the herds had been driven back from the track, singular hunting-parties were sometimes seen on the buffalo range. These hunters were capitalists connected with the newly constructed road, and some of them now for the first time bestrode a horse, while few had ever used firearms. On such a hunt, one well-known railroad director, eager to kill a buffalo, declined to trust himself on horseback, preferring to bounce over the rough prairie in an ambulance driven by an alarmed soldier, who gave less attention to the mules he was guiding than to the loaded and cocked pistol which his excited passenger was brandishing. These were amusing excursions, where a merry party of pleasant officers from a frontier post, and their guests, a jolly crowd of merchants, brokers, and railroad men from the East, started out to have a buffalo-hunt. With them went the post guide and a scout or two, an escort of soldiers, and the great blue army-wagons, under whose white tilts were piled all the comforts that the post could furnish—unlimited food and drink, and many sacks of forage for the animals. Here all was mirth and jest and good-fellowship, and, except that canvas covered them while they slept, the hunters lived in as much comfort as when at home. The killing of buffalo was to them only an excuse for their jolly outing amid novel scenes.

It was on the plains of Montana, in the days when buffalo were still abundant, that I had one of my last buffalo-hunts—a hunt with a serious purpose. A company of fifty or more men, who for weeks had been living on bacon and beans, longed for the "boss ribs" of fat cow, and when we struck the buffalo range two of us were deputed to kill some meat. My companion was an old prairie-man of great experience, and I myself was not altogether new to the West, for I had hunted in many territories, and had more than once been "jumped" by hostile Indians. Our horses were not buffalo-runners, yet we felt a certain confidence that if we could find a bunch and get a good start on them, we would bring in the desired meat. The troops would march during the day, for the commanding officer had no notion of waiting in camp merely for fresh meat, and we were to go out, hunt, and overtake the command at their night's camp.

The next day after we had reached the buffalo range, we started out long before the eastern sky was gray, and were soon riding off over the chilly prairie. The trail which the command was to follow ran a little north of east, and we kept to the south and away from it, believing that in this direction we would find the game, and that if we started them they would run north or northwest—against the wind, so that we could kill them near the trail. Until some time after the sun had risen, we saw nothing larger than antelope; but at length, from the top of a high hill, we could see, far away to the east, dark dots on the prairie, which we knew could only be buffalo. They were undisturbed too; for, though we watched them for some time, we could detect no motion in their ranks.

It took us nearly two hours to reach the low, broken buttes on the north side of which the buffalo were; and, riding up on the easternmost of these, we tried to locate our game more exactly. It was important to get as close as possible before starting them, so that our first rush might carry us into the midst of them. Knowing the capabilities of our horses, which were thin from long travel, we felt sure that if the buffalo should take the alarm before we were close to them, we could not overtake the cows and young animals, which always run in the van, and should have to content ourselves with old bulls. On the other hand, if we could dash in among them during the first few hundred yards of the race, we should be able to keep up with and select the fattest animals in the herd.

When we reached a point just below the crest of the hill, I stopped and waited, while my companion rode on. Just before he got to the top he too halted, then took off his hat and peered over the ridge, examining so much of the prairie beyond as was now visible to him. His inspection was careful and thorough, and when he had made sure that nothing was in sight, his horse took a step or two forward and then stopped again, and the rider scanned every foot of country before him. The horse, trained as the real hunter's horse is always trained, understood what was required of him, and with pricked ears examined the prairie beyond with as much interest as did his rider. When the calf of Charley's right leg pressed the horse's side, two or three steps more were taken, and then a lifting of the bridle-hand caused another halt.

At length I saw my companion slowly bend forward over his horse's neck, turn, and ride back to me. He had seen the backs of two buffalo lying on the edge of a little flat hardly a quarter of a mile from where we stood. The others of the band must be still nearer to us. By riding along the lowest part of the sag which separated the two buttes, and then down a little ravine, it seemed probable that we could come within a few yards of the buffalo unobserved. Our preparations did not take long. The saddle cinches were loosened, blankets arranged, saddles put in their proper places and tightly cinched again. Cartridges were brought round to the front and right of the belt, where they would be convenient for reloading. Our coats, tied behind the saddle, were looked to, the strings which held them being tightened and securely retied. All this was not lost on our horses, which understood as well as we did what was coming. We skirted the butte, rode through the low sag and down into the little ravine, which soon grew deeper, so that our heads were below the range of vision of almost anything on the butte. Passing the mouth of the little side ravine, however, there came into full view a huge bull, lying well up on the hillside. Luckily his back was toward us, and, each bending low over his horse's neck, we rode on, and in a moment were hidden by the side of the ravine. Two or three minutes more, and we came to another side ravine, which was wide and commanded a view of the flat. We stopped before reaching this, and a peep showed that we were within a few yards of two old cows, a young heifer, and a yearling, all of them to the north of us. Beyond, we could see the backs of others, all lying down.

We jumped on our horses again, and setting the spurs well in, galloped up the ravine and up on the flat; and as we came into view, the nearest buffalo, as if propelled by a huge spring, were on their feet, and, with a second's pause to look, dashed away to the north. Scattered over the flat were fifty or seventy-five buffalo, all of which, by the time we had glanced over the field, were off, with heads bending low to the ground, and short, spiky tails stretched out behind. We were up even with the last of the cows, and our horses were running easily and seemed to have plenty of reserve power. Charley, who was a little ahead of me, called back: "They will cross the trail about a mile north of here. Kill a couple when we get to it." I nodded, and we went on. The herd raced forward over the rolling hills, and in what seemed a very short time we rushed down a long slope on to a wide flat, in which was a prairie-dog town of considerable extent. We were on the very heels of the herd, and in a cloud of dust kicked up by their rapid flight. To see the ground ahead was impossible. We could only trust to our horses and our good luck to save us from falling. Our animals were doing better than we had supposed they could, and were going well and under a pull. I felt that a touch of the spurs and a little riding would bring us up even with the leaders of the buffalo. The pace had already proved too much for several bulls, which had turned off to one side and been passed by. As we flew across the flat, I saw far off a dark line and two white objects, which I knew must be our command. I called to my comrade, and, questioning by the sign, pointed at the buffalo. He nodded, and in a moment we had given free rein to our horses and were up among the herd. During the ride I had two or three times selected my game, but the individuals of the band changed positions so constantly that I could not keep track of them. Now, however, I picked out a fat two-year-old bull; but as I drew up to him he ran faster than before, and rapidly made his way toward the head of the band. I was resolved that he should not escape, and so, though I was still fifteen or twenty yards in the rear, fired. At the shot he fell heels overhead directly across a cow which was running by his side and a little behind him. I saw her turn a somersault, and almost at the same instant heard Charley shoot twice in quick succession, and saw two buffalo fall. I fired at a fat young cow that I had pushed my pony up close to. At the shot she whirled, my horse did the same, and she chased me as hard as she could go for seventy-five yards, while I did some exceedingly vigorous spurring, for she was close behind me all the time. To do my horse justice, I think that he would have run as fast as he could, even without the spurs, for he appreciated the situation. At no time was there any immediate danger that the cow would overtake us; if there had been, I should have dodged her. Presently the cow stopped, and stood there very sick. When I rode back, I did not find it easy to get my horse near her; but another shot was not needed, and while I sat looking at her she fell over dead. The three buffalo first killed had fallen within a hundred yards of the trail where the wagons afterward passed, and my cow was but little farther away. The command soon came up, the soldiers did the butchering, and before long we were on the march again across the parched plain.

Of the millions of buffalo which even in our own time ranged the plains in freedom, none now remain. From the prairies which they used to darken, the wild herds, down to the last straggling bull, have disappeared. In the Yellowstone National Park, protected from destruction by United States troops, are the only wild buffalo which exist within the borders of the United States. These are mountain buffalo, and, from their habit of living in the thick timber and on the rough mountain-sides, they are only now and then seen by visitors to the park. It is impossible to say just how many there are, but from the best information that I can get, based on the estimates of reliable and conservative men, I conclude that the number was not less than four hundred in the winter of 1891–92. Each winter or spring the government scout employed in the park sees one or more herds of these buffalo, and as such herds are usually made up in part of young animals and have calves with them, it is fair to assume that they are steadily, if slowly, increasing. The report of a trip made in January, 1892, speaks of four herds seen in the Hayden Valley, which numbered respectively 78, 50, 110, and 15. Besides these, a number of scattering groups were seen at a distance, which would bring the number up to three hundred.

In the far northwest, in the Peace River district, there may still be found a few wood buffalo. They are seldom killed, and the estimate of their numbers varies from five hundred to fifteen hundred. This cannot be other than the merest guess, since they are scattered over many thousand square miles of territory which is without inhabitants, and for the most part unexplored.

On the great plains is still found the buffalo skull half buried in the soil and crumbling to decay. The deep trails once trodden by the marching hosts are grass-grown now, and fast filling up. When these most enduring relics of a vanished race shall have passed away, there will be found, in all the limitless domain once darkened by their feeding herds, not one trace of the American buffalo.

21

Hunting the Deceitful Turkey

by Mark Twain

The great American humorist did some hunting, back in the days when places to hunt and game worth bagging were far more prevalent than today.

WHEN I WAS A BOY MY UNCLE AND HIS BIG BOYS HUNTED WITH THE rifle, the youngest boy Fred and I with a shotgun—a small single-barrelled shotgun which was properly suited to our size and strength; it was not much heavier than a broom. We carried it turn about, half an hour at a time. I was not able to hit anything with it, but I liked to try. Fred and I hunted feathered small game, the others hunted deer, squirrels, wild turkeys, and such things. My uncle and the big boys were good shots. They killed hawks and wild geese and such like on the wing; and they didn't wound or kill squirrels, they stunned them. When the dogs treed a squirrel, the squirrel would scamper aloft and run out on a limb and flatten himself along it, hoping to make himself invisible in that way—and not quite succeeding. You could see his wee little ears sticking up. You couldn't see his nose, but you knew where it was. Then the hunter, despising a "rest" for his rifle, stood up and took offhand aim at the limb and sent a bullet into it immediately under the squirrel's nose, and down tumbled the animal, unwounded, but unconscious; the dogs gave him a shake and he was dead. Sometimes when the distance was great and the wind not accurately allowed for, the bullet would hit the squirrel's head;

the dogs could do as they pleased with that one—the hunter's pride was hurt, and he wouldn't allow it to go into the gamebag.

In the first faint gray of the dawn the stately wild turkeys would be stalking around in great flocks, and ready to be sociable and answer invitations to come and converse with other excursionists of their kind. The hunter concealed himself and imitated the turkey-call by sucking the air through the leg-bone of a turkey which had previously answered a call like that and lived only just long enough to regret it. There is nothing that furnishes a perfect turkey-call except that bone. Another of Nature's treacheries, you see. She is full of them; half the time she doesn't know which she likes best—to betray her child or protect it. In the case of the turkey she is badly mixed: she gives it a bone to be used in getting it into trouble, and she also furnishes it with a trick for getting itself out of the trouble again. When a mamma-turkey answers an invitation and finds she has made a mistake in accepting it, she does as the mamma-partridge does—remembers a previous engagement—and goes limping and scrambling away, pretending to be very lame; and at the same time she is saying to her not-visible children, "Lie low, keep still, don't expose yourselves; I shall be back as soon as I have beguiled this shabby swindler out of the country."

When a person is ignorant and confiding, this immoral device can have tiresome results. I followed an ostensibly lame turkey over a considerable part of the United States one morning, because I believed in her and could not think she would deceive a mere boy, and one who was trusting her and considering her honest. I had the single-barrelled shotgun, but my idea was to catch her alive. I often got within rushing distance of her, and then made my rush; but always, just as I made my final plunge and put my hand down where her back had been, it wasn't there; it was only two or three inches from there and I brushed the tail-feathers as I landed on my stomach—a very close call, but still not quite close enough; that is, not close enough for success, but just close enough to convince me that I could do it next time. She always waited for me, a little piece away, and let on to be resting and greatly fatigued; which was a lie, but I believed it, for I still thought her honest long after I ought to have begun to doubt her, suspecting that this was no way for a high-minded bird to

334

be acting. I followed, and followed, and followed, making my periodical rushes, and getting up and brushing the dust off, and resuming the voyage with patient confidence; indeed, with a confidence which grew, for I could see by the change of climate and vegetation that we were getting up into the high latitudes, and as she always looked a little tireder and a little more discouraged after each rush, I judged that I was safe to win, in the end, the competition being purely a matter of staying power and the advantage lying with me from the start because she was lame.

Along in the afternoon I began to feel fatigued myself. Neither of us had had any rest since we first started on the excursion, which was upwards of ten hours before, though latterly we had paused awhile after rushes, I letting on to be thinking about something else; but neither of us sincere, and both of us waiting for the other to call game but in no real hurry about it, for indeed those little evanescent snatches of rest were very grateful to the feelings of us both; it would naturally be so, skirmishing along like that ever since dawn and not a bite in the meantime; at least for me, though sometimes as she lay on her side fanning herself with a wing and praying for strength to get out of this difficulty a grasshopper happened along whose time had come, and that was well for her, and fortunate, but I had nothing—nothing the whole day.

More than once, after I was very tired, I gave up taking her alive, and was going to shoot her, but I never did it, although it was my right, for I did not believe I could hit her; and besides, she always stopped and posed, when I raised the gun, and this made me suspicious that she knew about me and my marksmanship, and so I did not care to expose myself to remarks.

I did not get her, at all. When she got tired of the game at last, she rose from almost under my hand and flew aloft with the rush and whir of a shell and lit on the highest limb of a great tree and sat down and crossed her legs and smiled down at me, and seemed gratified to see me so astonished.

I was ashamed, and also lost; and it was while wandering the woods hunting for myself that I found a deserted log cabin and had one of the best meals there that in my life-days I have eaten. The weed-grown garden was full of ripe tomatoes, and I ate them ravenously, though I had never liked them before. Not more than two or three times since have I tasted anything that was so delicious as those tomatoes. I surfeited myself with them, and did not taste another one until I was in middle life. I can eat them now, but I do not like the look of them. I suppose we have all experienced a surfeit at one time or another. Once, in stress of circumstances, I ate part of a barrel of sardines, there being nothing else at hand, but since then I have always been able to get along without sardines.

22

The Sundown Covey

by Lamar Underwood

I wrote this story for the book Hunting Moments of Truth, *which my friend Jim Rikhoff published at Amwell Press back in 1972. Its publication in* Sports Afield *and other anthologies have proved it to be a reader favorite.*

NOBODY EVER USED THAT NAME, REALLY. BUT IT WAS THE COVEY OF bobwhite quail that we always looked for almost with longing, as we turned our hunt homeward in the afternoon. By the time we came to that last stretch of ragged corn and soybean fields where this covey lived, the pines and moss-draped oaks would be looming darkly in the face of the dying sun. The other events of the afternoon never seemed to matter then. Tired pointer dogs bore ahead with new drive; we would watch carefully as they checked out each birdy objective, sure that we were headed for a significant encounter before we reached the small lane that led to the Georgia farmhouse. I always chose to think of those birds as "the sun-down covey," although my grandfather or uncle usually would say something like "Let's look in on that bunch at the end of the lane." And then, more times than not, the evening stillness would be broken by my elder's announcement, "Yonder they are!" and we would move toward the dogs on point—small stark-white figures that always seemed to be chiseled out of the shadowy backdrop against the evening swamp.

There's always something special about hunting a covey of quail that you know like an old friend. One covey's pattern of movements between fields and swampy sanctuaries can be an intriguing and baffling problem. Another may be remarkably easy to find, and yet always manage to rocket away through such a thick tangle that you've mentally colored them gone, even before your finger touches the trigger. Another might usually present a good covey shot, while the singles tear away to . . . the backside of the moon, as far as you've been able to tell. My best hunts on more distant but greener pastures somehow have never seemed as inwardly satisfying as a day when a good dog and I can spend some time on familiar problems like these. Give me a covey I know, one that has tricked me, baffled me, eluded me—and by doing so brought me back to its corner of the woods for years.

In this sense, the covey we always hunted at sundown was even more special. As the nearest bunch of birds to the house, it was the most familiar. Here, trembling puppies got onto their first points. A lad learned that two quick shots into the brownish blur of the covey rise would put nothing into his stiff new hunting coat. A man returning from a war saw the birds running quick-footed across the lane and knew that he really was home again. The generations rolled on through times of kerosene lamps and cheap cotton to Ed Sullivan and soil-bank subsidies. And that same covey of bobwhites that had always seemed a part of the landscape still whistled in the long summer afternoons and hurtled across dead cornstalks that rattled in the winter breezes.

The hunters who looked for that covey and others in the fields nearby disciplined themselves never to shoot a covey below six birds. That number left plenty of seed for replenishment, so that every fall the coveys would again number fifteen to thirty birds, depending on how they had fared against predators.

Eventually, all that acreage moved out of our family. My visits to those coveys became less frequent as I necessarily turned toward education and then fields of commerce that were far away. But even during some marvelous quail-hunting days in other places, I often longed for return hunts to those intriguing coveys of the past. Would the swamp covey by the old pond still be up to their usual trick of flying into the field in the afternoon? Where would the singles from the peafield covey go now? Would the sundown covey still be there?

Finally, not long ago, the opportunity came for me to knock about a bit down in the home county. Several hunts with friends seemed as mere preludes to the long-awaited day when I got a chance to slip away alone to the old home grounds.

A soft rain had fallen during the night, but when I parked the truck by a thicket of pines just after sunrise, a stiff breeze had started tearing the overcast apart, and patches of blue were showing through the dullness. Shrugging into my bird vest, I ignored the shufflings and impatient whines that sounded from the dog box and stood a moment looking across a long soybean field that stretched toward a distant line of pines. I was mentally planning a route that would take me in a big circle to a dozen or so familiar coveys, then bring me to the sundown covey in the late evening. I unlatched the dog box, and the pointer, Mack, exploded from the truck and went through a routine of nervous preliminaries. I did the same, checking my bulging coat for shells, lunch, and coffee. Then I clicked the double shut and stepped into the sedge alongside the field, calling: "All right, Mack. Look around!"

The pointer loped away in that deceptive, ground eating gait that was his way of going. At age four, he had not exactly developed into the close worker I had been wanting. His predecessors who had run these fields in decades before were big going speedsters suited to those times. Controlled burning and wide-roaming livestock kept the woodlands open then. Now most of the forests were so choked with brush and vines that wide-working dogs brought a legacy of frustration. Mack was easy to handle but tended to bend out too far from the gun unless checked back frequently. I really hated hearing myself say "Hunt close!" so often, but I hated even worse those agonizing slogging searches when he went on point in some dark corner of the swamp a quarter-mile from where I thought he'd been working.

The sun was bright on the sedge and pines now, and the air winy crisp after the rain. Mack was a bouncing flash of white as he worked through the sedge and low pines. Once he started over the fence into the field, but I called him back. I wanted him to keep working down the edge. While the bean field seemed like a tempting place to catch a breakfasting bevy, the cover bordering it had much better chances—at least three to one, according to the quail hunting education I had received here as a youngster. I could still imagine the sound of my grandfather's voice as he preached:

"Never mind all them picture book covey rises in those magazines you read. It's only now and then you'll catch these old woods coveys in the open. Birds once had to range wide and root hard for their keep. Now all the work's done for 'em. Combines and corn pickers leave so much feed scattered in the field the birds can feed in a few minutes, then leg it back into the cover. That's where you want to work. First, if they haven't gone to feed, you're likely to find 'em. If they've walked into the field, the dog'll trail 'em out. If they've already been into the field and fed, you'll still find 'em. Only time you'll miss is when they've flown into the field and are still there."

I had seen this simple philosophy pay increasing dividends as the years wore on. As the cover became thicker and the coveys smarter, the clear shot had become a rare, treasured experience. To spend a lot of time working through the fields was to be a dreamer of the highest order.

Still in the cover, we rounded the end of the small field and headed up the other side. I was beginning to feel the bite of the day's first disappointment; Mack had picked up no scent at all. Where were they? This covey had always been easy to find. Maybe they had been shot out, I thought. Maybe the whole place has been shot out.

I decided to play out a hunch. I pulled down a rusty strand of fence and stepped out into the field. Mack leaped the wire and raced away at full gallop. Far downfield he turned into the wind and suddenly froze in one of the most dramatic points I've ever seen. I knew he was right on top of those birds, his body curved tautly, his tail arching. "Oh ho!" I said aloud. "So you beggars did fly to the field."

My strides lengthened and became hurried. I snapped the gun open and checked the shells in an unnecessary gesture of nervousness. Normally steady hands seemed to tremble a little and felt very thick and uncertain. My heartbeat was a thunderous throb at the base of my throat.

My tangled nerves and wire-taut reflexes scarcely felt the nudge of a thought that said, "Relax. You've done this before." The case of shakes I undergo every time I step up to a point makes it difficult to attach any importance to that idea. Covey-rise jitters are known to have only one cure: action.

On my next step, the earth seemed to explode. The air was suddenly filled with blurry bits and pieces of speeding fragments, all boring toward the pines that loomed ahead. I found myself looking at one particular whirring form, and when the stock smacked against my face, the gun bucked angrily. The brown missile was unimpressed. He faded into the swamp, along with a skyful of surviving kinsmen. My loosely poked second shot failed to drop a tail-ender.

Mighty sorry gathering up of partridges, I thought, using the expression that was my uncle's favorite on the occasions when we struck out on a covey rise. "Sorry, boy," I called to Mack, who was busy vacuuming the grass in a futile search for downed birds.

My elders would have thought that bevy's maneuver of flying out to the field was the lowest trick in the book. But now the practice had become so typical among smart southern Bobs that it was hardly worth lamenting.

I called Mack away from his unrewarding retrieve and headed after those singles. The woods ahead looked clear enough for some choice shooting if I could keep Mack close.

Thirty minutes later I emerged from those woods a frustrated, angry man. My estimate that the birds had landed in the grassy, open pinelands was about two hundred yards wrong. Instead they had sailed on into one of the thickest, darkest sweet-gum swamps I've ever cursed a bird dog in. It took Mack all of fifteen seconds to get lost, and when I found him on point after ten minutes of searching I proceeded to put the first barrel into a gum tree and the second into a screen of titi bushes. Then the heebiegeebies really took over as I walked over two separate singles that jumped unannounced. Finally, Mack pointed again, but as I fought through the tearing clutches of briers and vines to get to him, I bumped another single, which I shot at without a glimmer of hope. That action caused Mack to take matters into his own hands and send the bird he was pointing vaulting away through the trees. Then followed a lot of unnecessary yelling, and we headed for the clear.

I should have known better. Single-bird hunting in that part of Georgia had become a sad business. Now I was discovering that my old hunting grounds were in the same shape as the rest of the county. If you were going to mess with singles, you had to wait for the right type of open woods. Most were just too thick to see a dog, much less a six-ounce bird. The day's shooting was certainly not going to follow the patterns of the past when it came to singles. I would have to wait until I got a bevy scattered in a better place.

We cut away from the field into a section of low moss-draped oak trees. Mack ranged ahead, working smartly. My frustrations of the first covey slipped away as I began considering the coming encounter with the next set of old friends. This covey, if they were still in business, would be composed of dark swamp birds that lived in the edge of the creek swamp but used this oak ridge to feed on acorns during early mornings and late afternoons. They were extremely hard to catch in the open, sometimes running for hundreds of yards in front of a dog on point. But what a sight they always made as they hurtled up among the moss-draped oaks on the lucky occasions when we did get them pinned nicely.

This oak ridge was fairly open, so I let Mack move on out a little bit. When he cut through one thickish cluster of trees and did not come out right away, I knew he had 'em.

Incredible, I thought. *The first two coveys are still here, and we've worked 'em both.* Then the words turned into brass in my mouth as I eased up to the dog and past him. The thunderous rise I had been expecting failed to occur. I let Mack move on ahead to relocate. Catlike, he crept through the low grass for a few yards, then froze again. I moved out in front once more, and still nothing happened.

Then, suddenly I heard them. Several yards out front the dry leaves rustled under the flow of quick-moving feet. The covey was up to its old trick of legging it for the sanctuary of the swamp.

I hurried forward, crashing through the briers. Just ahead, the low cover gave way to a wall of sweetgum and cypress that marked the beginning of the swamp. Too late! I caught the sound of wings whirring. The birds had made the edge and were roaring off through the trees. They seemed to get up in groups of two and three. I caught an occasional glimpse of dim blurs through the screen of limbs and snapped a shot at one. Leaves and sticks showered down as Mack raced forward. Seconds later he emerged from the brush carrying a plump rooster bobwhite.

Had you seen me grinning over that bird, you might have thought I hadn't scored in five years. But the shot seemed mighty satisfying under the conditions. A few moments like this could make the day a lot more glorious than a coatful of birds ever could.

Now we followed an old lane that led down across the swamp and out beside a tremendous cornfield surrounded by pine and gallberry flats. I expected to find a couple of coveys here—and did, too, as the morning wore on in a succession of encounters with my old friends. A heart-warming double from a bevy Mack pinned along a fence row was followed by a succession of bewildering misses when we followed the singles into an open gallberry flat where I should have been able to score. Then we had the fun of unraveling a particularly difficult relocation problem when Mack picked up some hot scent in the corn, but could not trail out to the birds. The edge of the field sloped down to a grassy flat to an old pond with pine timber on the far side. I just knew those birds had flown across that pond to the woods to hole up for the day. When I took Mack over, he made a beautiful point, standing just inside the woods. I wish I could always dope out a covey like that.

We spent the middle of the day stretched out on the grass on the pond dam. The sandwiches and coffee couldn't have tasted better. The sun was warm and crows and doves flew against the blue sky. I thought about old hunts and old friends and couldn't have felt better.

In the afternoon we had a couple of interesting pieces of action, but failed to find some of my old neighbor coveys at home. My thoughts kept reaching ahead to the late-afternoon time when I would near the old now-deserted house by the lane and see the sundown covey again. Surely they would still be there. After all, we had been finding most of the old coveys. Who says you can't go home again? Who's afraid of you, Tom Wolfe?

The sun was dipping toward the pines and a sharp chill had come on when I skirted the last field and entered the stretch of open pine woods where I was counting on finding the covey of birds that I had carried in my mind all my life. Before I had gone 50 yards I had came on something that shocked me as though I'd walked up on a ten-foot rattlesnake. I newly cut stake had been driven in the ground, and a red ribbon tied to the top of it. Farther on there was another then another.

I had known that the new Savannah-Atlanta-Super-Highspeed-Interstate-Get-You-There-Quick Highway was to pass through this general area. But surely, a couple miles away. Not here. Not right here.

Gradually, my disbelief turned into anger. I felt like heading for the car right then and getting the hell out of there. Then suddenly three shots boomed in the woods some distance ahead.

Well, it was apparent that the sundown covey was still around. But an intruder had found them. I decided to go on up and talk to whoever it was. Actually, he probably had as much right to be here as I did now. I couldn't believe he was a regular hunter on this land though. The coveys I had been finding all day were too populous with birds to be gunned heavily.

I walked slowly through the pines for a few minutes without spotting the other hunter. Then his gun thudded again, this time from farther down in the swamp. He's after the singles now, I thought. I called in Mack and waited there opposite the swamp. The other fellow would have to come out this way.

During the next few minutes two more separate shots sounded. The sun sank lower, and the breeze blew harder in the pines. Finally, I heard the bushes shaking and a man came out of the cover. When Mack started barking he spotted me and headed my way. As he came up I saw that he was young, carried an automatic, and wore no hunting coat. He had some quail by the legs in his left hand.

"Looks like you did some good," I said.

"Yea, I got six."

"Where's your dog?" I asked.

"Oh, I don't have a dog. I spotted a covey crossing the road down there by the lane. I had the gun in the truck, so I went after 'em. Got three when I flushed 'ern and three more down in the branch. Tiny little covey, though. I don't think there were more than six when I first flushed 'ern. I imagine people been framin' into this bunch all the time." My heart sank when he said that. I didn't know what to say. He paused a minute, looking at Mack. "That's a nice dog. He any good?"

"Fair," I said. "Maybe you shouldn't have done that."

"What?"

"Shoot a small covey on down that way."

"Don't mean nothing. There's always a covey of birds along here. Every year. But there won't be for long. Interstate's coming through."

"Yea," I said slowly. "I see it is."

"Well, I gotta run. That's sure a nice-looking dog, Mister. See you around."

I watched him walk away. Then I leaned back against a pine, listening to the swamp noises. The wings of a pair of roost-bound ducks whispered overhead. An owl tuned up down in the swamp. Somehow I kept thinking that I would hear some birds calling each other back into a covey. Perhaps two or three had slipped away unseen from the roadside.

The night pressed down. Trembling in the cold, I started for the truck. Orion wheeled overhead. I started thinking about some new places I wanted to try. But never again did I hear that flutelike call that had sounded for me from that swamp so many times before.

A Drink for the Dog

by Tom Hennessey

It was a little past 9 a.m. when I turned off the Gouldsboro Point Road and pulled into Galen's yard. Leaning forward, I opened the door of the pickup and Coke, my chocolate Lab retriever, bounded out of the cab. When Galen came out the back door of his house, Gib, his young black Lab retriever, charged ahead of him and immediately the dogs began romping about the premises.

After we had loaded a skiff into the back of my truck and piled our duck hunting gear into it, Galen and I went into the house to wait for Mike, Kenny, Lewis, and Gary to show up. We had a little time to kill. The tides had worked around to where high water would occur about 1 p.m. It would be half tide—around 10 o'clock—before we could rig our decoys off the point where we planned to shoot.

While we sipped steaming cups of coffee, Coke and Gib raced past the windows, tumbling and snarling in mock anger. By the time the others arrived, both dogs were puffing and panting in good shape. I should have had the presence of mind to give Coke a drink of water right then. But in our anxiety to get to the gunning grounds we piled into two trucks and rumbled out of the yard. Because Galen's Gib was, at the time, plagued with a leg-muscle problem that cold water would aggravate, he was left home. The retrieving chores would be handled by Coke and Lewis's Bear, a black Lab pup that was showing a lot of promise.

For late-season duck shooting, the day was made to order. Shafts of sunlight sliced through layers of leaden clouds, and the breeze brisking up with the tide bobbed the decoys at the ends of their anchor lines. It was one of those once-in-a-while times when you could feel it in your bones that everything was just right.

We split into two groups. Galen, Gary, Coke, and I in a blind on one side of the point. Mike, Kenny, Lewis, and Bear on the other side. Hardly had we loaded our shotguns when Galen warned, "Watch it—buffleheads!" In diving-duck fashion—low and fast—they wheeled in and buzzed the formally dressed black and white decoys. When Galen and I hauled down, three ducks folded and spanked the surface. Gary was biding his time for black ducks. After fetching the buffleheads, Coke, to my shock and surprise, went to the water's edge and began drinking.

"No!" I yelled. He stopped, but then and there the damage was done. Shortly after, as he retrieved a drake whistler, I could hear Coke gulping salt water as he swam. With salt in his system his thirst became insatiable. When he came ashore his belly was bulging and I knew it would be only a matter of minutes before he'd be sick. The big retriever vomited violently. Water came out of him as though a fire hydrant had been uncapped. To my surprise, as soon as Coke had rid himself of the briny bellywash he seemed to be in good spirits. Wagging his tail, he bounded over to me and took my wrist in his mouth—his usual greeting and signal that all is well. It wasn't. As many times as we had hunted the coastal marshes, Coke had never attempted to drink salt water, I realized that the roughhouse romping with Galen's pup had overheated him, and I cursed myself for not having taken the time to give him a drink before we left.

The rush of primary feathers ripping air announced the arrival of a pair of black ducks. On set wings they scaled toward the dozen black duck decoys that we had set off separately to our right. A charge of No. 4 shot from Gary's long-barreled 12-gauge hauled feathers from the duck nearest us and it planed away in a long slanting dive. A white plume leaped from the surface as the wounded black struck far out in the bay. It would be a long, tiring retrieve, and as Coke churned after the diving, sculling duck I again heard him drinking.

Damn! How could I have been so negligent?

Swimming ashore slowly, the dog dropped the duck when he waded onto the gravelly point. Again the water gushed out of him. This time, however, he didn't run to me with assurances that he felt fine. This time he did what, I had never seen him do in four years of hunting. He lay down.

There was no need to tell Galen and the others that I was done hunting. Quickly we took up the decoys. Quickly we gathered our gear, and quickly we lit out of there. At Galen's house Coke drank a bowl of water dry and then curled up on the truck seat as we headed for Hampden. About the time we were driving through Holden, the dog began to get uneasy. Sitting up, he tilted his nose upward and breathed heavily. At home I immediately called the Penobscot Veterinary Hospital. "Bring him out," said Dr. Meiczinger after I had explained the situation.

"Will he be okay?" I asked as the vet poked two large pink pills down Coke's throat. "He'll be okay," was the welcome reply. "All that salt water was a shock to his system," Dr. Meiczinger continued, "that plus vomiting dehydrated him, took all the starch out of him. I'll give him a couple of shots that will help stabilize his system, then I'll need some X-rays to make sure there isn't any water in his abdomen." I noticed that Coke was breathing easier. The pills, the vet explained, had soothed the dog's intestinal tract which was raw and inflamed from the salt water. That was why Coke had tilted his nose upward. In that position the tract straightened and he could swallow air easier in an attempt to put out the fire.

No water showed in the X-rays. Dr. Meiczinger then informed me that he was going to start Coke on intravenous feeding and keep him overnight. "This guy needs some nutrition," he said. "Call me about nine in the morning and we'll see how things are shaping up." With that thought-provoking hook-up of bottle, tube, and needle attached to his right foreleg I left Coke in a kennel and went out into the dark.

Driving home, the thought drummed in my mind: all this for lack of a drink of water.

I wasn't popular at home. It wasn't bad enough that I felt as if I had betrayed my best friend; now my wife and kids were looking at me as if I'd spent the Christmas Club money on a new outboard motor. All that night I lay awake wondering how the best gun dog I've ever owned was getting along. He seemed so weak and lifeless when I left him. Would he really be all right? What if, somehow, the intravenous tube and needle became separated with the needle remaining in the dog's vein? Would he lose blood, or, worse, bleed to death? It was a long night.

Next morning, however, my worries were put to rest. Although still weak and wrung out, Coke was well enough to go home. For two days he ate and drank very little. When I spoke to him he would manage only one or two thumps of his tail. Seeing that big, burly dog in that condition depressed me and the thought plagued me—if I'd had water with me that never would have happened.

It upset and worried me that Coke wouldn't eat. No matter what I put in front of him, he refused it. Now it just so happened that my wife had roasted a turkey, and I remembered Coke actually drooling whenever a roast turkey appeared on the kitchen countertop. I went to the refrigerator and sliced off a slab of white meat. Coke ate it. In the next day or so, in fact, he ate that whole turkey, down to the last scrap of golden-brown skin. That seemed to be the turning point. The dog began eating regularly and in a week's time had bounced back to almost 100 percent.

After that unpleasant experience I vowed I would never again gun the coastal marshes without bringing along a drink for the dog. A retriever is sure to swallow some water while fetching ducks and you're well aware of the thirst that just a small piece of salty ham or corned beef can create. A quart plastic jug full of water and a small plastic bowl aren't much to lug in a packbasket, and you can bet your retriever will be mighty glad you brought it along if he or she develops a powerful thirst. Look at it this way: it might keep you from losing a night's sleep and a roast turkey dinner.

24

Dog Upon the Waters

by John Taintor Foote

If you have never had the opportunity to follow a good pointing dog in the pursuit of upland birds, your life's book of hunting experiences is missing a vital section. To watch a pointer, setter, or shorthair work the fields and cover, lock up on point, then fetch the bird you down is at the pinnacle of hunting exhilaration. If the dog happens to be yours, then the rush of excitement is positively breathtaking.

Finding, training, and caring for great gun dogs takes some doing. You don't pluck them off bushes like berries. That's why gun dog people are constantly running down news and even rumors of superstar dogs, and will go to the ends of the earth to find or breed that "dog of a lifetime." Few have ever enjoyed gun dogs more and written about them more eloquently than John Taintor Foote. A short story writer, playwright, and screenwriter, Foote's great dog stories are collected in the book Dumb-Bell and Others: The Great Dog Stories of John Taintor Foote. *His other sporting classic is* A Wedding Gift and Other Angling Stories, *published by Lyons & Burford. Most of Foote's stories were written during the 1920s and '30s, a period during which he was a close friend and field companion of Ray P. Holland, the legendary editor responsible for many of the most classic years of* Field & Stream's *growth. "Dog Upon the Waters" is the story of a very special setter named Myrtle, and how a lucky hunter learned she was "the one."*

MYRTLE IS DEAD. POOR FUNNY LITTLE SNIPE-NOSED MYRTLE. I LEFT her, bored to extinction, at a gun club in Maryland. Between shooting seasons, life to her was a void. It consisted of yawns, the languid pursuit of an occasional flea, the indifferent toying with bones and dog biscuits and a mournful, lackluster gazing at fields and thickets near by.

During these dreary months she was never chained or confined in any way. Self hunting, which spoils so many gun dogs, did not affect Myrtle. Occasionally, when the dragging days became more than she could bear, she would betake herself listlessly to quail cover, find a covey, point it for a moment, flush it and watch the birds whir off into the pines. She would then return, sighing heavily, to a twitching nap somewhat around the clubhouse.

She must have perished during one of these efforts to break the monotony of existence in a gunless world, because a letter from the club steward tells me that she was caught in a muskrat trap in the big marsh and drowned. The big marsh is perhaps a half mile from the clubhouse. Drowned! Except for Chesapeake and a spaniel or two, I never saw a better swimmer. And yet, in preventing a similar tragedy, she became my dog, body and soul. Also I learned to sniff audibly when scientific fellows announce in my presence that animals cannot reason.

And now, I fear me, I shall have to divulge a secret that has been closely kept for many a day. I am about to spread reluctantly on the printed page the one formula for securing the kind of quail dog that fills an owner with unspeakable joy from dawn to dark, year in, year out, come heat or cold, or drought or rain.

It has nothing to do with sending a check to a professional breeder and then waiting, all expectant, for a shipping crate to be delivered at one's door. It has nothing to do with raising endless litters of distemper-ridden puppies. If you want the rarest, the most perfect instrument for sport in all the world, and not the average plodder and flusher of commerce or home industry, stick to my formula. I set it down exactly as it was given to me by a wise man of the South many years ago.

Here it is: "A Georgia cracker will sell anything—his land, his mule, his house, his wife. By God, he'll sell a bird dog—a real one, I mean. Just show him cash money and he'll reach for it."

These words—after I had learned their true significance—accounted, some years ago, for my spending a winter in Atlanta. My string of gun dogs, so my handler told me, had petered out. I was looking for another string, and Atlanta is the clearing house for information about noteworthy setters and pointers located in various counties of south and central Georgia where the most quail and, ipso facto, the most good gun dogs are found.

Working out from Atlanta by motorcar, as rumors of dogs that knew their business drifted into town, I had secured four pointers. I had shot over perhaps fifty dogs in selecting them. The four were all fast, wide-going, covey finders. Class dogs are good for about three hours at top speed. I, therefore, had a pair for mornings and a pair for afternoons, but I needed something that would stay in closer and go slower and find singles—an all-day dog—to back up my four whirlwinds.

One evening a voice spoke over the telephone—a voice that I knew well. The voice said: "Listen. The foreman of our bottling plant was down below Macon last week. He got plenty birds. He's been telling me about a little setter bitch he saw work that sounds like what you're after. He says he can fix it for us to go down and shoot over her next Saturday. What say?"

"How far is it?"

"'Bout a hundred and twenty miles."

"Does your foreman know a good dog when he sees one?"

"Yep!"

"What does he say she's like?"

"He says she's a ball of fire."

"Doing what?"

"Finding singles—coveys too."

"All right, have him fix it."

Thanks to that telephone conversation, my glance rested upon Myrtle for the first time about eight o'clock the following Saturday morning. She came cat-footing from somewhere behind a paintless shack, set in three or four acres of cotton stalks, at her master's whistle. I took one look at her. Then my eyes swung reproachfully to the bottling-plant foreman who was responsible for, and had accompanied us on, a one-hundred-and-twenty-mile drive to see her.

"Never you mind," said he stoutly. "You want a bird dog, don't you?"

I did want a bird dog. I have ever been contemptuous of him who goes gunning with a silky-coated, bench-show type of setter calculated to drive a sportsman to undreamed-of heights of profanity with one hour's work in the field. But this specimen before me was—well, I felt that I could never bring myself to admitting the ownership of such a dog.

I had been told she was little. She was. She did not weigh much more than twenty pounds. She had a wavy black-white-and-ticked coat that gave her a claim on the setter family. Her muzzle was so pointed that her head suggested the head of a fox—a black fox—except for a pair of drooping bird-dog ears. Her tail was short, clubby and without any flag. She carried it drooping and a bit to one side. Her eyes were the yellow fox eyes that belonged in such a head. Her gait, as she had come loping to us, seemed more cat than fox, but it reminded me of both.

Delicacy made me omit the opening of the ritual expected at such a time. "How's she bred?" was never spoken. I inquired without interest about her age.

"Comin' three. Reck'n me an' you better stay together, an' yoh friends hunt their dogs."

"All right," I agreed feebly. I was in for it! A-hunting we must go!

And a-hunting we did go. My friend and the bottling-plant man with two of the former's dogs in one direction; my hapless self, with the unspeakable little setter and her lanky owner, in another. She had been named Myrtle, he told me, after his old woman. I had caught a glimpse of the "old woman" through the door of the shack ere we set forth. She was all of sixteen.

We walked in silence up a lane, and so came to fields and promising cover. "Get along, Myrt," said my companion, in a conversational tone, and Myrt drifted to our left into some high grass and disappeared. We found her presently, perfectly still, looking without particular interest straight before her. "She's got birds," I heard. And this, indeed, was true, if our finding a covey twenty yards ahead of her proved it. Accustomed to the tense rigidity on point of more orthodox shooting dogs, Myrt's method was disconcerting.

I shall not attempt to describe that day—my first day afield with Myrtle. She found, in her cat-fox fashion, twelve coveys, as I remember. After each covey find, she proceeded to point and promptly retrieve, when killed, every scattered bird of every covey—or so it seemed to me. And the day was hot, and the day was dry. Incidentally her master shot rings around me. Her final exhibition that evening would have settled my desire to call her mine if she had not already won me completely hours before. We had joined my friend and the bottling-plant foreman. They had found two coveys and a few singles, had killed four birds, and my friend's pair of pointers were the apple of his eye.

"There just weren't birds in the country we worked over," my friend explained. I saw the owner of Myrtle open his mouth to speak, then close it resolutely. We started down the lane to the house, my friend, with his dogs at heel, in the lead; Myrtle, cat-footing behind her master, in the rear.

The dusk had closed in softly about us. It was already too dark for decent shooting. The lane down which we plodded had a high wire fence on either side, with pine woods to the left and a flat, close-cropped field to the right. Suddenly I heard a whine behind me. I stopped and turned. Myrtle was trying to squeeze through the right-hand wire fence to get into the field beyond.

"Birds out yonder," said Myrtle's owner.

I called to my friend and explained. Now his dogs had just passed that way without a sign. Also, the field was almost as bare of cover as a billiard table.

"Out there!" he snorted. "Wait till we get back to Atlanta. Maybe we'll find a covey in the middle of Five Points."

Perhaps I should say here that Five Points is to Atlanta what Trafalgar Square is to London. Myrtle's owner met the insult by picking her up and dropping her over the fence. She went straight out into the field and stopped. There followed an exhibition of fence climbing against the watch by my friend and the bottling-plant foreman. They managed to scratch down two birds from the covey that roared up in the gloom somewhere out ahead of Myrtle.

Thirty minutes later she was stretched out on the back seat of the car on her way to Atlanta, too tired to wonder where she was going or with whom. She cost me—steady, gentlemen, don't throw anything; just observe the workings of the formula—forty dollars. The amount was simply spread carefully before her owner. The result was inevitable. And so I became the owner of Myrtle.

I made a point of feeding her myself. I brought her into the house and begged her to accept my favorite overstuffed chair. I petted her fondly. She accepted food and chair without enthusiasm. She barely submitted to the caresses. She was not interested in a mere owner. She wanted a master. She wanted the lanky cracker—that was clear. As to the matter of forty dollars changing hands, she completely ignored the transaction.

Having endured a few days of this, I accepted an invitation to go down with one of the best quail shots in the South to shoot with friends of his near Americus. I wanted birds smacked right and left over Myrtle. I wanted her to see shooting that was shooting, with the lanky cracker far, far away. This, I felt, might aid her perception of property rights. I loaded her into the car then, among a reassuring welter of gun cases, shell boxes and shooting coats, and, lest she be distracted while learning that forty dollars is forty dollars, I left the four whirlwinds straining at their chains, yelping prayers and curses after me, as we drove off.

Eventually we reached a plantation house and its broad acres, over which we were to shoot, to be greeted by two tall brothers who owned it all. A mincing, high-tailed pointer, who seemed to be walking on eggs, and a deep-muzzled, well-feathered setter helped to welcome us. They were a fine-looking pair of dogs. I opened the rear door of the car and Myrtle came forth.

Now our hosts were true gentlemen of the South. After a look at Myrtle, they spoke earnestly of the weather and the crops and of how hard it was to get hold of good corn liquor. The crack shot from Atlanta became absorbed in assembling his gun. All in all, the moment passed off well.

In due time we marched out over the fields, four guns in line. We had planned to separate into pairs when we reached wider country. This we never did. I do not like to shoot with more than one other gun. I wanted the crack shot to help me kill birds instantly and stone dead when Myrtle found them; but, in a surprisingly short time, the brothers showed little desire to leave us, despite their pair of dogs ranging splendidly through the cover. Myrtle, as we started, had run whining from one man to another for some moments. At last she stopped to stand and watch the other dogs quartering out ahead. She turned and looked deliberately at, or rather through, each of the gunners, myself included. Then with a last small whimper, she got to work.

It became clearer and clearer from then on that the place to kill birds that day was in the vicinity of Myrtle. That miniature, misbegotten what-not found covey after covey and heaven knows how many singles. Her work was marred, however.

When a bird fell, she would find it at once and pick it up. She would stand uncertain for a moment and whimper, then start with the bird in her mouth for the nearest man. Having visited all four of us, she would begin to move in a vague circle, whining and looking about. Once she dashed for a high black stump in a field, to return dejectedly with the bird still in her mouth. I blew my whistle at such times. She never seemed to hear it. I would go toward her, calling her name, and ordering her to "Bring it here!" She only retreated from me, whimpering as I advanced. Getting to her at last, I would take hold of the bird and persuade her to let go of it. All this took time. It was also, to me, her legal owner, somewhat mortifying.

I shared my lunch with Myrtle. She accepted a sandwich, then withdrew a little from the rest of us, to stand looking off into the distance.

Later that afternoon a covey scattered in a narrow thicket along the bank of the river. The river was in flood—a wide, tawny plain with hummocks of fast water in the middle and still reaches of backwater at its edges. Myrtle pointed a single within inches of the water. The bird, when flushed, swung out over the river. The deadly gun from Atlanta cracked. The bird came down in the backwater just at the edge of the current. Myrtle was in the river swimming for the bird the moment it fell. She got to it quickly, but an eddy or the wind had carried it out into the current. As she turned to come back with the bird in her mouth, the force of the river took her, and downstream she went. There was a bend just there, curving away from our side. We four stood helpless on its outer rim and watched her work slowly shoreward, going downstream ten feet for every foot she gained toward the backwater and safety.

I remember yelling, "Drop it, Myrt—drop it!" knowing that she could make a better fight without that wretched bird. She did not obey. She struggled on until she came at last to the backwater with the bird still in her mouth. We all breathed sighs of relief and watched her swim swiftly toward us when free from the drag of the current. "Good girl! Bring it here!" I called, and got out a cigarette with shaking fingers. I began to bask in exclamations I heard along the bank: "Hot damn! That's the baby!" And "Come on home with the bacon, gal!" At least I was her owner. But trouble swiftly met that small swimmer.

There were cat briers growing below her in the flooded ground. One of the longer of these through which she swam fastened in her collar— the new collar I had bought her only the day before. Swim as she might, it held her fast. Her stroke became less smooth. She began to paw the water with her front feet—splashing as she did so. My shooting coat, filled with shells, came off and in I went.

No swimming, I found, was required. I was no more than up to my armpits in icy water when I reached Myrtle. For this I was duly thankful. Myrtle was showing fright and exhaustion by now. She was no longer swimming. She was dog-paddling frantically to keep her head above water. The quail was still in her mouth. I disengaged the brier from her collar and carried her to shore. Then I sat down to empty my hunting boots. I thought I felt the rasp of a pink tongue on the back of my hand as I did so. I can't be sure, for I was pretty cold.

The day was well along and my bedraggled state demanded the plantation house and a fire. We started toward both, hunting as we went. I was at the left end of the line. Myrtle stopped on point, out in front and to the right. It was evidently a single, since flushed birds had gone that way. I called, "Go in and kill it!" And stood to watch the shot. The bird fell at the report of the gun. Myrtle went into some brambles to retrieve. She emerged with the bird in her mouth.

"Bring it here!" I heard from the man to whom it rightfully belonged. If Myrtle heard him, she gave no sign. Nor did she give that whimper of uncertainty that I had heard throughout the day, as she had stood with a recovered bird in her mouth. She came to me on a straight line, running eagerly, to lay the dead quail in my extended palm.

Her eyes had that look—half pride in work well done, half love and faith and companionship—which is characteristic of a shooting dog as a bird is brought to the master's hand. "Here it is, boss!" that look seemed to say. "It's yours. And I am yours—to slave for you, to adore you, as long as I shall live."

Although my teeth were chattering, I was warmed suddenly from within. Myrtle rode back to Atlanta that night, curled in my lap, a weary but contented little dog.

Sources

The stories "Tracks to Remember," "Homebodies," and "A Drink for the Dog," by Tom Hennessey are from the book *Feathers 'n Fins*, Amwell Press, 1989, reprinted by permission of Nancy Hennessey.

"All-In' for Doves," by Lamar Underwood, from *Athlon Outdoors*, reprinted by permission of the author.

"That Twenty-Five-Pound Gobbler," by Archibald Rutledge, from *Outing*, 1919.

"On Seeing Whitetails," by Stewart Edward White, from *The Mountains*, 1904.

"'Yonder They Are!'" by Lamar Underwood, from *Athlon Outdoors*, reprinted by permission of the author.

"An Elk Hunt at Two-Ocean Pass," by Theodore Roosevelt, from *The Wilderness Hunter*, 1893.

"The Man-Eaters of Tsavo," by Lt. Col. J. H. Patterson, DSO, from *The Man-Eaters of Tsavo*, by Lt. Col. J. H. Patterson, DSO, 1907.

"The Plural of Moose Is Mise," by Irvin S. Cobb, from *Field & Stream* magazine, 1921.

"Whitetail Hunting," by Theodore Roosevelt, from *The Wilderness Hunter*, 1893.

"Red Letter Days in British Columbia," by Lieutenant Townsend Whelen, from *Outdoor Life*, 1906.

"The Road to Tinkhamtown," by Corey Ford, from *Field & Stream* magazine, November, 1970. Reprinted with the permission of Dartmouth College Library.

"The Mountain Goat at Home," by William T. Hornaday, ScD, from *Camp-Fires in the Canadian Rockies*, 1906.

"The Oregon Trail," by Francis Parkman Jr., from *The Oregon Trail*, 1847.

"My Most Memorable Hunting Dog," by Archibald Rutledge is from the book *Bird Dog Days, Wingshooting Ways*, edited by Jim Casada, University of South Carolina Press, 2016, reprinted by permission of Jim Casada.

"Hunting the Grisly," by Theodore Roosevelt. This text was prepared from a 1902 edition, published by G. P. Putnam's Sons, New York and London. It was originally published in 1893. It is part two of *The Wilderness Hunter*.

"Bob White, Down 't Aberdeen," by Nash Buckingham originally appeared in *Field & Stream* magazine, 1913.

"The White Goat and His Country," by Owen Wister, from *American Big Game Hunting*, 1893.

"The Forest and the Steppe," by Ivan Turgenev, from *A Hunter's Sketches*, 1917.

"The Last Buffalo," by George Bird Grinnell, from *American Big Game Hunting*, 1893.

Sources

"Hunting the Deceitful Turkey," by Mark Twain, from *The Mysterious Stranger and Other Stories*, which was written in 1898 and never finished.

"The Sundown Covey," by Lamar Underwood, from *Hunting Moments of Truth*, Amwell Press 1972. Published in *Sports Afield* magazine and other anthologies. Reprinted by permission of the author.

"Dog Upon the Waters," by John Taintor Foote, from *Dumb-Bell and Others: The Great Dog Stories of John Taintor Foote*, 1946.